Justice, Responsibility and Reconciliation in the Wake of Conflict

Boston Studies in Philosophy, Religion and Public Life

Volume 1

Aims and Scope

Boston University Studies in Philosophy, Religion and Public Life is an interdisciplinary scholarly series which publishes seminal papers on topics of pressing and perennial interest at the intersection of philosophy, religion and public life. The series is especially interested in interdisciplinary work that illuminates questions of value, truth, reality and meaning, as well as topics in the relevant fields which have a particular intersection with public life (for example, philosophical and religious perspectives on contemporary issues in ethical and political philosophy). In addition, the series serves as a prominent forum for important academic work emerging within the specific sub-discipline of the philosophy of religion.

Cover Image

The "Free at Last" sculpture stands in the midst of Boston University's Marsh Plaza, and is a memorial to the life and work of BU's most famous students of philosophy and religion, the Reverend Dr. Martin Luther King, Jr.

For further volumes:
http://www.springer.com/series/8881

Alice MacLachlan • Allen Speight
Editors

Justice, Responsibility and Reconciliation in the Wake of Conflict

 Springer

Editors
Alice MacLachlan
Department of Philosophy
York University
Toronto, ON, Canada

Allen Speight
Institute for Philosophy and Religion
Boston University
Boston, MA, USA

ISBN 978-94-007-5200-9   ISBN 978-94-007-5201-6 (eBook)
DOI 10.1007/978-94-007-5201-6
Springer Dordrecht Heidelberg New York London

Library of Congress Control Number: 2012945629

Printed on acid-free paper

Springer is part of Springer Science+Business Media (www.springer.com)

Acknowledgments

This is the first volume in a new—in fact, renewed—series, *Boston Studies in Philosophy, Religion and Public Life*. It represents a commitment on the part of the series editors to give a voice both to issues and contemporary thinkers whose work has a bearing on questions of value, truth, reality and meaning, as well as topics which have a particular intersection with public life (for example, philosophical and religious perspectives on contemporary issues in ethical and political philosophy). In addition, the series serves as a prominent forum for important academic work emerging within the specific sub-discipline of the philosophy of religion. These are issues which over the years shaped the Institute for Philosophy and Religion's predecessor book series, under the editorships of Leroy Rouner and M. David Eckel, and continue to inform the aims and mission of the Institute under its present leadership.

We would particularly like to thank the editors at Springer who have worked with us, Sasha Goldstein-Sabbah and Anita Fei van der Linden, as well as Willemijn Arts, who initially commissioned the series. Strategic ongoing support from the Boston University Humanities Center and the office of the Dean of the College of Arts and Sciences at Boston University made possible the lecture series and conferences from which the papers in this initial volume grew.

Support from the Social Sciences and Humanities Research Council of Canada was crucial for editorial assistance in preparation of the volume. We would also like to thank York University graduate research assistants Olivia Sultanescu and Christina Konecny, Institute graduate assistant Lynn Niizawa and interns Chrissy Anderson and Ryan Stelzer for their invaluable help.

Contents

Chapter 1
Introduction

Alice MacLachlan and C. Allen Speight

1.1   The Wake of Conflict: Charting the Terrain

What are the moral obligations facing participants and bystanders in the wake of conflict? How have theoretical understandings of justice, peace, and responsibility changed in the face of contemporary realities of war?

Recent years have seen a wide discussion among academics and policy makers concerning issues such as the nature of just war, the ethics of killing, and the responsibilities of agents within and beyond the immediate theater of conflict. Yet there remain large and under-explored facets of the modern experience of conflict and its aftermath that require conceptual and practical attention.

Some of these questions may seem to be quite basic – but are, given the experience of the last few years, still the most resistant to easy conceptual formulations. What in fact is *meant* by "peace" and "conflict"? What are the relevant conditions for discerning that agents or victims are within one or the other? How can they be distinguished from intermediate stages such as truces or states of emergency – and what governs the normative relationships in each? There is still much to be thought through in considering the various relevant roles – those of participants, victims, bystanders, third parties, witnesses, etc. – in conflict and post-conflict situations.

A. MacLachlan (✉)
York University, S418 Ross Building, 4700 Keele Street, Toronto, ON M3J 1P3, Canada
e-mail: amacla@yorku.ca

C.A. Speight (✉)
Department of Philosophy, Boston University,
745 Commonwealth Avenue, Boston, MA 02215, USA
e-mail: casp8@bu.edu

A. MacLachlan and A. Speight (eds.), *Justice, Responsibility and Reconciliation in the Wake of Conflict*, Boston Studies in Philosophy, Religion and Public Life 1,
DOI 10.1007/978-94-007-5201-6_1, © Springer Science+Business Media Dordrecht 2013

A further concern animating this volume is the wide range of differing idioms within the contemporary discussion of conflict and post-conflict situations. First, there is the familiar (yet increasingly challenged) just war tradition, in which a distinct theory of *jus post bellum* remains – despite much new work – still a *desideratum* alongside the more worked-out areas of traditional concerns with the justice of the cause of war (*jus ad bellum*) and its just conduct (*jus in bello*). While just war theory has roots dating back at least to Augustine, it has been taken up with renewed interest by philosophers and political thinkers in the last generation in large part as a response to new challenges posed by the nature of conflict and warfare in the post-World War II world. Michael Walzer's *Just and Unjust Wars* (Walzer 2000), for example, was shaped in particular by his response to Vietnam and has been a central text in this period of reshaping just war theory (see, among others, Elshtain 1992, 2004; Johnson 1984). More recently, Jeff McMahan's *Killing in War* (McMahan 2009) has raised new questions about Walzer's formulations of the separation in traditional just war theory between *jus ad bellum* and *jus in bello*, as well as more broadly the separation between the morality of killing in war and the morality of killing in other circumstances. The question of war's *aftermath*, however – the territory marked out but much less developed within traditional just war theory in terms of *jus post bellum* – has remained very much an open one, as the papers in the first section of the volume will attest.

Second, there is the growing field of literature on moral repair, both material and symbolic (Spelman 2002; Walker 2006), as well as evolving attempts to understand the goals of moral and political reconciliation (Prager and Govier 2003; Schaap 2005; Eisikovits 2010; Murphy 2010). These theorists treat war alongside a much longer list of conflicts, disruptions, displacements, and transitions, ranging from historical injustices, postcolonial legacies, and authoritarian rule to more recent atrocities of genocide and crimes against humanity, as well as the violence of civil and ethnic conflict. Their concerns in each case lie both with the repair of damaged or oppressive political relationships, and with the establishment of appropriate criteria for recognizing and sustaining morally and politically appropriate ones. Yet appropriate relationships rely as much on the growth of mutual trust and respect, as they do on the fulfillment of specific, measurable obligations. As a result, work on moral repair has brought new focus and attention to the potential *political* role for phenomena such as apology (Tavuchis 1991; Smith 2008; Celermajer 2009), forgiveness (Digeser 2001; Govier 2002; Griswold 2007), amnesty (Villa-Vicencio and Doxtader 2003) and pardons (Moore 1997). Optimism regarding these newly politicized phenomena varies widely. In the case of forgiveness, for example, some, like Trudy Govier, argue that forgiveness as we typically understand it has an important role to play in collective contexts, while others, like Peter Digeser and Charles Griswold, distinguish between interpersonal or moral forgiveness, on the one hand, and related political concepts. Still others, like Jeffrie Murphy (2003) and Thomas Brudholm (2008), are suspicious of "boosterism" about forgiveness in politics, fearing that it undermines legitimate claims of political injustice. In other words, the literature of moral repair not only raises issues regarding the nature and methods of repair; it also challenges whether norms of repair are always appropriate – asking whether some relationships are better left broken.

Finally, a third literature has grown around numerous recent attempts to consider the specific structure of certain moral, cultural, and political norms for post-conflict responsibilities and obligations. Many such attempts fall under the relatively new category of transitional justice. In the wake of conflict or regime change, political actors confront questions of individual and collective responsibility – and thus, the need for accountability and legal justice – without stable, recognizable sources of legal and political authority to draw upon. Furthermore, in many cases, responsibility for wrongdoing is both convoluted and widespread across wide segments of the population, making it hard to know how, and whom, to punish appropriately. Familiar institutions like criminal trials and punishment give way to (or are supplemented by) other mechanisms, such as truth commissions, public inquiries, formal apologies and negotiated amnesties and pardons. The seemingly distinctive nature of the claims that arise in transitions from conflict to peace, or from authoritarianism to democracy – as rapidly changing political and legal structures seek to deal with the legacies of past wrongdoing – have led some, most notably, Ruti Teitel, to argue that transitional justice represents a unique and distinct *kind* of justice (Teitel 2000). Others, like David Dyzenhaus, are skeptical of this apparent uniqueness, arguing that the transitions that typically follow large-scale conflict are merely new, complicated forums for employing nevertheless familiar norms of political and legal justice (Dyzenhaus 2003).

The concern fueling both advocates and skeptics of transitional justice appears to be the understandable unease felt by proponents of liberal justice, when norms and values unfamiliar to so-called "ordinary" legal justice (at least, conservatively conceived) are invoked – for example, talk of reconciliation and forgiveness, truth telling and amnesty. Indeed, these values have led some to argue that transitional justice is not justice at all, but euphemistically describes an uneasy compromise, in which the demands of justice are not given their usual priority, but are weighed against other social priorities – priorities that are "just" in name only (Ash 1997; Kiss 2000). The drive to define transitional justice as a unique and distinctive kind is motivated in part by the need to defend it (and the measures associated with it) as something other than a corruption or dilution of justice proper, while still asserting its status as *something appropriately like* justice, as we typically understand it.

In each of these three distinct yet interconnected literatures – that is, just war, moral repair, and transitional justice – familiar moral and political issues come to the fore, albeit couched in very different terms. These include tensions between individual freedoms and collective cooperation, the allocation of moral and political responsibilities, the importance of recognition and respect in political life, the resolution of political disagreements, and the limits of civil discourse. Ultimately, theorists and practitioners in all three are concerned to determine how we ought to see and remember what has taken place within a given conflict, the agents involved, relevant norms of reconstruction, the short and long term *meanings* given to the conflicts and their aftermath, and – most significantly – how to prevent their repetition. It is our belief that bringing key theorists together, across contexts, debates, and disciplines, furthers each of these ultimate investigations. Furthermore, the answers garnered in one debate hold important implications for each of the others. For instance, just what combatants on each side of a conflict are willing to accept as "justice," following the cessation of hostilities, will depend in part on the trust and recognition garnered by symbolic acts of apology and healing, or by the reinstatement of democratic and other community norms.

This volume's aim is to bring together new papers from leading scholars in these differing idioms within the fields of philosophy, political theory, international law, religious studies, and peace studies with an eye to pursuing essential questions about conflict and its aftermath in an interdisciplinary way. The origin of the collection lies in a year-long lecture series and conference hosted by the Institute for Philosophy and Religion at Boston University in 2008–2009 around the theme "Justice in Conflict – Justice in Peace." The focal conference of the series, on "Reconciliation, Moral Obligation and Moral Reconstruction in the Wake of Conflict," was held in March 2009 and provided an initial interdisciplinary forum for many of the participants in this volume to share ideas and seek common approaches.

1.2 Structure and Aims of the Volume

The volume is divided into three parts, each of which corresponds to a key theme emerging from the conference and lecture series. These include the nature of conflict in Part I, the responsibilities it invokes in combatants, bystanders, and survivors in Part II, and the practices of truth-telling, apology, and reparation which, taken together, begin to shape post-conflict reconciliation, in Part III. Each part contains several distinct voices, each of which offers a different frame, perspective, or method for tackling crucial questions arising in the wake of conflict. In placing such diverse voices in conversation, we have had three broad purposes in mind. The first of these, mentioned above, is to bring together philosophical and theoretical conversations that – while mutually significant – have tended to remain distinct: i.e. just war/ conflict, political reconciliation, and historical responsibility. Second, we have tried to seek out new *tools* for furthering these conversations, whether across topics or within a given theme. Such tools range from the introduction of new political concepts and categories (for example, Nir Eisikovits' proposed "truce thinking") to new frames for now familiar concepts, including François Tanguay-Renaud's analysis of emergency, and the theoretical frames for political apologies provided by Lynne Tirrell and Alice MacLachlan. We have also looked for work that invites new connections: whether between themes, as in Margaret Walker's work on symbolic and material reparations, or between thinkers, as in Gregory Fried's comparison of Heidegger and Gandhi. Equally significant are new and challenging *disconnections*, like the disconnect between peace and reconciliation proposed by Anat Biletzki. Ultimately, we have tried to highlight what we take to be the most important questions being raised by leading voices in each field, whether these concern the obligation to rebuild a nation destroyed by war, as discussed by Brian Orend and

Paul Robinson, how to assign individual responsibility following periods of social chaos, raised by Colleen Murphy, or the role of freedom in transitional justice, taken up here by Ajume Wingo.

Part I, "What is War? What is Peace?," opens with a series of papers by Eisikovits and Biletzki, both of which challenge how we typically frame the narratives we tell about conflict and its resolution, and instead invite us to find new frames for distinguishing war from peace, and conflict from resolution. In "Truce!", Eisikovits invites us to expand our political imaginations by taking seriously the concept of truces. Typically viewed either as a "mere" stepping stone to something better and more lasting or as a kind of false promise, the truce actually represents a political category in its own right: a state that is neither war nor peace, but that is preferable to the former, and more achievable than the latter. By asking what an approach to conflict organized around "truce-thinking" would look like, Eisikovits draws out key advantages of looking lower and more locally, when it comes to ending conflict. Ultimately, close analysis of truces suggests we make more progress towards curtailing violence, when we do not assume that the only escape is the utopian hope of perfect peace.

In "Peace-less Reconciliation," Anat Biletzki also takes issue with conventional wisdom about peace: in this case, her target is the time-line of transitional justice, as typically told, and the problematic expectations around peace and reconciliation that this storytelling creates. Biletzki subjects the related practices of peacemaking and reconciliation to a Wittgensteinian contextual analysis. Typical timelines insist that reconciliation comes only after a period of stable, just peace – and, at the same time, hold the absence of reconciliation up as a reason why such a peace cannot be found, with the pessimistic result that both appear illusory, even paradoxical. Instead of presuming that a just peace is a necessary condition for any real reconciliation *and* that reconciliation is required for the establishment of a just peace, Biletzki argues, we must open ourselves to the possibility of "peace-less reconciliation": that is, genuine steps towards a very real and rich reconciliation, achieved between formerly warring peoples, even before the cessation of formal military action and other violence. Biletzki's focus is the Israeli-Palestinian conflict. Like Eisikovits, Biletzki's analysis encourages us to look lower and more locally, finding new appreciation for smaller, and possibly more tentative, even fragile, signs of resolution and relief, as a new strategy for engaging productively with the seemingly endless reality of violent conflict.

Not only peace but also conflict is re-framed in the first section of the volume. In "Heidegger and Gandhi on Conflict," Gregory Fried argues that, despite their widely differing views on philosophical issues such as the nature of truth and its relation to the social and political, both thinkers nonetheless can be said to have a distinctly *particularist* standpoint according to which finitude – and hence conflict – is an inevitable part of the human experience. Fried's essay suggests ways in which an understanding of both Heidegger's notion of *polemos* (Greek for "war" or "conflict") and Gandhi's notion of *satyagraha* (often translated "truthforce," and crucial for his practice of nonviolent political action) may offer important insights within the contemporary discussion of the nature of conflict.

The final piece in this section, François Tanguay-Renaud's chapter, "Basic Challenges for Governance in Emergencies," widens the theoretical frame with which we examine the political, moral, and legal issues found in the wake of conflict, by reminding us that violent conflicts share features with certain other public emergencies. These include the particular challenge to good governance posed by conflict, and the ways in which *emergencies*, in particular, shape – and ought to shape – the decision-making of those in authority. Viewing conflict through the lens of history and theory can sometimes prevent us from grasping the effects of uncertainty and urgency on political decision-making. In presenting and defending a typology of emergency justifications for action, Tanguay-Renaud provides theoretical resources for evaluating decisions made during wars and other emergencies, and for understanding how these either exacerbate or mitigate ongoing violent conflict.

In Part II, "Framing Responsibilities," we turn from the nature of war and conflict to the responsibilities engendered by both. The topic of *jus post bellum*, or post-war justice, has only recently been taken up widely by theorists, no doubt inspired in part by questions of reconstruction efforts in Iraq and Afghanistan. In "At War's End: Clashing Visions and the Need for Reform," Brian Orend presents his case for a brand new Geneva Convention that would outline principles and guidelines for those looking to resolve armed conflicts and deal with the inevitable aftermath, fairly and decently. Given that we have an impressive number of international laws and rules intended to guide the initiation and conduct of war, Orend argues, it only makes sense we supplement these with others whose focus is on completing it. Furthermore, the project of drafting these would draw international attention to the growing problem of unresolved post-conflict devastation. Orend defends his proposal against possible objections by hypothesizing the need for a rehabilitation vision for conflict termination, rather than the familiar (and often punitive) vision fueled by revenge.

Not everyone is convinced that *jus post bellum* requires new norms of active engagement by former combatants. In "Is there an obligation to rebuild?", Paul Robinson argues *against* the kind of approach exemplified by Orend. Robinson is wary of efforts to create a new international norm, whereby victorious states must rebuild those whom they have defeated. Such a norm, Robinson claims, rests on false assumptions about the nature of rebuilding efforts, the legitimacy of the wars themselves, the abilities of states to engage in this kind of work, and the compatibility of such a norm with the Western just war tradition. Indeed, he concludes, recognizing this obligation might require us to abandon the concept of a just war altogether, deciding instead that wars inevitably involve injustice of some kind.

Some of the most complex responsibilities that arise in the aftermath of conflict concern individuals, and not states. In times of peace, the task of holding individuals responsible for acts of injustice and wrongful harm falls to the legal system. But what of those times when the legal system, and the surrounding society, have fallen into disarray? In "Political Reconciliation, Responsibility and Grudge Informers," Colleen Murphy takes up this crucial question, focusing on the infamous case of the grudge informer, and – by providing a critical survey of various justifications for punishment and their potential application – uses this case to articulate and defend a conception of just political relationships, found within a just political order. She ultimately concludes that punishment of grudge informers may well contribute to the establishment of both, and that it may be justified in part on these grounds. In doing so, Murphy reminds us that grand questions of *jus post bellum* and the responsibilities of states, combatants, and international actors should not be disconnected from concrete cases of individual responsibility. The latter may play a crucial role in providing resources for viable solutions to the former.

Finally, in Part III, "The Shape of Reconciliation," we take up questions of justice, responsibility and reconciliation as these play out in the longer term. We do so by turning from broad themes and principles to three *practices* of reconciliation: truth commissions, official apologies, and reparations. In each case, the nature, purpose, and functioning of the practice is brought into sharp focus, drawing out the ways in which these practices shape how we think about and engage in political and social reconciliation, more generally.

Truth Commissions are the practice most often associated with the growing field of transitional justice. As Ajume Wingo notes, in "Freedom in the Grounding of Transitional Justice," following the success of South Africa's Truth and Reconciliation Commission – and the crucial role many attributed to it, in avoiding a period of bloody civil war, following the end of apartheid – truth commissions have gained an international reputation as effective tools for social healing and reconstruction in a wide variety of contexts. What are we to make of this reputation – that is, how might we go about *measuring* the effectiveness of truth commissions as methods for dealing with conflict and injustice? Any empirical investigation would require that we first establish what, conceptually, are the relevant markers, and this in turn requires that we understand how the populations and peoples in question understand notions such as justice, responsibility, truth, and peace. In particular, Wingo argues, truth commissions are not conceptually neutral when it comes to the crucial concepts of individual freedom and social cooperation; we can identify and understand the successes and limitations of particular truth commissions best when we acknowledge this. Wingo articulates two distinct concepts of freedom, and concludes that truth commissions may function best in societies that privilege relational freedom over negative liberty.

Truth commissions are not the only mechanism for important truth telling about past conflicts and injustices. The practice of political apologies has also grown in popularity, over the last 50 years, leading some to hypothesize the arrival of an "age of apology." Lynne Tirrell and Alice MacLachlan both examine political apologies as performed speech acts, though drawing on very different examples. In "Apologizing for Atrocity: Rwanda and Recognition," Tirrell paints a vivid and compelling picture of the harms of genocide, harms which President Clinton's later apology for US inaction was intended to address. While, Tirrell notes, apology is the practice *least likely* to appear sufficient for addressing the world-changing harms of genocide, she argues that without apology, humanitarian aid and reparations are insufficient for important reparative practices of acknowledgement, recognition, and healing, and, ultimately, for reconciliation. Tirrell draws on contemporary philosophy of language, including J. L. Austin's speech act theory, to illustrate the power of a *good* apology in cases like Rwanda.

In "Government Apologies to Indigenous Peoples," Alice MacLachlan considers the extreme reactions political apologies invoke in recipients and commentators, noting that these range from excessive piety to damning, global cynicism about the practice altogether. She suggests that a critical analysis somewhere between the two can be found by reconsidering the multiple potential functions of a political apology, and draws particular attention to the narrative and commitment functions, alongside the apology's power to *disavow* wrongdoing. By taking as her examples two 2008 apologies made by the Canadian and Australian governments, MacLachlan advocates particularistic, contextual assessment of each function, noting that this requires theorizing individual apologies both as performed speech acts and as essentially political action. While Tirrell theorizes apologies primarily in terms of language, MacLachlan emphasizes their political and active nature, describing a framework inspired by the political thinking of Hannah Arendt.

As both Tirrell and MacLachlan note, the symbolic nature of apologies can lead some to suggest that they are acts of cheap grace, at least when unaccompanied by financial and material compensation. This is especially true in cases of genocide, as Tirrell concludes. But should the division between symbolic and material reparation be so sharply divided? In "The Expressive Burden of Reparations: Putting Meaning into Words, Money and Things," Margaret Urban Walker suggests that we need not think of apologies and reparations as separate practices, at all. This too-easy division emerges because the normative literature on reparative justice has been dominated by a juridical or tort paradigm. If, instead, we conceive of reparations politically and relationally, then the categorical distinction between material and symbolic starts to disappear. Material reparations are importantly expressive; they communicate important norms, such as the recognition of human dignity or equal citizenship and they can potentially express new forms of respectful, trustworthy and mutually accountable relationships. Walker presents a normative theory of reparations that emphasizes their dual nature, and which goes beyond tort notions of compensation and restitution to suggest the need for broader, moral and political, reordering.

1.3 Conclusions: Justice, Responsibility and Reconciliation?

If the diverse group of theorists, perspectives, themes, and disciplines represented in this volume share a common belief, it lies in the overwhelming and irreducible complexity of the conceptual and normative issues emerging from situations of conflict, and their immediate aftermath. Few of the questions raised – whether they concern the distinctions we draw between war and peace, conflict and reconciliation, the nature and limits of victors' obligations, the appropriate tools for allocating and enforcing political and legal responsibility, or the methods, tools and practices of reconciliation – are likely to find definitive and conclusive resolution, in the near future. Yet the voices gathered here are useful not only for the advances they make towards such resolution, but also for their ability to clarify and reframe what such resolution might look like. Furthermore, in drawing out new conceptual tools, theoretical frameworks, and thematic connections, they set the stage for other, further advances within crucial fields in philosophy, political theory, international relations, and law.

Finally, the discussions in this volume point unmistakably toward the conceptual interdependence of the three political values chosen as its title; we see, reflected again and again in the following pages, just how closely connected what it is that we take to be our responsibilities, and what it means to meet them, are tied both to the nature of justice, as we conceive it, and to the possibility of reconciliation. At times, this interdependence can appear vicious – as when reconciliation appears a distant, faint, hope without basic conditions of justice, even as the latter seem to require the kind of mutual trust and respect between former combatants that only reconciliation can generate. But it is our hope, and the hope of our contributors, that ultimately the conceptual and causal connections are virtuous: that is, that by better understanding how to know and fulfill our responsibilities, and by learning how to trust former enemies to do the same, we – as theorists, and in the wider world – come closer to the twin goals of justice *and* reconciliation, in the wake of conflict.

References

Ash TG (1997) True confessions. In: New York review of books, 17 July, pp 16–17

Brudholm T (2008) Resentment's virtue: Jean Amery and the refusal to forgive. Temple University Press, Philadelphia

Celermajer D (2009) The sins of the nation and the ritual of apologies. Cambridge University Press, Cambridge

Digeser P (2001) Political forgiveness. Cornell University Press, Ithaca

Dyzenhaus D (2003) Judicial independence, transitional justice and the rule of law. Otago Law Rev 10:345–369

Eisikovits N (2010) Sympathizing with the enemy: reconciliation, transitional justice, negotiation. Martinus Nijhoff, Dordrecht

Elshtain JB (2004) Just war on terror: the burden of American power in a violent world. Basic Books, New York

Elshtain JB et al (1992) But was it just? Reflections on the morality of the Persian Gulf War. Doubleday, New York

Govier T (2002) Forgiveness and revenge. Routledge, New York

Griswold C (2007) Forgiveness: a philosophical exploration. Cambridge University Press, Cambridge

Johnson JT (1984) Just war tradition and the restraint of war: a moral and historical inquiry. Princeton University Press, Princeton

Kiss E (2000) Moral ambitions within and beyond political constraints. In: Rotberg RI, Thompson D (eds) Truth v. justice: the morality of truth commissions. Princeton University Press, Princeton

McMahan J (2009) Killing in war. Oxford University Press, New York

Moore K (1997) Pardons: justice, mercy, and the public interest. Oxford University Press, New York

Murphy J (2003) Getting even: forgiveness and its limits. Oxford University Press, New York

Murphy C (2010) A moral theory of political reconciliation. Cambridge University Press, New York

Prager CAL, Govier T (2003) Dilemmas of reconciliation: cases and concepts. Wilfrid Laurier University Press, Waterloo

Schaap A (2005) Political reconciliation. Routledge, New York

Smith N (2008) I was wrong: the meaning of apologies. Cambridge University Press, Cambridge

Spelman E (2002) Repair: the impulse to restore in a fragile world. Beacon, Boston
Tavuchis N (1991) Mea Culpa: a sociology of apology and reconciliation. Stanford University Press, Stanford
Teitel R (2000) Transitional justice. Oxford University Press, New York
Villa-Vicencio C, Doxtader E (2003) Restorative justice: ambiguities and limitations of a theory. In: Villa-Vicencio C (ed) The provocations of amnesty: memory, justice and impunity. David Philip Publishers, Cape Town
Walker MU (2006) Moral repair: reconstructing moral relations after wrongdoing. Cambridge University Press, New York
Walzer M (2000) Just and unjust wars. Basic Books, New York

Part I
What Is War? What Is Peace?

Chapter 2
Truce!

Nir Eisikovits

Abstract We have not thought enough about truces. Our political imagination is committed to a false dichotomy between war and peace. Since truces are neither, we don't pay them serious attention. When we do think about truces we consider them as "mere truces": stepping stones in the transition beyond themselves, to something better and more durable – a permanent peace. Truces are acceptable for a while, but then they must be left behind. Staying in one for too long signifies failure. It is time to take truces much more seriously. By dismissing them and continuing to focus on the war-peace dichotomy we are denying ourselves a useful descriptive tool that could help us make sense of the way many conflicts actually subside. Furthermore, by insisting that the only acceptable and legitimate ending of a war is a lasting, stable peace with justice we may be putting ourselves at risk of fighting longer and harder than we have to. Finally, Political Islam has a nuanced theology and jurisprudence of truces. Given the history of tensions between Islam and the West, it is problematic that the former has a way of curtailing violence that we in the West have not thought about.

> Truce, truce. A time to test the teachings: can helicopters be turned into ploughshares?
> We said to them: truce, truce, to examine intentions.
> The flavour of peace may be absorbed by the soul.
> Then we may compete for the love of life using poetic images.
> – Mahmoud Darwish/A State of Siege

N. Eisikovits (✉)
Department of Philosophy, Suffolk University, 8 Ashburton Place, Boston, MA 02108, USA
e-mail: neisikovits@suffolk.edu

A. MacLachlan and A. Speight (eds.), *Justice, Responsibility and Reconciliation in the Wake of Conflict*, Boston Studies in Philosophy, Religion and Public Life 1, DOI 10.1007/978-94-007-5201-6_2, © Springer Science+Business Media Dordrecht 2013

War ends with a kiss. On August 14th, 1945, Edith Shain, a 27 year old nurse at Doctors Hospital in New York, left her shift and ran into the street to celebrate the surrender of the Japanese. A few moments after she reached Times Square, a sailor embraced her. "Someone grabbed me and kissed me, and I let him because he fought for his country," She told the Washington Post many years later.[1] A snapshot of the kiss, taken by Alfred Eisenstaedt and published by Life Magazine, became one of the most famous images of the last century. Ms. Shain's explanation for its popularity is as good as any: [The picture] "says so many things: hope, love, peace and tomorrow. The end of the war was a wonderful experience, and that photo represents all those feelings."[2] This is how wars come to a close. Men stop killing each other and start kissing pretty nurses instead. We leave the fighting behind. Permanently. We demobilize. We go back to work. We go back to school. We start families and have babies. Violence is replaced by its opposite.

***

At a luncheon given in 1916 to honor James M. Beck, author of a book about Germany's moral responsibility for "the war of 1914," the host, Viscount Bryce, had the following to say about calls circulating in America to end the war: "Peace made now on such terms as the German Government would accept, would be no permanent peace, but a mere truce. It would mean for Europe constant disorder and alarm… more preparation for war, and further competition in prodigious armaments."[3] Peace denotes permanence. A "mere" truce is dangerous, unstable, temporary, a dishonest cover under which to prepare for more war.

***

In a "fireside chat" broadcast over the radio in December of 1943, soon after his return from the Teheran and Cairo Conferences, President Roosevelt dismissed the "cheerful idiots" who thought that Americans could achieve peace by retreating into their homes: "The overwhelming majority of all the people in the world want peace," he asserted. "Most of them are fighting for the attainment of peace – not just a truce, not just an armistice – but peace that is as strongly enforced and as durable as mortal man can make it."[4] War ends with a stable peace. Real peace, not "just a truce." As lasting as men can make it. Nothing else is worth dying for.

***

Three days after Israel and the Hamas-led government of the Palestinian Authority reached a ceasefire in November of 2006, Israeli writer Amos Oz had the following to say about the agreement: "If it lasts, the cease-fire that Israel and the Palestinians announced…is a first step. At least three more steps need to be taken in its wake… We need direct negotiations. Negotiations about what? … Not about a *hudna* or a *tahadiya*, the Arabic words for the temporary armistice or truce that Palestinian leaders have suggested. We need an all-inclusive, comprehensive, bilateral agreement

---

[1] Brown (2010).

[2] Brown (2010).

[3] *New York Times*, July 6, 1916, p. 3.

[4] Roosevelt (1943).

that will resolve all aspects of the war between Israel and Palestine."[5] War ends when we bury the hatchet. When there is nothing at all left to fight about. Not with a *hudna*, not with a *tahadiya*. These are just temporary fixes.

Why do we think that war ends only when its opposite – peace – is ushered in? How did the idea of peace come to mean durable, fair, stable agreements involving the resolution of all controversies, mutual recognition, and the complete repudiation of violence? Do wars really end like that? What are the risks of sticking to this way of thinking about war's end? We have not thought enough about truces. Our political imagination is committed to a false dichotomy between war and peace. Hobbes tells us that "during the time men live without a common power to keep them all in awe, they are in that condition which is called war." He then goes on to add, laconically: "all other time is peace." In the years leading up to World War I the political and intellectual elites of Europe divided their enthusiasms between two popular books. The first, published in 1910 and promptly translated into a dozen languages, was titled *The Great Illusion*. Its author, Norman Angel, argued that war had become obsolete due to the financial interdependence of modern states. A year later the prominent German military theorist von Bernhardi published *Germany and the Next War* in which he insisted that war was "a biological necessity," expressing the laws of evolution in human affairs.[6] The same dichotomy was replicated by the debate, more than 80 years later, between Francis Fukuyama and Samuel Huntington. The former held that liberalism and its attendant commercial peace represented the final stage of historical development. The latter retorted with the thesis of the Clash of Civilizations, predicting that cultural conflict, primarily along religious lines, would dominate the post Cold-War world.

Historical, economic, or cultural necessities dictate that we must have peace. Or they dictate that we must have war. Since truces are neither, we don't pay them serious attention. As the brief but representative excerpts above suggest, when we do think about truces we consider them as "mere truces": stepping stones in the transition beyond themselves, to something better and more durable – a permanent peace. Truces are acceptable for a while, but then they must be left behind. Staying in one for too long signifies failure. When we do find ourselves in a long-term truce we tend to obscure that reality by employing the terminology of war and peace all the same. The US and the Soviet Union had a *"Cold War"* for more than 40 years although they never fought directly. The Americans and the Russians were not at war. And they were not at peace. Why don't we have a clear way of thinking about that in-between state?

It is time to take truces much more seriously. By dismissing them and continuing to focus on the war-peace dichotomy we are denying ourselves a useful descriptive tool that could help us make sense of the way many conflicts actually subside. More significantly, by insisting that the only acceptable and legitimate ending of a war is a lasting, stable peace with justice we may be putting ourselves at risk of fighting longer and harder than we have to.

---

[5] Oz (2006).

[6] For an interesting discussion of both books see Tuchman 2004, Chapter 1.

In regular usage the term "truce" denotes an agreement (formal or informal) between belligerents to stop hostile acts without terminating the war itself. The cessation of hostilities may be total or partial extending to some fronts of the combat zone, some purpose (such as the collection and burial of the dead), or some period of time. In this paper I will introduce and legitimize the idea of "Truce Thinking": contrary to the spirit of the examples cited above, sometimes political leaders *should* focus on the reduction of violence, its partial abatement, its temporary cessation. Sometimes they *should* prefer these to permanent, just and lasting peace agreements. That we have failed to conceptualize and accept unsatisfying, less than completely stable indeterminate ideas about the end of war is problematic both theoretically and practically. The paper has two sections. The first makes the case for taking truces more seriously. The second characterizes Truce-Thinking – the state of mind involved in seeking and making them.

2.1 The Case for Truces

2.1.1 The Peace That Kills

Our tendency to posit lasting and stable peace as the only acceptable way of ending a war makes wars longer and more brutal than they have to be. What Wilson called "the war to end all wars" has a good claim on intensity, given the promised benefit.

In the Luncheon mentioned earlier, Bryce described World War I thus: "... We are fighting for great principles – principles vital to the future of mankind, principles which the German government has outraged and which must at all costs be vindicated to defeat militarism... This is a conflict for the principles of right which were violated when innocent noncombatants were slaughtered in Belgium and drowned on the Lusitania. The Allies are bound and resolved to prosecute it till a victory has been won for these principles and for a peace established on a sure foundation of justice and freedom."[7]

A peace that establishes "the principles vital to the future of mankind" can justify, perhaps even consecrate, a lot of suffering and carnage.[8] In a recent book about the Napoleonic Wars, American historian David Bell reminds us that we have inherited from the enlightenment the idea that peace is our birthright, that war and violence are irrational aberrations to be uprooted. But such an uprooting, by the very fact that is it seen as the eradication of an abnormality, precisely because it promises to return us to our original state of peace, gains a substantial claim on violence. Bell writes: "A vision of war as utterly exceptional – as a final cleansing paroxysm of violence – did not simply precede the total war of 1792–1815. It helped,

---

[7] *New York Times*, supra note 3.

[8] I am grateful to James Carroll for several conversations on this point.

decisively, to bring it about. Leaders convinced that they were fighting "the last war" could not resist committing ever greater resources to it, attempting to harness all their societies' energies to a single purpose, and ultimately sacrificing lives on an industrial scale so as to defeat supposedly demonic enemies."[9]

When war is understood as an anomaly or disease rather than as an inescapable human reality – when we think of peace as our birthright, then the battle that is meant to restore peace becomes very vicious indeed. But this suggests that it is harmful, deadly harmful, that we don't know how to aim lower than "ending all war." That, children of the enlightenment, abhorring war, we can't imagine more modest, limited alternatives to it than peace. What if we legitimized truces as a possible way of halting war? Bell's analysis suggests that there are cases where this would have a mitigating effect on the intensity of fighting.

An analogous argument can be made about Roosevelt's insistence on the Axis Powers' "unconditional surrender". The demand, issued after the Casablanca Conference (in spite of Churchill's skepticism), was supposed to prevent Germany from rearming as it did after World War I. Roosevelt was, in effect, telling the Nazis and the Japanese that there was only one kind of peace the allies would accept, that it involved very harsh conditions, and that it was not negotiable. The war could only end with an *absolute, thoroughgoing, unambiguous* victory for the allies. Did this demand prolong the fighting unnecessarily? Did it take the wind out of the sails of Hitler's opposition? Did it force the Germans into a desperate fight, which they may have given up earlier had the possibility of a negotiated surrender been open to them?

"Unconditional surrender," writes James Carroll in his *House of War*, "meant that the enemy would have no reason to mitigate the ferocity of its resistance. It was an invitation to the Germans and the Japanese, as their likely defeat came closer, to fight back without restraint."[10] Reflecting on Churchill's resistance to the idea, Carroll adds: "Churchill understood that by foreclosing any possible negotiations towards surrender, the allies were making it more likely that the axis powers would fight to the bitter end at a huge cost to lives on both sides, resulting on a level of devastation that would itself be the seedbed of the next catastrophe…"[11]

Carroll's analysis, like Bell's, raises a haunting question: what if we had a richer repertoire for thinking about how wars wind down? What if we were in the habit of accepting that they do not always end once and for all with a Kantian or Wilsonian peace or with a harshly imposed, long-lasting Pax Americana a la Roosevelt? Would our wars be shorter? Would they become less bloody?

The tortured history of the Israeli-Palestinian Conflict provides another illustration. In the summer of 2000, the parties were on the verge of a historic breakthrough. President Clinton issued invitations for a summit in Camp David. Before departing

---

[9] Bell (2007: 316).

[10] Carroll (2006), 8.

[11] Carroll (2006), 9.

for the talks, Israel's Prime Minister, Ehud Barak, declared that there were only two possibilities. Either he would return with a "final status" agreement ending "all claims" between the parties, or he would "expose" the Palestinians and their leader as obdurate opponents of peace, in which case war would ensue. The rest is history. The Palestinians did not accept Barak and Clinton's proposals for ending the conflict and war did follow. But was the dichotomy that Barak set up helpful? Were there really no options between lasting peace and war? And wasn't the positing of this dichotomy one of the reasons that war broke out?[12]

2.1.2   Truces Can Keep Us Safe Too

We assume that peace is required to keep us safe. That's part of its allure. We speak of a "lasting" or "stable" peace supposing that once we have achieved it (even if at a considerable price) we could finally begin living as private men and women focusing on our work and families. At peace, the liberal nation finally fulfills its *telos* and becomes an enabler rather than a taker of lives.

But a cursory glance at history suggests that peace is not always necessary to keep us safe. The policy of Détente between the U.S. and the Soviet Union was essentially a truce, and for all of its cynicism and amorality, it kept them from destroying the world, until the conditions ripened for a more principled and ambitious relationship.

For more than 30 years Israel has had a peace treaty with Egypt and an armistice with Syria. It is far from clear that its northern border is more dangerous than its southern one. There have been almost no direct confrontations over the last decades on both fronts. While the Syrians have enabled Hezbollah to arm itself to the teeth, the Egyptians looked away while Hamas used their territory to smuggle munitions into the Gaza strip. There is certainly no dramatic evidence that peace with Egypt has kept Israel much safer than its long-term truce with Syria.

To look back much further, the so called "Concert of Europe" created after the end of the Napoleonic Wars was an attempt to enforce the agreements reached in the Vienna Conference – primarily the preservation of the balance of power between European powers, and the containment and reintegration of France. This was much more of a truce than a principled Kantian peace – the parties had little concern for mutual attitudes, forms of government, or international norms of conduct. And yet, the arrangement kept Europe quiet for almost a century.[13]

Examples can be multiplied but the point should be clear: formal, ambitious peace agreements that purport to end conflict fairly once and for all often guarantee

---

[12] Some good accounts of the Camp David meetings and their aftermath include: Ross (2004), Ben Ami (2006), Enderlin (2003).

[13] On this see Howard (2000), 43.

the security of the parties who sign them. But such agreements do not represent the only alternative for obtaining stability. In some cases the interests, capabilities and ideologies of the parties bode well for prolonged calm even in the absence of formal peace agreements.

2.1.3 How Wars Actually End

War rarely ends with a clear-cut victory followed by a stable peace. The Treaty of Paris remaking Europe after the defeat of Napoleon and the victory parades to mark the vanquishing of the Nazis are the exception rather than the rule. This is especially true if we adhere to the Clausewitzian definition of war as an instrument of policy (and of victory in war as the ability to impose our policy aims on our enemies). On such an understanding, the American Civil War did not end with the unambiguous victory of the North because, within a decade, the South was able to frustrate the northern vision of extending political rights to blacks. World war I did not end with the unambiguous defeat of Germany. In spite of America's desire for a swift and clearly determined confrontation, the first Gulf War ended with Saddam Hussein still in power, slaughtering the same insurgents the Americans had encouraged to rise up against him. Israel's 1982 war in Lebanon has, in one permutation or another, never ended, morphing from a brief, intense war with the PLO, to a war of attrition with the PLO and later with Hezbollah in Southern Lebanon, to a series of cross border skirmishes with Hezbollah, to another brief intense war against Hezbollah, back to the heightened cross border tensions obtaining as of this writing.[14]

These "ragged endings"[15] have become more noticeable after World War II. Since the late 1940s, most military conflicts have become asymmetrical.[16] They typically involve a competition between a technologically capable military power with an orderly chain of command and a weaker, loosely organized force that relies on guerilla tactics. Guerillas exhaust conventional armies by turning indigenous populations against them and inflicting enough damage to weaken the regulars' domestic political support.

Anyone following recent conflicts in Iraq, Afghanistan, Lebanon and Palestine can see these dynamics in play. Asymmetrical warfare defies our notions of clear military victory and the establishment of lasting peace. As David Kilcullen argues in a recent book, the only effective strategy for fighting such wars is isolating the ideological hard core of the enemy from its incidental supporters by providing security and economic opportunity to the indigenous population. The execution of

---

[14] The historical survey presented here is based on Jeb Sharp's excellent five part series (2008) for PRI titled "How Wars End".

[15] I borrow the term from Ms. Sharp.

[16] For a good discussion of the growing significance of such conflict see, e.g. Van Creveld (1991).

such a strategy takes a long time and a great degree of persistence. Success is not stable even when it is finally achieved. It is hard to defeat guerillas. Even when we do, the outcome is not best described as peace. Asymmetrical conflicts are kept at bay, stabilized, managed until they are brought to a bearable level.

All of this suggests that the traditional dichotomy between war and peace is too simplistic for thinking about contemporary armed conflict. Winning and the institution of peace have traditionally meant that one side can impose its political agenda on another. But guerilla warfare upsets this Clausewitzian view of war, often rendering it irrelevant. A party which has been defeated in conventional warfare can switch to guerilla tactics (as did the Taliban, the Iraqis and, according to some historians, the Southern Democrats after the American Civil War) in order to make sure the stronger side cannot obtain their political goals militarily.[17] When this happens the very aims of war often change to stabilization, the reduction of killing, the restoration of some degree of public order. None of these achievements presupposes a permanent, just end to conflict and all of them are closer to our definition of truce than they are to the classical idea of peace.

2.1.4   Truces in Political Islam

From Palestine to Afghanistan to Iraq much of the (largely asymmetrical) fighting Western powers have been doing lately has been with Muslims. An important advantage of introducing truces into our thinking is that Islamic Jurisprudence devotes a good deal of attention to them. The first truce in the Islamic tradition can be traced back to the Treaty of Hudaybiyah signed in 628 AD between Mohammad and the people of the tribe of Quraysh who controlled the city of Mecca. Mohammad and his followers wanted to perform a pilgrimage to Mecca but the local inhabitants did not welcome them. In order to avert a bloody confrontation, the parties reached a 10-year armistice regulating future pilgrimages. This agreement is the source of legitimacy of truces in Islam.[18]

An Islamic truce or "hudna" consists in the suspension of the duty of Jihad against non-believers. It is permissible for Muslims to enter into such an agreement under a variety of circumstances – ranging from the perceived military weakness of the Muslim army through the remoteness of the battlefield to the scarcity of resources necessary for fighting.[19]

Muslim thinkers allow for a wide range of *hudnas* – some lasting only a few days, intended primarily for rest and rearmament, others enduring 6 or, as in the

---

[17] See Stephen Biddle, *Interview with Jeb Sharp*, supra note 14.

[18] As one scholar puts it: "the treaty signed by the Prophet with the Meccans at Hudaybiyah … was adopted as a model to be followed in respect to its stipulations, implementation and for the reason of its eventual revocation." See Weigert (1997, 400–401).

[19] Weigert (1997, 400).

case of Hudaybiyah, 10 years. Furthermore, most Sunni scholars accept the idea of unlimited *hudnas* when it is clear that the Muslim army cannot defeat its enemy.[20]

The historical record provides numerous examples of truces between Muslims and "infidels." Saladin and the Crusaders signed eight such agreements in the twelfth century (4 initiated by the Crusaders, 4 prompted by Saladin). Only one of these was broken.[21] The French and their Algerian foes under the command of Abd Al-Qadir signed two hudnas in the 1830s,[22] and the Spanish and the Moroccans signed a hudna in 1860 that eventually developed into a full-blown peace agreement.[23]

Hudna is not the only term in Islamic jurisprudence denoting a temporary cessation of hostilities. The related notion of tahadiya shares the identical Arabic root h-d-n, denoting quiet or calm. While a tahadiya is usually a short, informal, often unilateral ceasefire, *hudnas* are formal, binding agreements between two parties and it is rare for them to be broken, as their stability and endurance are tied with the honor of the signatories: "Hudna," writes one scholar, "denotes something sacred, although it is not a religious notion *per se*. Once a person has signed or shaken hands on a *Hudna* agreement for a certain period of time, he might not renew it, but he will not resume fighting before the term of the agreement is over. There is a belief among Muslims that whoever breaches a *Hudna* will be punished by the almighty: one of the breaching party's family members may die or contract an incurable illness. If one breaches a cease-fire that is not a *Hudna*, there will be no retribution from Heaven. The annulment of other terms or agreements, even of a peace treaty, is not as severe as the annulment of a *Hudna*."[24]

Muslims take *hudnas* seriously. They view such agreements as a way of curtailing, sometimes even permanently ending wars. Western powers have been doing a lot of fighting with Muslims. Shouldn't these powers think more carefully about a method of conflict reduction central to the political tradition of their enemies?

Consider the recent history of the Israeli Palestinian conflict. Ever since the early 1990s moderate Israelis have been claiming that they want to reconcile with the Palestinians – to reach a peace accord ending all mutual claims and involving mutual recognition. The operative terms are Kantian – perpetual peace with justice and recognition. But these terms are foreign to a good deal of Islamic jurisprudence. Instead, Hamas, and increasingly other Palestinian factions, have claimed that they cannot recognize Israel as a Jewish State but would, rather, sign a long-term *hudna* with it. The Israelis, in turn, have taken such statements as evidence of Palestinian rejectionism. But what is it that is being rejected? Could it be that what is being rejected is the metaphysical baggage that comes with the idea of permanent peace and recognition rather than the reality in which people commit to stop killing each

---

[20] Weigert (1997, 402).

[21] See Ginat (2006, 255).

[22] Ginat (2006, 257).

[23] Ginat (2006, 258).

[24] Ginat (2006, 254).

other? And if people really are willing to stop killing each other for a long time can their enemies be justified in rebuffing them because of their refusal to label the new state of affairs "peace"?

A famous commentary on the truce of Hudaybiyah by Az-Zuhri tells us that "when the truce came and war laid down its burdens and people felt safe with one another, then they met and indulged in conversation and discussion."[25] There is, according to this account, no need for a formal and final peace agreement in order for the combatants to talk (even "indulge" in talking) with each other. A reliable setting down of the burdens of war can suffice. The emphasis is not placed on the rationality of peace, nor on the rights of former combatants and their need to have their political identity reaffirmed, but on what happens when we focus on the more modest goal of easing – not completely and not forever – the rigors of battle.

2.1.5 War's Allure

War has its attractions. It is easy to sell the "old lie" that "Dulce et decorum est pro patria mori" to "Children ardent for some desperate glory"[26] because, on many levels, the lie is appealing.

The psychologist Lawrence LeShan tells us that war is appealing because it fulfills two conflicting human needs: for individuation on the one hand, and for merging into something greater than ourselves on the other. War provides a "means of resolving the tension between our…needs for singularity and group identification… [it] sharpens experience, heightens perception, and makes one more and more aware of one's own existence. At the same time, war allows us to become part of something larger and more intense… The Way of the One and the Way of the Many are followed simultaneously and each intensifies the other."[27]

War is appealing because it provides an outlet for our aggressive instincts. "Men are not gentle creatures who want to be loved, and who at the most can defend themselves if they are attacked," Freud notes in *Civilization and its Discontents*. He continues, famously, bleakly: "they are, on the contrary, creatures among whose instinctual endowments is to be reckoned a powerful share of aggressiveness. As a result, their neighbor is for them not only a potential helper or sexual object, but also someone who tempts them to satisfy their aggressiveness on him, to exploit his capacity for work without compensation, to use him sexually without his consent, to seize his possessions, to humiliate him, to cause him pain, to torture and to kill him. *Homo homini lupus*. Who, in the face of all his experience of life and of history, will have the courage to dispute this assertion?"[28] In a later correspondence

---

[25] See Pickthall (2004), Surah 48, 557.

[26] The quotes are from Wilfred Owen's famous poem "Dulce et Decorum est."

[27] LeShan (2002, 28).

[28] Freud (1961, 69).

with Einstein, Freud blames this aggressive, destructive impulse (which he describes as co-equal with our erotic instinct to "conserve and unify") for the ease with which men can be "infected with war fever."[29]

War is appealing because it is exhilarating. In Act IV, Scene V of *Coriolanus* Shakespeare has one of the serving men declare: "Let me have a war, say I: it exceeds peace as far as day does night; it's spritely, waking, audible, full of vent. Peace is very apoplexy, lethargy, mulld, deaf, sleepy, insensible; a getter of more bastard children than war is the destroyer of men." A soldier stationed in Ramadi, Iraq makes a similar point with rather fewer flourishes:

> There's a rush that comes on the heels of a significant event here. After the IED explodes, or the RPG whistles overhead, or the shot cracks past, there's a moment of panic as you process the fact that you are still alive – that this time, they missed you. After that second's hesitation, the rush hits. No one really knows what it is, exactly, but we all feel it. It's physical. It's emotional. For some, it's spiritual. Some say it's endorphins or adrenaline; some say it's rage, or hate, or joy. Some say it's safety – the knowledge that someone is watching out for you. It's different for everyone, but it's always there. For me, the rush is mostly exhilaration. It's a feeling of invulnerability. I've heard the unforgettable sound of an RPG somewhere very, very near my little sector of space, and stood a little taller yelling 'Missed me, you bastards!' as I spun the turret and looked for the shooter. The first time I got blown up, I had to remind myself to get up and look around for the trigger man, or possible gunmen set to take advantage of the confusion. I felt like I was floating through a world where time stood still. There's something about looking directly at an artillery shell, and seeing it vanish with a sharp crack and rush of dust and debris, that changes you. My brain was yelling at me 'This isn't normal! You shouldn't be alive and thinking right now!,' and my body was yelling back 'Well, I'm definitely alive, so hoist your doubting ass up into the turret!' I've never felt more alive than I do in the moments after a near miss. I feel the same way after a big jump skiing, or after jumping off a bridge, but here the feeling is magnified a hundredfold. It's incredible when you do something that you shouldn't live through, but do. Some might call me sick, or crazy. I assure you that I am sane, and very much alive.[30]

We have been trying to eradicate war for five millennia. Part of the reason we have not been able to is that war, in addition to being horrific and absurd can also be (often at the same time) satisfying, interesting and exciting. It presents challenges, friendships, attachments and achievements that the combatants, if they are not too maimed or psychologically broken, often think back to nostalgically for the rest of their lives.

Here then is an additional, troubling reason to introduce the notion of truce into our thinking about international affairs: the dichotomy between war and peace suggests that the only acceptable alternative to war is its complete elimination. But war is too irresistible to be eliminated. There is strong historical, psychological and literary evidence suggesting that war cannot be done away with. It cannot be permanently removed or cured. We may be better off thinking about ways to contain, reduce and control it. There are many areas of political life in which we can, as Freud reminds us, "expect gradually to carry through such alterations in our

---

[29] *Why War? A Correspondence between Einstein and Freud (1931–1932).*

[30] http://acutepolitics.blogspot.com/2007/03/war-cocaine.html

civilization as will better satisfy our needs and will escape our criticisms." But not all areas are like that: "we may also familiarize ourselves with the idea that there are difficulties attaching to the nature of civilization which will not yield to any attempt at reform."[31]

2.2   Truce Thinking

The arguments offered in the preceding section are not necessarily of equal weight. It may well be that some of them are more persuasive than others. Perhaps war's allure is, with great effort, resistible. Perhaps we should be exporting our Kantian ideas about fair and final peace arrangements to the rest of the world rather than importing less perfect concepts. Perhaps, taking the very long view, peace agreements are the best way to keep ourselves safe. But the cumulative effect of the arguments in part 1 is to shift the burden of proof to those who argue that nothing less than a final, permanent and just peace should be accepted as the appropriate way to think about the end of war. The case for truces, like most cases that can be made in political philosophy, is provisionary. Before we rest it let us characterize the state of mind involved in making truces: what are some of the most important assumptions involved in accepting truces as part of the legitimate repertoire for mitigating political conflict?

2.2.1   *Optimism About the Passage of Time*

An old Jewish story tells of a despot who decides his dog must learn to speak. He reviles the Jewish community living under him but admires their Rabbi for his wisdom and erudition. One evening the tyrant summons the rabbi. "You are one of the smartest people around," the tyrant begins. "I don't like you or your people, but I need help," he continues. "See this dog at my feet– I need you to teach him to talk. If you succeed I will be kind to your people. If you fail – God help you all." The Rabbi strokes his beard for a long moment. "Teach your dog to talk… not easy…it will take a long time and a lot of money…give me five years and three thousand Dinars and I will do it." The tyrant agrees, but not before he repeats his threat. The Rabbi goes home and knocks on the door with excitement. "Bluma," he tells his wife, "look! I have three thousand Dinars!" "That's wonderful!" She exclaims. "How did this happen?" The Rabbi tells her. Bluma's face turns grey. "What have you done? You can't teach a dog to speak! We are done for." "Slow down, Bluma" The Rabbi replies. "Five years is a long time. Maybe the dog will die, maybe the tyrant will die, or maybe the Messiah will come. We'll see."

---

[31] Freud (1961, 74).

Truce Thinking emphasizes immediate benefits – temporary relief, rest, quiet over more abstract considerations regarding the rights of the parties, mutual acknowledgment and settling questions about distributive justice. More precisely, Truce Thinking suggests that it is worthwhile pursuing immediate benefits even when we have absolutely no idea if the more permanent concerns can ever be addressed. Like the Rabbi, the Truce Thinker wants to buy us time. During that time circumstances may change. The dog or the tyrant could die, or the Messiah might come: new, more moderate political parties could come to power, the balance between the global political parties supporting each of the combatants could shift, a manmade or natural cataclysm could put local tensions into perspective. Or the very fact of quiet and rest could generate stakes in continued quiet and rest. People could get used to not killing each other and hesitate to return to it.

Peace Thinking is future oriented. The references to "the future of our children" pervade most great peace speeches. "We want our children and your children to never again experience war;"[32] "for the generations to come, for a smile on the face of every child born in our land, for all that I have taken my decision to come to you…to deliver my address;"[33] "I do not believe that you want Northern Ireland to ever again be a place where tomorrow's dreams are clouded by yesterday's nightmares."[34] Truce Thinking, by contrast, is oriented towards the present. It deemphasizes the future. It leaves some of the hard work for the next generations. If the Israelis and the Palestinians can stop shooting at each other for 5 years without resolving questions about borders, the status of Jerusalem, or the "right of return," so be it. A lot could happen in 5 years. If the Sunnis and Shiites can recreate a vibrant commercial life in Iraq without resolving the constitutional arrangement dividing power between them, and without completing the accounting for Saddam's Hussein's crimes, so be it. Commercial life and the fact of quiet have their own dynamic. The constitutional difficulties and the crimes of the past will still be there to be addressed at a later time.

2.2.2 Aim Low

A time-tested negotiating strategy recommends that we aim higher – ask for more – than we would settle for: set a high asking price for your home so there is room to go down, demand a bigger raise than you would be satisfied with, push your children for straight A's in math so they can bring home a B+ average and so on.

[32] Benjamin Netanyahu, speech at Bar Ilan University, June 14th, 2009. English version available online: http://www.haaretz.com/hasen/spages/1092810.html

[33] President Anwar Sadat's address to the Israeli Knesset, November 20th, 1977.

[34] President Bill Clinton on Northern Ireland's Good Friday Agreement, December 13th, 2000. Available online: http://www.independent.co.uk/news/uk/home-news/clinton-urges-peace-in-farewell-ulster-speech-626328.html.

The strategy has a diplomatic correlate: articulating ambitious goals as part of a process of conflict resolution in hope that the parties will be pressured into making more progress. Aim at reconciliation and you end up with coexistence. Aim at coexistence and you end up with the status quo.

The setting of ambitious diplomatic goals may be less the product of tactical calculation than the expression of strategic vision – the conviction that extraordinary effort is required to break out of a prolonged stalemate. Some historians have claimed that President Carter's ambitious agenda for the Middle East in the late 1970s resulted from his disappointment with the skepticism of his advisors who urged him not to pressure Begin and Sadat to make peace.[35] Contemporary commentators argue that it is a similar desire to redefine the playing field, which is behind President Obama's bold early push in Middle East diplomacy.

High expectations can, indeed, motivate a negotiating partner. But they can also paralyze her. They can signal that she is bound to disappoint and, as a result, instill a sense of helplessness. The risk is not limited to a specific party bowing out of the negotiation. Setting goals too high may well create a sense of cynicism about the activity itself. Buyers may stay away from our home altogether; our children may simply give up on math. The combatants may decide that "if this is what peace is about – if this is what we have to do for it – we have no interest."

Truce Thinking works in the reverse direction. It aims low in order to strike high. It seeks to generate a measurable, visible reduction of war. To give combatants a "taste" of peace, hoping that the taste will create an appetite, hoping, to use the words of Darwish, that "the flavor of peace may be absorbed by the soul."

The Freeze movement ignited by Randall Forsberg in the 1980s provides a striking example of the power of aiming low. A two paragraph proposal to first "decide when and how to achieve a mutual and verifiable freeze on the testing, production and future development of nuclear warheads" and later to "to pursue… verifiable reductions" in the number of such warheads caught on like a brush fire in the United States, sweeping up scores of civic and professional organizations, city councils and state legislators. Within 2 years of its publication, the Freeze proposal became the most "successful American grassroots movement of the twentieth century."[36] It brought out millions into the streets, was adopted by the House of Representatives and, eventually, convinced President Reagan that his policy of preparing for, rather than trying to avoid, a nuclear war with the Russians had to be reversed. Part of the reason why the Freeze movement was so effective lay in its modesty. The proposal was a quintessential example of Truce Thinking –it stated an obtainable, tangible goal which regular people who knew nothing about international security could relate to. Rather than "banning the bomb" or ending the state of war with the Russians, Forsberg and her followers called for freezing nuclear weapons at their current levels. They demanded a truce in the nuclear arms race

---

[35] Stein (1999, 40).

[36] The assessment appears in Carroll (2006). For an excellent overview of the Freeze movement see pp. 385–397.

rather than pushing for ending it all together. The effect, however, was to begin the process of arms reduction. Eight years after the publication of Forsberg's manifesto the Cold War was over.

2.2.3   Irreconcilable Enemies Don't Have to Fight

It is possible to avert war with those who will not make peace with us. Israel and Hamas are genuinely irreconcilable. The Soviets and the Americans were genuinely irreconcilable during much of the Cold War. But the realization that others are radically, wildly different from us, that they see the world in terms that we can never accept, does not have to lead to belligerence.

In early 1946, the American Diplomat George Kennan sat down at his desk in Moscow to write a reply to a query sent by the State Department. His superiors wanted to know why the Soviets refused to join the World Bank and the International Monetary Fund. Kennan's response, which became known as the "Long Telegram," (it was 8000 words long and opened with an apology for "burdening the telegraphic channel") went far beyond the question. It took up the future of the relationship between the two powers in the broadest terms.[37] Kennan argued that the radical difference between American and Soviet ideologies did not imply that military confrontation was inevitable. First, because Soviet ideology itself did not dictate war: "we are going to continue for long time to find the Russians difficult to deal with. It does not mean that they should be considered as embarked upon a do-or-die program to overthrow our society by a given date. The theory of the inevitability of the eventual fall of capitalism has the fortunate connotation that there is no hurry about it. The forces of progress can take their time in preparing the final *coup de grâce*."

Second, because ideological difference alone neither starts nor sustains a war – "[World War II] has added its tremendous toll of destruction, death and human exhaustion. In consequence of this, we have in Russia today a population which is physically and spiritually tired… There are limits to the physical and nervous strength of people themselves."

Kennan reminds us that those who are, in theory, ready for a "duel of infinite duration" with us do not have to become our enemies in practice. An opposing political entity can stand on the other side of an ideological abyss and yet harbor no tangible desire to harm us. The ideology itself, simple exhaustion or a combination of both may well bode for quiet.

There is a gap, Kennan suggests, between ideological difference and military action. And we can exploit that gap; we can buy time, perhaps even a lot of time.

---

[37] The Telegram was later revised and published anonymously in Foreign Affairs. It became known as the X Article. I quote from the Foreign Affairs version of the essay. It is available online at: http://www.historyguide.org/Europe/kennan.htm.

And during that time, if we become the best, most principled example of ourselves, if we show off the ways in which our own ideological and cultural commitments are more benign than those of the competition, things may change in our favor. For Kennan, "containment," the term he became famous for, was mainly a cultural, diplomatic project. Prevailing in the contest with the Russians depended largely on whether the US could "measure up to its own best traditions and prove itself worthy of preservation as a great nation."

Tragically, Secretary of Defense Forrestal, who initially encouraged Kennan to rewrite his telegram as an essay for *Foreign Affairs*, badly misread his protégé's argument. Focusing exclusively on the discussion of the unbridgeable ideological difference between the Soviets and Americans, he concluded that the Soviets were, by definition, an enemy and had to be met with equal force anywhere they made military headway. It was this militarized understanding of containment that, to a large extent, animated the American involvements in Korea and Vietnam.

Forrestal distortion notwithstanding, Kennan's essay embodies an important facet of Truce Thinking. Long term quiet and real enmity are compatible. Though it would certainly be nice, we do not have to stop hating, fearing or disagreeing with others in order to prevent war. The very ideologies we balk at can become the source of calm. Marxism did not require a War of Armageddon with the West. Neither does Political Islam. There are openings. There are cracks. The question for the Truce Thinker is not whether we can make friends out of our enemies. It is, rather, whether we can get to know our enemies well enough, as Kennan did, to find ways of not fighting them.

2.3 Conclusion

Truce Thinking suggests that some of the problems of international relations can't be resolved. It accepts that political conflict can take the form of a chronic disease to be managed rather than cured. Just as doctors treating a patient with such a condition focus on managing her symptoms and maximizing her quality of life, it is sometimes the task of political leaders to make our lives bearable rather than peaceful. The trick, of course, is learning to distinguish between the conflicts that can be resolved and the ones that must be managed. But that is not a task for philosophers. It is a purely practical matter, determined by the circumstances and political history of each conflict.

In the final analysis, peace cannot always be had, there are circumstances when seeking it at all costs can be harmful, and yet, the fact that some conflicts are unsolvable does not suggest that life for those living through them must become unbearable.

There is, of course, much more work to be done. One would need to consider objections. Two major concerns come to mind. The first is that legitimating truces promotes appeasement in international relations – that the willingness to reach accommodations with unsavory actors who reject basic tenets of political decency can encourage and empower them. A second, related objection is that truces stunt political progress – by favoring quiet and the immediate alleviation of local tensions they divert attention from the dramatic, long-term, structural changes that must be made in order for stable peace to take hold. There are also further conceptual questions to explore. One of the most important ones concerns the dynamics of trust involved in making a truce. Truces represent the first limit or curtailment on war. Why would anyone trust an enemy enough to enter into one? What does it take to develop such trust under conditions of belligerence? A careful focus on reciprocity? A unilateral gesture which creates what Thucydides called "a debt of honor to be repaid in kind"? These questions will have to wait for a closer, more detailed consideration.

Acknowledgments Earlier versions of this paper were presented at a conference on the aftermath of war at Boston University and at the Political Theory workshop at the University of Haifa. I am grateful to participants in both events for their comments. James Carroll, Gregory Fried, Maria Granik, David Lyons, Fred Marchant, David Matz, Jeffrey Lipshaw, David Roochnik and Michael Soolkin provided valuable feedback. Thanks are also due to the students in my seminars on truces at Suffolk University. Our discussions were instrumental for thinking through many of the issues discussed here. Michael McDonough, Peter August and Jack Rotondi have provided valuable research assistance for this paper. Finally, I owe a debt of gratitude to The National Endowment for the Humanities for its generous support of this project and to Suffolk University for granting me a summer research stipend to work on it.

References

Angell N (2009) The great illusion: a study of the relation of military power to national advantage. Cornell University Press, Ithaca

Anonymous (1 Mar 2007) War cocaine: blog entry. In: Acute politics. http://acutepolitics. blogspot.com/2007/03/war-cocaine.html. Accessed 22 Nov 2011

Brown E (2010) "Edith Shain, nurse kissing Navy man in Eisenstaedt's WWII photo, dies at 91" Washington Post. http://www.washingtonpost.com/wp-dyn/content/article/2010/06/23/AR201 0062305311.html. Accessed 24 June 2010

Bell D (2007) The First Total War: Napoleon's Europe and the birth of warfare as we know it. Houghton Mifflin, Boston

Ben Ami S (2006) Scars of war, wounds of peace: the Israeli-Arab tragedy. Oxford University Press, New York

Carroll J (2006) House of war: the Pentagon and the disastrous rise of American power. Houghton Mifflin, Boston

Enderlin C (2003) Shattered dreams: the failure of the peace process in the Middle East, 1995–2002. Other Press, New York

Freud S (1961) Civilization and its discontents. Norton, New York

Freud S, Einstein A (1931–1932) Why war? A correspondence between Einstein and Freud. http://pagesperso-orange.fr/chabrieres/texts/whywar.html

Fukuyama F (1993) The end of history and the last man. Harper Perennial, New York

Ginat J (2006) Hudna: origins of the concept and its relevance to the Arab-Israeli conflict. In: Podeh E, Kaufman A (eds) Arab-Jewish relations: from conflict to resolution. Sussex Academic Press, East Sussex

Howard M (2000) The invention of peace. Yale University Press, New Haven

Huntington SP (1998) The clash of civilizations and the remaking of world order. Simon & Schuster, New York

Kilcullen D (2009) The accidental guerilla: fighting small wars in the midst of a big one. Oxford University Press, New York

LeShan L (2002) The psychology of war: comprehending its mystique and its madness. Helios Press, New York

Oz A (2006) By the light of a truce. In: The globe and mail. Nov 29 edn. http://www.theglobeandmail. com/servlet/story/LAC.20061129.COMIDE29/TPStory/Comment

Pickthall M (2004) The glorious Qur'an: text and explanatory translation. Tahrike Tarsile, Elmhurst

Roosevelt FD (1943) Fireside Chat 27: on the Tehran and Cairo conferences. http://millercenter. org/scripps/archive/speeches/detail/3333. Accessed 22 Nov 2011

Ross D (2004) The missing peace: the inside story of the fight for Middle East peace. Farrar, Straus and Giroux, New York

Sharp J (2008) How wars end. Five part audio series. http://www.pri.org/theworld/?q=how_wars_end

Stein K (1999) Heroic diplomacy: Sadat, Kissinger, Carter, begin and the quest for Arab-Israeli peace. Routledge, New York

Tuchman B (2004) The guns of August. Ballantine Books, New York

Van Creveld M (1991) The transformation of war. The Free Press, New York

von Bernhardi F (1912) Germany and the next war. Edward Arnold, London

Weigert G (1997) A note on Hudna: peace making in Islam. In: Lev Y (ed) War and society in the Eastern Mediterranean, 7th-15th centuries. Brill Publishers, Leiden

Chapter 3
Peace-less Reconciliation

Anat Biletzki

Abstract Reconciliation is commonly viewed either as a step toward peace, taken in the aftermath of violent conflict, or as a closing note of the move from war to peace, constituting a definitive feature of a just peace. This article posits an alternative role for reconciliation *during* times of conflict and suggests that, in certain cases, it may be a necessary first step out of hostilities. We suggest three elements – recognition of asymmetry, determination of victimhood, and, most crucially, a narratively based acknowledgment – to distinguish such peace-less reconciliation from its more conventional counterpart in the context of transitional justice. Using the Israeli-Palestinian ongoing, violent conflict as an illustrative case in point, we investigate these factors at work in current attempts at reconciliation before the cessation of violence and claim that the dearth of such efforts may explain the persistence of that unattenuated enmity. Whether the specific idiosyncrasies of the Israeli-Palestinian story can be generalized to a more comprehensive theory of peace-less reconciliation remains an elusive question.

A. Biletzki (✉)
Philosophy, Tel Aviv University, Tel Aviv, Israel

Philosophy and Political Science, Quinnipiac University, 275 Mount Carmel Ave.,
Hamden, CT 06518, USA
e-mail: anatbi@post.tau.ac.il

Justice brings peace, not the other way around.
(group e-mail from Muhammed Jabali, one of the young leaders
of the "Tent Revolution," Tel Aviv, August 2011)

3.1   Introduction

One's ruminations, even if they be submissions of theoretical and conceptual
deliberation, are born of a time and place; my thoughts arise in and from a place –
Israel-Palestine – in current, dire times. This does not, however, condemn such
reflections to the status of a "case-study," purporting to be an instance of a generalized
theory of reconciliation. Rather, the aim of this exercise is to broach the issue of reconciliation and, using the experience, the insights, and the convolutions that go with a
place and a time, submit a nuanced reading of what reconciliation is, what it can be,
and what it should be. This last, however, does not pretend to be a prescriptive agenda
advising other times and places; it is, rather, a particular description – in Wittgensteinian
mode – of an undeniably contextual reconciliation. Wittgenstein, one of the twentieth
century's most enigmatic philosophers, in what is known as his later period, believed
that philosophy should be done in a different way than it had been traditionally
pursued. Instead of looking for some version of a theoretical truth, we should instead
look at how language is used ordinarily, describe these uses, and thereby acquire
insights into the meanings of our words and our human behavior. He says: "We can
only describe and say, human life is like that" (1967), enjoining philosophers to
refrain from explanations and general theories (to be kept for scientists). With
Wittgenstein, who also says that understanding can be had by "seeing connexions"
(1953, 122), this professes to throw light on other cases; *pace* Wittgenstein, it may
even lead to a theory of reconciliation being developed in conjectural provinces.

This is the conventional wisdom: First, war or violent conflict, then cessation of
hostilities (termed cease-fire, truce or armistice), then a somewhat-peace, then a
transitional period during which warring parties aspire to arrive at justice – i.e., to
make the peace a just peace (usually posited as the attainment of "democracy").
Accordingly, successful transitional justice procedures may lead to varying degrees
of a just peace. The conventional assumption that accompanies such wisdom holds
that *during* a time of war, *during* violent conflict, there are no normal, explicit mani-
festations of peaceable relational co-existence between the parties. It is after war, in
post-conflict time, during a period that aspires, perhaps, to peace though not yet a just
peace, that reconciliation makes its entrance. And, indeed, the way the tale of transitional justice is recounted, it is up to reconciliation to ensure that final stage of just
peace. Reconciliation is, in a sense, a necessary condition of just peace and, in that
same sense, it must precede the ultimate end-point, by a temporal, procedural or even
formal hair-split. In some renditions, apposite, authentic reconciliation is precisely
definitive and constitutive of that final end-point. In others it is only one means –
others being an interim truce, negotiations, peace-treaties, democratic institutions,
longer-term education, a period of calm – on the way to that end of just peace. In all
versions, however, before the beginning-point of this progress, i.e., still in the time

of conflict, reconciliation is absent. That, in fact, is the defining trait of violent conflict – it is devoid of the compassionate understanding, the elements of forgiving, the thoughtful give-and-take of human intercourse that are demanded by reconciliation. In other words, no matter where in the time line between violent warfare and a true, just peace one places reconciliation, whether simultaneous with that peace, immediately pre-peace, or on the way-to-peace, reconciliation does not take place in wartime. There is a presupposition at work here – that reconciliation can only manifest itself after violent conflict has been put to rest: in the *wake* of conflict.[1]

I put on offer a different time line; more significantly, I attempt to sidestep questions of time or temporal necessity in the investigation of genuine reconciliation. Initially counter-intuitive, the proposal here entertained is that reconciliation, although relevant to a fully realized, just peace, is not dependent on the cessation of violence; reconciliation does not need to wait for even a semblance of peace, a quiet on the front, a truce, a cease-fire, peace negotiations or treaties. In some cases – paradigmatically in the Israeli-Palestinian case – reconciliation might be, instead, a necessary step in the ending of war itself. This choice of formulation, then, posits an integrated process between reconciliation and (even preliminary) peacemaking. Though the two, reconciliation and peacemaking, should be distinguished – and a differentiation between several types of peacemaking with attendant value judgment as to their very different contributions to authentic peace will ensue – it is here submitted that the latter, the so-called "peacemaking" that heralds cease-fires, truces, or even veritable peace treaties, does not necessarily come before the former, that is, reconciliation. Whether reconciliation can stand alone – that is to say, whether we can broach ante-peace or peace-less reconciliation – is the further question to be raised here; a final query will try to assess this variety of reconciliation.

3.2 Preliminary Clarifications

Admittedly, the reconciliation being addressed here is political reconciliation, in the very categorical sense that its purported absence is due to political conflict.[2] Nevertheless, a number of additional clarifications are called for; certain conceptual truisms must be exposed and either accepted (as true) or rejected (as inappropriate or, sometimes, fallacious).

---

[1] *The International Journal of Transitional Justice*, puts its agenda "to effect social reconstruction in the wake of widespread violence." The *Stanford Encyclopedia of Philosophy*, under the entry "Transitional Justice," makes it even more explicit. It begins with a temporal description, "Once violent conflict between two groups has subsided," and goes on to *define* transitional justice as a field which is involved with an "investigation of the aftermath of war." Most writers on reconciliation and forgiveness or reconciliation as being a mainstay of transitional justice invariably use that coinage – "aftermath of war/conflict" – in any analysis of reconciliation.

[2] I do not refer here to the minimalist sense of political reconciliation that Griswold (2007, 193) mentions.

First, although the idea of *re*conciliation appears semantically distinct from conciliation – reconciliation assumes an earlier togetherness, before the onset of violence, which is to be *re*constituted after cessation of conflict[3] – our use of the term, in keeping with ordinary usage, will be indifferent to this supposition. Indeed, political reconciliation as we understand it and as we charge it to function is forward looking and future-oriented. This is not to say that the work of reconciliation does not require a very demanding look at the past, soon to be elaborated on; rather, its *re*institution as an earlier state of peaceful co-existence between warring partners is not necessary or obligatory. Sometimes, oft-times, the history of a conflict does not include any such earlier state, and reconciliation must bring about a novel, hitherto unknown and perhaps unimagined state of affairs.

Secondly, in contrast to several models of political reconciliation that focus on and emphasize ritual and apology, indeed, the ritual itself of apology, this investigation will be invigorated primarily by a cognitive view of reconciliation rather than any procedural one.[4] Differently put, we are pursuing the idea of *ideal* reconciliation, an essential conciliation between persons, rather than any performative version of such. Again, this is not to say that such reconciliation does not permit or sometimes even require certain formal elements, which will soon be suggested; it is only to say that these are not necessarily a matter of apology or other performatives.

An additional element to be elucidated concerning the phenomenon of reconciliation is the relative status of the parties to be reconciled. There is no *a priori* demand concerning the parity of social, political or economic status and behavior – or, for that matter, their absence – between the factions. To be sure, one can imagine reconciliation between parents and children, between bosses and their underlings, between masters and slaves, between rich and poor. Still, we are often witness to a common, very conventional *mantra* demanding equality and mutuality of recognition that are needed for true reconciliation to occur. We will (again with Wittgenstein), contrary to these normative attitudes, descriptively note and emphasize differences of status and, furthermore, ask about their significance for the achievement of reconciliation. At the very least, these disparities hold great import for the *process* of reconciliation.

Finally, genuine personal reconciliation has often been conceptually analyzed as essentially involving forgiveness.[5] It is important to note that we are here speaking

---

[3] See e.g., Griswold (2007, xxv). Long and Brecke (2003) talk of "*reconciliation* – mutually conciliatory accommodation between former antagonists," but interestingly, in an earlier working-paper version of their book (Brecke and Long 1998), they had written "*reconciliation* - returning to peace, harmony, or amicable relations after a conflict." See also Walker (2006, 384) on restorative justice – rather than reconciliation, but still dealing with "re" – as not "assuming a morally adequate status quo ante."

[4] This personalized nature of reconciliation does not preclude its political character. It may be somewhat similar to Alice MacLachlan's (2013b) elaboration of "political forgiveness," applying the structure of her type (2), and perhaps then type (3), political forgiveness to political reconciliation.

[5] But see "Reconciliation without apology?" in Griswold (2007, 206–210). See also Derrida (2001).

of personal, political reconciliation; i.e., the reconciliation effected between political, warring groups that happens between individual members of the group (though not necessarily all the members). So, although intuitive understanding maintains that, on a personal level, one can only sincerely reconcile with one's enemies after having forgiven or after being forgiven, the order of things here will be interrogated: political reconciliation is a process which may include individual acts and states of mind of forgiveness, but which does not, of necessity, come to pass after the forgiveness. Reconciling, in our sense, means undergoing processes of change of heart and mind with and *vis à vis* an-other, which may consist of forgiveness but need not inevitably do so. Certainly one – and definitely a group – can find oneself at a certain stage of reconciliation without yet having forgiven or been forgiven. An essential replacement for forgiveness will be considered here and will serve the express purposes of political reconciliation, sometimes beyond the personal.

3.3 Vagaries of the Israeli-Palestinian Conflict

Wittgenstein admonishes us to look at the particular instance rather than the general type. What is the engine of the particular story of reconciliation in Israel-Palestine? Our story is clearly, in this case, about political reconciliation. Traditionally, standard categorizations of political reconciliation recognize two main types: international as opposed to civil reconciliation.[6] Within the grouping of civil reconciliation there is an additional sub-categorization distinguishing between civil conflicts where warring parties are various ethnic, religious, or racial groups, with the conflict defined by their variety, and civil conflicts between colonizing and indigenous groups. Quintessential international conflicts are the long-term rift between Germany and France or the shorter-term wars of history (the Spanish-American War, the Sino-Japanese War, the World Wars; the list is endlessly populated). Prototypical civil conflicts of recent times are the Rwandan atrocities, the Baltic wars of the 1990s, and the horrors of Sudan. Conflicts arising from processes of (de-)colonization are the paradigmatic struggle of Native Americans or the more current contests in India and Indochina. And there are, certainly, conflicts which are not facilely categorized or that may inhabit multiple categories; such were, for example, both the South African and the Irish imbroglios.

How are we to categorize the Israeli-Palestinian conflict? Usual parlance places it as an international conflict between two national groups, originally perceived as

---

[6] More precisely, scholarship on political reconciliation takes one of two directions: (a) the categorization of civil and international reconciliation based on traditional political thought, international relations, and history. See e.g., Long and Brecke (2003), who provide separate treatments of "international war and reconciliation" and "civil war and reconciliation"; (b) the very contemporary and up-to-date discussion which appears to be focusing on reconciliation within societies (e.g., Schaap 2005).

Israelis and Arabs, later recognized as Israelis and Palestinians. The former perception is problematic in ascribing to Arabism, per se, a national identity; the latter was tardy in recognizing the national aspirations of the Palestinians. In some discussions these two national groups are already viewed as two state-groups, one a real, existing, functioning state – Israel, the other a state-in-the-making – Palestine. There is a whiff of disingenuousness in this depiction if one considers that an important ingredient of the Palestinian agenda in this conflict is specifically the creation of a Palestinian state. In contrast to the international categorization, the Israel-Palestine conflict has also been depicted as a civil war between either two ethnic groups or two religious groups, both vying for power over and ownership of the same real estate. When presented in such civil terminology, the Israel-Palestine problem has, appropriately but very imprecisely, been termed the Jewish-Palestinian or even the Jewish-Muslim conflict.[7] Other internal-civil portrayals of the conflict in which these two groups are embroiled hinge on the ideology, advent and success of Zionism as a colonialist project which has usurped the land, rights, lives and even identity of the indigenous group – the Palestinians. In this case one will hear it called the Zionist-Palestinian conflict.

This variation in categorizing the conflict – international, civil, colonial – results in a name-change, of course (the Arab-Israeli problem, the Palestinian-Israeli conflict, the Jewish-Muslim clash; the Jewish-Palestinian war; the Zionist-Palestinian conflict), but in much more than that. Distinct categorizations lead to different narratives, indeed to different dates marking the beginning of the conflict, from the end of the nineteenth century, i.e., the beginning of Zionism, through 1948, the establishment of the State of Israel, to 1967, the beginning of the – or that particular – occupation of Palestinian lands. Lest you think that the title of the conflict, its narrative, or the date of its inception brings its identification to closure, note the further complication deriving from Palestinians who *are* citizens of Israel – in other words, self-perceived members of the Palestinian nation who are citizens of the State of Israel, marking a well-known, but no less tricky, divorce between nation and state in the Jewish nation-state. So, although emphatically recognized as a matter for political reconciliation, the Israel-Palestine conflict is not easily put in any of the slots of international, civil, or colonial contexts of conflict.[8]

There is call here for a methodological confession alluded to above: I will be adopting, throughout, a stance of uniqueness in describing this particular conflict and its attendant, still non-existent, reconciliation; but this distinctiveness will optimally carry further implications for the idea of reconciliation. The claim of distinctiveness in this particular (perhaps international, perhaps civil) situation is what invigorates the allegation that standard analyses of reconciliation need refinement or change

---

[7] Indeed, one of the most common but, to my mind, supremely inadequate explanations for the conflict's persistence holds that it is extreme, fundamentalist, religious elements on each side to the conflict that are ultimately to blame for its intractability.

[8] I continue to name this conflict the "Israeli-Palestinian" conflict – merely for convenience of usage, adopting conventionality for ease of reference. In essence it is the Zionist-Palestinian war.

and that this is true especially concerning their placement of reconciliation at the post-conflict point. In other words, it is the vagaries of the Israeli-Palestinian conflict that will be called upon to illuminate the more general concept of reconciliation. There is still and always the lingering doubt that perhaps we are all contextually bound to the conflicts we know or are a part of. Perhaps any analysis of any particular conflict is destined to be unique and particular. Perhaps all we can do, in Wittgensteinian manner, is describe, not explain or fall prey to the "craving for generality" (1958, 17). In that case, however, the added value of the theoretical terminology (categories, narratives, labels) of conflict, resolution and reconciliation with which we are engaging is called upon to serve a different purpose: a particular description, not explanation, of what must take place if reconciliation is to be achieved.

3.4 Reconciliation During Conflict

There have been 44 or 63 or over 100 years of conflict between Zionists and Palestinians (neither uniquely national nor ethnic; neither particular states nor religions): wars, blood-letting, killings, suicide-bombings, regular bombings, targeted assassinations, terrorist activities, invasions, and sieges. There have been periods of intense physical violence; there have been periods of what is termed in Israel "low scale violence"; there have been wars, usually marked by a beginning and end date[9]; there have been uprisings and invasions; and there have been periods of calm – some touted as bespeaking a "peace-process," though never as peace.[10] But since there has been continuous oppression and occupation, it is reasonable to opine that the conflict has been with us for decades, not ever letting up or reaching anything akin to a period of even transitional peace. A typical, divergent opinion describes the years between 1993 and 2000, usually called the Oslo years, as such an endeavor of peacemaking; I hope to dispel that illusion. For the proposition on offer here is that the lack of any progress that would lead to a long-lasting truce, treaty, period of transitional peace, or, of course, a semblance of a real, just peace is the result of no real moves being made towards reconciliation. It is my further thesis that such reconciliation requires a number of elements that have rarely been promoted during 63 years of the State of Israel. Without such elements of reconciliation, pursued or attained *during* such conflict, any gestures of tentative peace are either spurious or, even if naïvely construed as authentic, doomed to fail.

It is imperative to clarify: this is not a list of necessary and sufficient conditions for reconciliation to materialize. It is rather an investigation of moments of

---

[9] It is an oft-remarked truism that at any time in the past 60 years, any 20-year old could report on five wars that she had personally lived through.

[10] See Biletzki (2007) for a view of the inanity and insignificance of that specific term, "peace-process."

reconciliation that are necessary for the begetting of peace. Remarkably, in specific conflicts – South Africa, for instance – some of these points were reached, in public and global consciousness, while the conflict was raging. I submit that, since *none* of them has surfaced in any substantial form and that, in fact, they are all vehemently and consensually denied in Israel, it has proven impossible to even begin to consider a germination of peace.[11] While the first two functions below, recognition of asymmetry and identification of victimhood, are contingent situations whose ascertainment may be context-dependent, the third – narrative and acknowledgment – is a *sine qua non* of reconciliation, whether during or post-conflict. This last, however, is seductive and paradoxical precisely in that it does not require peace (or any version of less- or non-conflictual situations dubbed "peace") for its embodiment. What, then, are the desirable elements of reconciliation that ought to emerge *during* conflict?

3.4.1 Recognition of Asymmetry (When It Is the Fact of the Matter)

The semantics of several or most of the terms in our repertoire of war and peace – especially "war," "conflict," and "compromise" – presupposes symmetry between the warring sides. Interestingly, apology and forgiveness are not prey to this default. Indeed, in the analysis of reconciliation which claims apology and forgiveness as essential elements of reconciliation, there must be, at the very least, a recognized wrongdoer and a recognized victim of the wrongdoing if apology and forgiveness are to take place. But just as interesting is the conceptual possibility that reconciliation can travel both ways: it has no *a priori* commitment to either a differential of status between reconciling sides or, alternatively, to equality of status between them. So one can surely imagine a situation where both sides to a conflict are wrongdoers and both sides are victims. If we try to entertain a process of reconciliation that, as we conceive it, does not necessarily entail apology and/or forgiveness, it is not implausible to think of the sides of such reconciliation as equals and of the reconciliatory relation as symmetrical. Such has been the lot of political common wisdom on the Israeli-Palestinian conflict – positing two sides, each guilty of wrongdoings, each victimized by the other, each needing to compromise, and both equally culpable for the creation and subsistence of the conflict.

It is our wont to question this conventional wisdom.[12] Since the diagnostics of a wrongdoing is a necessary point of analysis in any reconciliation, assessing the relationship between conflicted parties correctly as symmetrical or asymmetrical is mandatory for the reconciliation to be true conciliation. Now, the *bon temps* of

---

[11] A political history of the last two decades can discern the deterioration – from the 1993–2000 supposed peace-period of the Oslo accords (which included nary a sign of the elements at issue here) to shorter and shorter periods of "cease-fires," "truces," and other fictional attempts at "peace."

[12] See Biletzki (2008).

contemporary peace-discourse invigorates several factors leaning towards symmetry. Clearly, it is manifest that both sides have perceptions of wrongs having been done to them. Additionally, contemporary political fashion embraces the idea of third parties as "unbiased mediators" showing no (justified or unjustified) partiality to either side of the conflict. And, on the whole, political audiences, as opposed to political players, are more amenable to "there are two sides to every story" than to a one-sided culprit-victim ontology. However, in spite of this general proclivity for symmetry, it is critical for the purpose of *bona fide* reconciliation to arrive at the cognizance that, in a particular story, the descriptive – but no less essential for that – truth might be one of asymmetry: one side may be more in the wrong than the other, one side may have suffered more profusely than the other, one side violated the rights of the other more grievously – one side was more a victim than the other.

3.4.2   Who Is the Victim?

At this point in the argument we do well to distinguish between interpersonal reconciliation and political reconciliation – the latter being effected between a state/group/community, or its representatives, and a state/group/community or an individual. There are various structural options in the distinctive brand of political reconciliation but its definitive trait involves a reconciling public entity (state/group/ community or its representatives) on at least one side of the reconciliation. Now, in the case of Israel-Palestine, it is abundantly clear that both Jews and Palestinians, as individuals, have been wronged by individuals of the other group; that is to say, they have been victims. But the pertinent question before us concerns the victimhood of a whole group. And here we come across an interesting variation within the common discourse of reconciliation: Jews justly profess to victimhood of 2,000 years, to a history of anti-Semitism, and to the ultimate victimhood, bar none, during the Holocaust. Indeed, it is a universally accepted platitude, and no less correct for that, that the State of Israel was established – that is, it was voted on by the United Nations General Assembly and legitimized by the global community[13] – as a result of the genocide perpetrated against the Jews in the Holocaust. Palestinians, on their part, point to a victimhood of a little over a century (since the establishment of the political movement of Zionism in the late nineteenth century), to a history of Zionist colonization, and to their ultimate victimhood in the *Naqba*, the Catastrophe of 1947–1948, when about two-thirds of indigenous Palestinians living on their land in Palestine were expelled from their homes to become refugees in a grand operation of ethnic cleansing that, many claim, has been going on ever since.

---

[13] The *de facto* founding of the state was a domestic decision of local powers that be in the Jewish community in Palestine (under the British Mandate); the international establishment of the new state is legally ambiguous since General Assembly decisions, such as that of the partition of Palestine, are not binding, but *de facto* recognition (custom) by the international community is, as is the General Assembly's acceptance of Israel as a member of the U.N.

In what way is this a variation on the ordinary reconciliation-discourse of victimhood? The symmetrical form of reconciliation, based on a (possibly false) presupposition of symmetry, involves wrongdoing by each side of a conflict towards the other; each is a wrong-doer but, more importantly and more pertinently for apology or forgiveness, each is a victim of the other. Yet engaging with reconciliation that involves recognition of the other side's suffering, i.e., the other side's victimhood, one cannot help but notice the strangeness of the supposed symmetry in the Israeli-Palestinian case. Both peoples are victims, with a history and evidence to buttress their respective claims of victimhood. But the Jews are victims of history, anti-Semitism, and the Germans; the Palestinians are victims of the Jews. Lacking the symmetry of the victimizer-victim relationship between Jews and Palestinians, it is incongruous to posit equal victimhood for them. *Grosso modo*, and again contrary to conventional wisdom, although there are recognizable, particular cases of individual victimizers and victims on both sides, there is group victimhood, political victimhood – between Jews and Palestinians – on one side only.[14]

The issues of symmetry and victimhood and their accurate identification are circumstantial: circumstances of diverse situations admit various versions of symmetry, asymmetry, and victimhood. There may be mutuality involved (in, e.g., causation of suffering) but this does not imply moral equivalence. So it is incumbent on participants in reconciliation to get "the story" right, or as right as is possible for the forward-looking orientation of reconciliation. In that sense, then, the possibility of reconciliation, which is dependent on Truth – who did what to whom, is indifferent to its positioning during or in the wake of conflict. The corollary is that it could just as well be emphasized (for our purposes) that the end of conflict is not a requirement for these two features of reconciliation. But, given asymmetry and determination of victimhood, there is then a normative condition of the move to reconciliation that is far better placed during an ongoing conflict. Simply put: without the correction of narrative and the pursuant acknowledgment there is less chance of climbing out of the depths of violent, historically weighty conflict. This kind of reconciliation cannot wait for peace, for it is its midwife.

3.4.3 Narrative and Acknowledgment

Narrative and changes of narrative have become staples of the conversation. Griswold's (2007) emphasis on narrative functions significantly in his explication of forgiveness; I do the same for reconciliation. Added to the above insistence on admission of asymmetry and dissimilar victimization, the narrative that challenges

---

[14] There are interesting complexities here having to do with the option of indirect victimhood. For instance, Van Evera (Memory and the Arab-Israel conflict: time for new narratives, unpublished manuscript, 2003) has written that Palestinians are *indirect* victims of Christian anti-Semitism, since Zionism was a reaction to and a result of anti-Semitism. The unsurprising vernacular rejoinder has the Palestinians saying "why should we pay for what the Germans did to the Jews?".

us is the Jewish narrative rather than the Palestinian one. In other words, and again in contradistinction to the conventional approach, this thesis does not call for a mutual recognition, by both sides to a conflict, of the other side's narrative. It rather makes a new, strident demand on one side's narrative.[15]

In telling the story of victimhood, Jews point to history and anti-Semitism. This part of Jewish-Israeli identity carries forward with stupendous consistency, almost inertia, into the story of the establishment of the State of Israel. The narrative on that specific piece of history – from 1945 until 1949, the establishment of the state, aka as the War of Independence and sometimes even the War of Revival – includes the mythological structure reminiscent of the whole of Jewish history: the few against the many. The "many" of this particular story are the millions of Arabs surrounding the Jews of Israel or the several Arab states attacking the State of Israel. Astoundingly, nowhere do Palestinians, the indigenous people of the land, figure in the conventional Israeli story. Or, if they are present in the tale, they are depicted as hapless locals who were enticed to leave by other Arab states with promises of victorious return to their homes and lands after the war.

Nowhere is mention made, in the Israeli narrative, of hundreds of villages devastated, demolished, and desecrated – or of hundreds of thousands of people driven out to a refugee existence of over 60 years that has burgeoned into one of the world's longest and greatest refugee crises. The striking point is that these untold facts, making up the essential core of Palestinian story-telling (and therefore automatically suspected, by Israelis, of being a Palestinian myth), have been meticulously chronicled since the 1980s by a group of *Israeli* historians, the New Historians, bent on "outing" the data in Israeli archives. These contrary-to-the-received accounts have now become authoritative history. It is therefore all the more striking that in Jewish-Israeli (not to mention American) common discourse, in elementary school education, in song and story, and in popular media there is no *Naqba*. The professionals' history has changed; the national, cultural narrative has not. Explanation for such a discrepancy between what has been entertained and then accepted in certain professional quarters as history and what functions as the common narrative is straightforward and hinges on these being two very different contexts: the academic-historical context and the popular cultural-political life of a society. When do those contexts meet? When does that known history become the received narrative? Differently put, how can the story of history become a deep narrative of a people?

The essential step is that of *acknowledgment*, an acknowledgment that must accompany the historical account to make it deep, i.e., to make it significant for reconciliation.[16] It is not enough to tell the "unrelated-to-us" story of the *Naqba*; its significance is such that Jewish Israelis must take responsibility for it if it is to change from a historical tale carrying no moral weight to a people's narrative that is

---

[15] See Jacob Schiff (2008) for a compelling connection between narrative and acknowledgment (albeit in the context of structural injustice).

[16] This is reminiscent of MacLachlan (2013a) where acknowledgment is called upon to negate the founding myths of a state.

part of a common identity – with accountability attached to actions. That kind of acknowledgement-carrying-narrative carries political risk; but only acknowledgment can give rise to reconciliation. Neither apology alone, forgiveness alone, or apology and forgiveness together can function as this necessary facet to usher in political reconciliation. Only acknowledgment.[17] On multiple occasions I have encountered Palestinians who are eager to begin and then continue the process of reconciliation; arrestingly, their demand has always been "only acknowledge."

The normativity of the requirement of acknowledgment is not unrelated to the earlier elements – precise appraisal of asymmetry and consciousness of obvious victimhood. One could even say that such appraisal and consciousness may be a necessary part of acknowledgement; or more expressly, that we may be called on to *acknowledge* asymmetry and specific victimhood. I think, however, that this belies an important aspect of the reconciliation-during-conflict that is at issue here. The descriptive, truth-telling assessment of asymmetry and victimhood – even when carried out in the time of conflict, perhaps especially when carried out then – does not acknowledgment make. A paradigmatic example of such (historical!) truth telling *sans* acknowledgment is the case of Benny Morris (1988), one of Israel's New Historians, who is to be credited for exposing the previously uncovered facts of Israeli malfeasance during the Arab-Israeli war of 1948 and its aftermath. Morris's project is, indeed, a matter of doing history, not a case of conducting political or human intercourse or, for that matter, professing value judgments on those historical events. When asked, several years after his shattering findings, about Israeli culpability and wrongdoing, he famously said that not only were Palestinians "transferred" out of their lands but that "the non-completion of the transfer was a mistake" (Shavit 2004). This was admission, but quite the contrary of acknowledgment. The acknowledgment of wrongdoing harbors accountability. Buttressed by recognition of asymmetry it is, instead of a multiplicity of neutral, mutually told narratives, a one-sided taking-of-responsibility for the victimhood of the other side. The deep-rooted seeds of conflict cannot be extracted without such narrative acknowledgment. For that same reason, the conflict itself cannot be truly ended before an explicit act of acknowledgment is enacted.[18]

3.5   A Note on Peacemaking and Reconciliation

We have been witness, mostly in the past two decades, to several "peacemaking" projects; that is to say, groups of Palestinians and Jewish Israelis collaborating in mutual and common ventures whose professed agenda is "peacemaking." We speak

---

[17] See Trudy Govier (2003) for a view of apology as a form of acknowledgment. As explained above, we focus on the cognitive, epistemic essence of acknowledgment, rather than its performativity as evidenced in apology.

[18] There are affinities, to be investigated elsewhere, between this view of acknowledgment and Hannah Arendt's political forgiveness.

here not of programs that involve formal political negotiations or culminate in signed treaties – that is left for diplomats and politicians, i.e., for the official authorities. These peacemaking groups are, to be sure, worthy candidates for reconciliation as adumbrated above. First there are the professionals: groups of doctors from both the Israeli and Palestinian sides who work together to alleviate suffering; teachers from both sides who develop joint educational programs; psychologists, architects, engineers, social workers, and students of just as many disciplines – all organizing in professional groups in order to engage in a semblance of co-existence which, they believe, can either lead to peace or take its place when it tarries. (An abiding question inquires how this kind of engagement inter-relates with the official political engagement and negotiations.) Then there are several organizations that gather children and youth from both sides to participate in sports together, or go to camps (sometimes abroad) together, or play in orchestras together. There is the paradigmatic Israeli-Palestinian Science Organization (IPSO) established by Sari Nusseibeh, President of Al-Quds University in Palestine, and Menachem Yaari, Chair of the Israel Academy of Sciences, devoted to developing cooperative scientific projects by Israelis and Palestinians in concert. And most advertised, there are now cooperative economic projects, launched by Israeli and Palestinian businessmen, carrying forward the new Gospel – attributed, among others, to Prime Minister Benjamin Netanyahu – that joint business enterprises will usher in the long-dawdling peace.

The ironic voice ascertained above is intentional: these are all so-called peacemaking programs, but do they harbor reconciliation? What would be a criterion to demarcate projects of reconciliation from those of opportunistic "peacemaking"? Do we envision one and can we formulate it? If, as I now suggest explicitly, a process of reconciliation must be at work before any talk of a just peace can ensue, does it not become obligatory to distinguish between specious peacemaking – games and shows of peace – and authentic reconciliation? [19]

Recall that the necessary pre-conditions of reconciliation were, first, the recognition of asymmetry in order, secondly, to acknowledge a real victim. Much is demanded of such recognition. The asymmetry of the conflict, what has been termed the "differential of power" and what we have ascertained as inequity in history, must enter into authentic peacemaking – predicated on genuine reconciliation – by its explicit negation: that is to say, an unequivocal insistence on formal, semantic and behavioral equality in any and all activities of joint peacemaking programs must be mandated and championed. This may be difficult to accomplish but is vital if such enterprises are not to fall, again, into the historical asymmetry, inequality, and one-sided control that has been at the essence of the conflict. A fitting example is given in IPSO guidelines, seemingly naïve in focusing on numbers, which dictate that all its projects be peopled by a precisely equal number of Palestinians and Israelis. Other organizations are more lax about more than just numbers. For example, we find more ambiguity in financial and business ventures, where income and investments

---

[19] By "authentic" I do not make a turn here from political reconciliation to the personal reconciliation between (all) individuals of the warring sides. Authentic reconciliation is acknowledgment-bearing.

make their way to Palestine, specifically to Palestinian businessmen, but financial control and profits are decidedly on the Israeli side. This might be, indeed, an intangible criterion – unequivocal parity as the manifestation of the recognition and repair of asymmetry – but it is key to our analysis: disregarding the asymmetry reinforces the historical, political and economic imbalance of power that has accompanied Israeli-Palestinian relations *ab initio*.

Recognition of asymmetry was posited as the first step, with one-sided identification of the victims a second necessary point of reconciliation. In this puzzle of distinguishing between *bona fide* projects and organizations of reconciliation and what I have elsewhere called "the peace industry" (Biletzki 2008), acknowledgment now plays a subtle role. Should one celebrate or view as insidious the impressive peace institutions in splendid buildings, which cost millions of dollars to plan and construct, and which hold as many receptions and peace banquets as programs for Israeli and Palestinian children or business meetings for Israeli-Palestinian "partners"? Is past asymmetry replaced, in these cases, by current impartiality? Is there any true acknowledgement of past wrongs? An abstruse case in point is an institution like the Peres Center for Peace, Israel's most grandiose peace spectacle. Going through its multitudinous publications – pamphlets, invitations, reports, position papers, etc. – one cannot but be struck by the absence of any mention of the word "Occupation." If Occupation, which is the formal, legally accepted status of the Palestinian Territories, is ne'er to be found in the words of a peace center, it is no surprise that the *Naqba*, the constitutive narrative of the Palestinians that must be acknowledged, is absent as well. This is a peace-center devoid of acknowledgment or reconciliation and cannot therefore aspire to peacemaking. More significantly, bogus peacemaking is not only divorced from acknowledgment-based reconciliation; it rather preserves the continued oppression and current occupation of Palestinians by Israelis.

3.6   Conclusion – A Curious Twist of Symmetry

Is there a noticeable instance of acknowledgment for the sake of true reconciliation? Two fascinating groups in Israel-Palestine provide not only exemplars but also, in the case of the second, somewhat of a foil to the whole theoretical exercise which has engaged us here.

The first is an organization called *Zochrot*. Translated into English, this means "remembering" – in the plural, female voice, in various bodies. No more explicit acknowledgment is imaginable: we or they or you, as women, remember the *Naqba*. The organization, made up of Israelis (both Jewish and Palestinian, both men and women), has adopted the objective of remembering, and more so of reminding, the Israeli public of the Palestinian catastrophe of 1948. Its venue involves Palestinian villages – their inhabitants, their culture, their art, their music, their stories, their tragedies – destroyed during the *Naqba*. It organizes trips and tours to villages and towns that no longer exist, led by guides who know Hebrew and Arabic and by inhabitants who know and remember local history. It publishes articles and interviews on the Palestinian narrative of the *Naqba* years. It holds lectures, symposia, and exhibitions on the *Naqba*. Poignantly, yet effectively, it hangs up road signs all over the land of Israel, marking localities with Palestinian names long ago obliterated. This is physical, cultural, historical, emotional acknowledgment. For *Zochrot*, "acknowledging the past is the first step in taking responsibility for its consequences."[20] This is a case of real reconciliation, constituted of acknowledgment, conducted in these times of dire conflict.

A second reconciliatory group is *Combatants for Peace*. Made up of 600 fighters – quite literally fighters, i.e., Israeli soldiers who have been in battle situations in the killing fields and Palestinian combatants, some even called "terrorists" by the Israeli authorities – this group has decided to "put down our guns, and to fight for peace."[21] They hold meetings discussing how to support peacemaking. They give talks in schools and community centers, enjoining youth and young adults to eschew battle appointments. They build playgrounds where Israeli and Palestinian children play together. And they mutually acknowledge the wrongdoings that they have perpetrated. But there's the rub.

Given a non-ending conflict and also, more so, given an ongoing show of "peacemaking" that has made no headway in the past 44 (or 63 years), it behooves us to think out of the conventional box – particularly the box holding worn-out mantras of peace-processes and negotiations. It has been proposed, above, that one reason for the lack of progress in orthodox peacemaking is the misplacing of reconciliation near the end of the process, specifically in the wake of violence, instead of at its beginning, during on-going strife. Reconciliation, we have said, as opposed to many other games of peacemaking, involves most emphatically the acknowledgment of wrongdoing and admission of its imbalance. But looking at *Combatants for Peace*, who have become almost an icon of reconciliation, one cannot deny that one of the linchpins of *their* concept of reconciliation – which is undeniably a sincere reconciliation – is the insistence on *mutual* acknowledgment of equal wrongdoing and equal victimhood on both sides. This is not to say that *Combatants for Peace* do not recognize the Palestinian *Naqba* or the Israeli Occupation of Palestinian lands: they explicitly make reference to both in explicating their purposes and ends (the end of Occupation and a just peace). Yet they embrace an equal self-recrimination, a well-managed story of symmetry, as the pragmatic means to those ends.

So we conclude with casting doubt. Reconciliation, as carried out by actors like *Zochrot* and *Combatants for Peace*, must start during conflict, it cannot wait for politicians and negotiators, and it is, as such, a peace-less reconciliation. But in cases such as that of Israel-Palestine, when the roots of conflict are so implacably strong and the mythology of identity so rooted and pervasive, changing the received narrative by providing acknowledgment of a one-sided wrongdoing might be a political blunder instead of a courageous, risky political undertaking. Perhaps

---

[20] http://www.Naqbainhebrew.org/index.php?lang=english

[21] http://cfpeace.org/?page_id=2

peace-less reconciliation, precisely due to its convolution within the conflict, requires the pragmatism of a less-than-unequivocal one-sided acknowledgement. Perhaps it needs subtlety in its formulation, and, yes, even a modicum of pragmatism almost to the tune of cynicism. Perhaps we must, with Wittgenstein again, take note of the idiosyncrasies and distinctiveness of various cases, come "back to the rough ground," (1953, 107) and be satisfied with a description, not a theory, of reconciliation without peace.

References

Biletzki A (2007) The language-games of peace. In: Webel C, Galtung J (eds) Handbook of peace and conflict studies. Routledge, London/New York, pp 345–354

Biletzki A (2008) Much ado about nothing: the Israeli-Palestinian peace process. In: Audit of the conventional wisdom. MIT. http://web.mit.edu/cis/editorspick_biletzki08_audit.html

Brecke P, Long WJ (1998) War and reconciliation. Consortium on negotiation and conflict resolution, Georgia Institute of Technology, Working papers series #98-1

Derrida J (2001) On cosmopolitanism and forgiveness. Routledge, London/New York

Govier T (2003) What is acknowledgement and why it is important? In: Parger CAL, Govier T (eds) Dilemmas of reconciliation: cases and concepts. Wifrid Laurier University Press, Waterloo, pp 65–90

Griswold CL (2007) Forgiveness: a philosophical exploration. Cambridge University Press, New York

Long WJ, Brecke P (2003) War and reconciliation: reason and emotion in conflict resolution. MIT Press, Cambridge

Morris B (1988) The birth of the Palestinian refugee problem, 1947–1949. Cambridge University Press, Cambridge/New York/Melbourne

MacLachlan A (2013a) The philosophical controversy over political forgiveness. In: Stokkom BAM et al (eds) Public forgiveness in post-conflict contexts. Intersensia Press, Cambridge, pp 7–64

MacLachlan A (2013b) Government apologies to indigenous peoples. In: MacLachlan A, Speight CA (eds) Justice, responsibility and reconciliation in the wake of conflict. Springer, Dordrecht

Schaap A (2005) Political reconciliation. Routledge, London/New York

Schiff J (2008) Confronting political responsibility: the problem of acknowledgment. Hypatia 23(3):99–117

Shavit A (2004) Survival of the fittest, interview with Benny Morris. Haaretz. http://www.haaretz.com/hasen/pages/ShArt.jhtml?itemNo=380984. Accessed 9 Jan 2004

Walker MU (2006) Restorative justice and reparations. J Soc Philos 37(3):377–395

Wittgenstein L (1953) Philosophical investigations. In: Anscombe GEM, Rhees R (eds) (trans: Anscombe GEM). Blackwell, Oxford

Wittgenstein L (1958) Blue and brown books. Blackwell, Oxford

Wittgenstein L (1967). Remarks on Frazer's golden bough. In: Rhees R (ed) Synthese 17:233–253

Chapter 4
Heidegger and Gandhi: A Dialogue on Conflict and Enmity

Gregory Fried

Abstract While Heidegger and Gandhi share the conviction that conflict is an inevitable feature of the human condition, they differ on what that conflict entails and what it may accomplish. For Gandhi, human finitude means that any individual and any culture will have only a partial perspective on the truth, whether in religious matters or in questions of justice, and therefore conflict is the necessary result of these differences. Although Heidegger also argues that we are finite beings, he would disagree with Gandhi's view that we may critique ourselves and our institutions in the light of a truth that, if only partially glimpsed, transcends our particularity. For Heidegger, there is no transcendence to a world of timeless principles and ideals, only the immanence of historical belonging. This means that while Heidegger believes that conflict plays a role in refining a community's sense of its own historical destiny, he would condemn as nihilism Gandhi's view that conflict can invite us to transcend ourselves. For Heidegger, genuine conflict reveals the opponents as incommensurable enemies; for Gandhi, the goal of conflict must always be the possibility of reconciliation, and conflict must unfold in a way to promote this. The essay argues that Gandhi's position on what I call soft enmity offers a more promising understanding of the dialectic between our rootedness in historical traditions and our need to judge those traditions by standards that go beyond them.

Heidegger—*and Gandhi*? Gandhi—*and Heidegger*? The conjunction might seem improbable, even preposterous. After all, Heidegger was a thinker's thinker,[1] one of the most difficult and profound (his detractors would say obscure) philosophers of the twentieth century, whereas Gandhi frequently repudiated the title of thinker

---

[1] Hannah Arendt called Heidegger "the hidden king" of German philosophy in the 1920s; see Arendt (1978).

G. Fried (✉)
Department of Philosophy, Suffolk University, 8 Ashburton Place, Boston, MA 02108, USA
e-mail: gfried@suffolk.edu

A. MacLachlan and A. Speight (eds.), *Justice, Responsibility and Reconciliation in the Wake of Conflict*, Boston Studies in Philosophy, Religion and Public Life 1, DOI 10.1007/978-94-007-5201-6_4, © Springer Science+Business Media Dordrecht 2013

or scholar, preferring to identify himself as a man of action and of devotion to his faith. Indeed, some might take offense at the juxtaposition of Gandhi and Heidegger. After all, Heidegger was—at least for a time—an ardent supporter and promoter of National Socialism, one of the most violent and racist regimes in human history, whereas Gandhi dedicated his life to nonviolent action as the way to uphold principles of universal justice and human equality. Nevertheless, there are many ways in which their respective thought addresses common concerns, and it is precisely because of their differences that the comparison will be fruitful. Both Heidegger and Gandhi view the modern world as in crisis: Heidegger discerns the root of this crisis in what he calls nihilism, and while Gandhi does not use that term, his view that humanity is on the verge of self-destruction through nuclear war and an overreliance on technology intimates as well a sense that nihilism stalks our modern age.[2] Both argue that the human condition is grounded in facing up to the challenge presented by one's own community's historical situation, and both hold that a kind of critical fidelity to one's own tradition is essential to authentic human life. Heidegger and Gandhi also share a suspicion of technology and modern science as the putative salvation for our woes and as the high road to a true understanding of the human condition. But just what it is that constitutes our era's nihilism, and how human conflict plays into that crisis, is what will provide the ground for the dialogue and the disagreement between Heidegger and Gandhi.

4.1   Beginning with Being: Finitude and the Ethics of Conflict

As Heidegger emphasized many times over the course of his career, the central focus of his thought was "the question of the meaning of Being" (*die Frage nach dem Sinne des Seins*).[3] While Heidegger's work has the reputation (not without reason) of being terribly difficult, his motivating question is in fact quite simple. In German, the word *Sein* is a nominative composed from an infinitive: *sein*, in English, *to be*. The English "Being" obscures what Heidegger is asking about, because "Being" gives the impression that we are inquiring about some *thing*, some fundamental reality that underlies everything else real, a "supreme being," or God, or the equation $E = mc^2$, or what have you. But Heidegger's question is simply about what it means for something, anything, *to be*, not about what explains the substance of all reality. When we say that something *is*, what does that mean? One might be tempted to say that when we say that something *is*, we mean that it endures, that it

---

[2] In 1946, Gandhi wrote about the "cataclysmic changes in the world" brought about by the atom bomb and that "without the recognition of this truth [namely, truth of *satyagraha* as a moral force in each of us], and due effort to realize it, there is no escape from self-destruction." The truth he means is the realization that every human being bears within, even if only dormant, the twin spiritual force of truth and non-violence. See Gandhi (2003, 279–80).

[3] See Martin Heidegger (1962, 1).

exists as present and in some way as meaningful to us. For Heidegger, then, Being itself is *no thing*, but rather how it is that *any* thing that is, in any sense of that little word "is," can be intelligible to us. But that is not yet an answer to the question of the meaning of Being itself; it is only a clarification of the question's scope and domain. Heidegger takes his clue from our sense that what is *endures*, that it is in some sense (however attenuated) *present* to us *in* and *through* time. For Heidegger, *time* is the horizon for the understanding of Being, and we as human beings (what he calls Dasein) have the distinction of being the being for whom Being itself arises as a question. But Heidegger also insists that Being is not simply enduring presence, even if that has become our dominant Western understanding of it, because Being is not merely static presence, as if (again) it were a thing. Rather, Be-*ing* is verbal; it is a *presencing* that also entails *absence*—the coming in and going out of presence.

This may all seem tremendously abstract and infinitely distant from the nitty-gritty of Gandhi's nonviolent political action, but it helps to recall that Gandhi titled his autobiography *The Story of My Experiments with Truth*. That wording is important, and Gandhi meant it with the utmost seriousness. Let's start with "Truth," which is a translation of the Sanskrit *satya*. English and Sanskrit, as well as modern Hindi, German, and ancient Greek, among many other languages, all share a common archaic parentage in the Indo-European language. *Satya*, truth, whose stem, *sat-*, has its ancient root in the Indo-European stem *es-*, which is cognate with the German *ist*, the Greek *esti*, the French and Latin *est*, and the English *is*, among many other related languages.[4] So here we have the link: for both Heidegger and Gandhi, their life's work may be understood as an endeavor to understand this *is*, or Being—although we should be on guard against assuming that they understand or answer the question of Being in the same way. In Gandhi's case, he insists on calling his nonviolent action his *experiments* with truth because he shares a conception of *satya* that is common to the Hindu tradition: *satya* is the absolute Truth,[5] the final reality that transcends all transient phenomena and serves as their source and support. Drawing on the tradition of the Sanskrit mantra, *om tat sat*, Gandhi declares:

> Truth is not a mere attribute of God, but He is That. He is nothing if He is not That. Truth in Sanskrit means *Sat*. *Sat* means *Is*. God is, nothing else is. Therefore the more truthful we are, the nearer we are to God. We *are* only to the extent that we are truthful.[6]

For Gandhi, precisely because this ultimate Truth, as the essence of what is, transcends the world of becoming to which we belong, even if it undergirds it as well, he stresses again and again in his writings that human beings, who are themselves transient elements of the world, may never grasp this final Truth in its entirety while they exist in their present form. (As a Hindu, he leaves open the possibility of *moksha*, a transcendent liberation of the human spirit from the illusions of the world and from the cycle of birth and death, a final and complete unification of the limited

---

[4] See the entry for *es-* in Watkins (1985, 17).

[5] We will render *satya* as capitalized *Truth* to emphasize its distinctive importance in Gandhi's thought; this is consistent with conventions for translating key Hindu terminology.

[6] Quoted in Bondurant (1965, 19).

self with Truth, or Brahman, the true Self.) What this means for Gandhi is that while human beings may have faith in this ultimate Truth, the best we can achieve is to attain glimpses and intimations of it, but we cannot lay claim to authoritative and complete possession of the Truth. Gandhi therefore distinguishes between *absolute* Truth and *relative* truths:

> I worship God as Truth only. I have not yet found him, but I am seeking after Him. I am prepared to sacrifice the things dearest to me in pursuit of this quest. Even if the sacrifice demanded my very life, I hope I may be prepared to give it. But as long as I have not realized this Absolute Truth, so long must I hold by the relative truth as I have conceived it.[7]

For Gandhi, Truth as Absolute is beyond us, even if we catch glimpses of it that illuminate our existence; but because these are only glimpses, they are partial and refracted by the contingent circumstances of the lives that we and our communities are leading, here and now.[8] Gandhi is not a relativist in the sense of a relativism that holds that all truths are relative to historical circumstances and that there is no "Truth" beyond those contingencies. His relativism is a plea for a kind of modesty, in opposition to what we might call an epistemological arrogance: we must concede that the truths to which we have access, though intimations of the absolute Truth will always be distorted by our own biases, desires, and misunderstandings. To take a characteristic quote:

> Finite human beings shall never know in its fullness Truth and Love, which is in itself infinite. But we do know enough for our guidance. We shall err, and sometimes grievously, in our application.[9]

We might call this a *constructive skepticism*, because it is optimistic rather than petulantly deconstructive or hubristically dogmatic. Our finitude makes absolute knowledge of the Absolute virtually impossible, but our finitude is nevertheless illumined by what transcends it, and therefore guided by it, however haltingly. Hence Gandhi's emphasis on "My Experiments" with Truth: what we *hold to be true*, we must also always *hold open to question* through experiences and arguments that challenge these convictions, and we must be ready to adjust our positions as the Truth shows itself in a new light. They are *"My"* experiments, because each of us must come to such challenges to our understandings of the truth from the unique starting place by which we each must start his or her "Story."

---

[7] Gandhi (1957, xiv).

[8] I would argue, though I do not have space to do so here in full, that Gandhi's notion of being a *seeker* after Truth has a great deal in common with Plato's understanding of the nature of the philosophical life. See Fried (2006), where I argue that Plato distinguishes between *zetetic* and *echonic* philosophy, where the former understands truth as a goal to strive for, the latter as a possession to be owned. In my reading, Plato comes down decisively in favor of philosophy as zetetic: as guided by heuristic ideals, as constructively skeptical and non-dogmatic, and yet still able to make claims about justice.

[9] Gandhi (1982, 67), quoted from *Young India*, April 27, 1927.

Heidegger shares with Gandhi the sense that human existence is, as it were, *storied*: that we each inevitably begin with the sheer fact that we are always already born into a specific time and place that gives our world meaning in a richly particular way and that points us in the direction of distinct but bounded horizon of possibilities for our future. He calls this givenness of meaning our *thrownness*, which in turn is part of the *historicity* of our human existence, namely, that we understand our own Being in terms of time. But Heidegger parts company with Gandhi in denying that there is any transcendent reality beyond the historicity of human meaning, beyond the time that we are given and the world that we inhabit as historical beings. Heidegger takes his stand in radical opposition to a Platonism that asserts that what truly *is*, what is most in Being, is a world that is absolute, eternal, unchanging, and complete, a world beyond the shadows and messiness of this world. Furthermore, for Heidegger, Platonism is responsible for a fundamentally distorted interpretation of Being that has had repercussions for the whole history of Western thought and life:

> The entire spiritual existence [Dasein] of the West is determined to this day by [Plato's] doctrine of ideas. Even the concept of God arises from the idea, even natural science is oriented toward it. Christian and rationalist thought are combined in *Hegel*. Hegel, in turn, is the foundation for currents of thought and world views, above all for *Marxism*. If there had been no doctrine of ideas, there would be no Marxism. So Marxism cannot be defeated once and for all unless we first confront the doctrine of ideas and its two-millennia-long history.[10]

Heidegger holds Plato responsible, more than any other philosopher, for the *nihilism* of the West that has culminated in its contemporary crisis, a nihilism he discerns in both the Christian faith in a transcendent God and in the atheist's faith in reason. At the root of this nihilism is a conviction that Being is equivalent with what truly is, and that true Being is something that exists as an *idea* (or perhaps even beyond the Platonic ideas), eternal and accessible to reason, beyond the historical jumble of worldly phenomena. Heidegger attributes the nihilism of Western thought to what he calls its *metaphysics*, by which he means an interpretation of Being that treats Being as simply another being, a thing, rather than the temporal unfolding of a field of meaning within which things in general become meaningful to us.

Heidegger wants to distinguish between *Being* (as the unfolding source of how things are meaningful to us) and *beings* (things, entities, or simply what is), and he argues that forgetting this distinction is what underlies the millennia-long history of Western metaphysics that treats Being as a being. Heidegger would probably argue that Gandhi (like the Greeks) tends to identify Being, truth, and that-which-is (or at least the *supreme* entity). If *satya* means "is-ness," or *Sein*, then it can't be absolute and separable from us, according to Heidegger, even though some entities (mathematical objects, for example) might be. For Heidegger, there is no eternal Truth; instead, there are only epochal *unconcealings* of what the world means to

---

[10] Heidegger (2010, 118), translation amended.

historical human beings. Truth, for Heidegger, is grounded not in a trans-historical reality, but rather in what makes the world open and accessible to us as historically situated beings.

Heidegger famously engaged in dialogues with Eastern thought, but these tentative encounters were with East Asian traditions—the Taoism of China, and the Zen of Japan[11]—not with the myriad traditions of South Asian thought from the Indian subcontinent. Although Heidegger never discussed Gandhi, as far as I know, it is probably fair to say that he would have placed him squarely within the company of Western metaphysics, and he might have attributed this affinity to the Indo-European roots of Hindu metaphysics, which would link it linguistically with the metaphysics of the Greeks. In Gandhi's reading of Hinduism, there are unmistakable parallels to what Heidegger takes to be the nihilism of Platonism: the notion that Being is beyond time and the phenomena of this world, that it is absolute and timeless, perfect and unchanging. That Gandhi often said things such as quoted above—that "I am prepared to sacrifice the things dearest to me in pursuit of this quest" for Absolute Truth, that he would wish to reduce himself to zero, that he strives to attain *moksha* (which he defines as "absolution from the need to have an embodied existence"[12]), and thereby release from the cycle of life and death[13]— Heidegger would take as further signs of a nihilistic understanding of Being. Heidegger draws upon Nietzsche's understanding of nihilism as a retreat into a notion of Being that is hostile to life and all its Becoming, and whether it is a fair characterization or not, he shares with Nietzsche the notion that pining for release from the wheel of life's suffering is a nihilistic attitude: "No Buddhism—the opposite!"[14]

This point leads us directly to the *politics* of Being for Heidegger and Gandhi. In a lecture course delivered in 1933–1934, Heidegger proclaimed:

> For us, the issue is whether we can arrive at an essential understanding of the essence of truth through [Plato's] doctrine of ideas. If we talk of the doctrine of ideas, then we are displacing the fundamental question into the framework of ideas. If one interprets ideas as representations and thoughts that contain a value, a norm, a law, a rule, such that ideas then become conceived of as norms, then the one subject to these norms is the human being—not the historical human being, but rather the human being in general, the human being in itself, or humanity. Here, the conception of the human being is one of a *rational being in general.*

---

[11] For a discussion of this connection, see Parkes (1987).

[12] Gandhi (2003, 273).

[13] For example, in speaking of his experiments with Truth and how far he still has to go: "I must reduce myself to zero." And: "Not until we have reduced ourselves to nothingness can we conquer the evil in us." And: "The first step towards *moksha* is freedom from attachment. Can we ever listen with pleasure to anyone talking about *moksha* so long as our mind is attached to a single object in this world?" See Gandhi (1982, 35, 62) and Gandhi (2003, 81, 28–29, 170).

[14] Heidegger (1989, 171). For a discussion of this passage, see Polt (2006, 174). Heidegger is obviously referring to Buddhism's goal of release in nirvana from life's cycle of suffering, rather than Hinduism's deliverance through *moksha*, but I believe it is fair to say that he would see both notions as closely related and nihilistic, because they seek to nullify the tragic nature of existence through an escape to something beyond it.

In the Enlightenment and in liberalism, this conception achieves a definite form. Here all of the powers against which we must struggle today have their root.

Opposed to this conception are the *finitude, temporality,* and *historicity* of human beings. The confrontation in the direction of the future is not accidental either…[15]

Heidegger spoke these words at the moment of his most ardent activism for National Socialism, when the movement had just arrived at power in Germany and when he was serving as rector of his university as a Party member. For Heidegger, "all of the powers against which we must struggle today" are summed up in the *universalism* of the Enlightenment and of liberalism, a universalism that Heidegger reads all the way back to Plato, and which he traces through Christianity and the secularized versions of Christianity in liberal democracy and international socialism. This universalism, wedded to the notion of *ideas* that transcend particularity, forms the core of the idea that fundamental rights and principles of justice apply generally to all human beings, irrespective of time and place. In this sense, even Marxism, with its projection of an endpoint to all human history that would encompass humanity on a planetary scale, is a form of Platonizing idealism. I mean *idealism* in the following sense here: the focus on an ideal beyond what now is as the criterion for the moral evaluation of what merely *happens to be* in light of what might or *should be.*

When Heidegger opposes this liberal universalism in the grand sense to his conception of "the *finitude, temporality,* and *historicity* of human beings," he means that what is most important to what it means to *be* human is our connection to a *particular* history and a *particular* community rooted in a *particular* homeland. For Heidegger, this belonging is not fungible; it is not something one may simply *choose,* it is something one already is, because it is the source of how the world makes sense to us as bearers of a specific history that *owns* us and binds us within a horizon of meaning. Nevertheless, this same finitude of our identity means that this very identity is always open to question and must be revisited as a question throughout a people's history. Heidegger's opposition to liberal universalism is rooted in his view that a people cannot discover its own identity by measuring it against some transhistorical categories of inalienable rights, human nature, and so forth. Instead, Heidegger argues that each people works out its identity through a constantly renewed confrontation with the meaning of its own past as the foundation for its future. In practice, this meant for Heidegger the absolute rejection of the classic enterprises of liberalism, such as the universal rights of man or the notion of a global "league" of nations, in favor of each people working out its destiny for itself. As I have put it elsewhere, what Heidegger supported was a form of multiculturalism and pluralism—but among nations, not within them.[16]

It is remarkable that Heidegger and Gandhi begin with the premise of the radical finitude of human beings and yet arrive at such different conclusions about what this means for politics. For Heidegger, our finitude precludes universalism; for Gandhi,

---

[15] Heidegger (2010, 127).

[16] See Fried (2000, 19, 233).

the former requires the latter. For Gandhi, our finitude is grounded in our at once being connected to the Truth, the Absolute, while at the same time being unable to grasp that Truth completely as a whole; for Heidegger, our finitude is grounded in his rejection of the very existence of a trans-temporal, eternal, unchanging Reality: all we have is our bounded passage through time, and this is what we must come to terms with; Being is the ground of finitude, not of our link to the infinite. For both Gandhi and Heidegger, finitude means that *conflict* is an inevitable part of the human experience, since both hold that it is not possible for us to grasp the whole. Where they differ is in *how* that conflict should be engaged.

For Gandhi, conflict is inevitable because both individual persons and entire cultures each have, at best, only a partial (or "relative") perspective on the Truth. And yet that Truth undergirds all partial perceptions of it. Because of this, we will inevitably clash over decisive questions, whether religious, philosophical, social, political, or economic—and for Gandhi, these are all bound together—but there are also grounds for hope that these very clashes will bring us closer to the Truth, and to each other. In Gandhi's form of skeptical idealism, his experimental pragmatism, such conflicts are not simply inevitable, they are essential, because they provide the opportunity for us to analyze, refine, and develop our necessarily limited understanding of the Truth. When Gandhi says that "all religions are true,"[17] he does not mean that every detail of each religion's doctrine is correct, for that would be absurd; he means, rather, that given our finitude, each of the world's great religions is equally on a pathway to the Truth, that each has its insights, as well as its blind spots. His political practice of *satyagraha* is meant to open both contending parties in any conflict to make progress on that pathway.

As the polestar of transformative political and social action, from the most humble personal dispute to campaigns for decolonization, Gandhi insists that conflict must be carried out in a spirit of love and nonviolence, or *ahimsa*. On the one hand, we have a duty to take a stand based on our present understanding of the Truth; on the other, we must simultaneously acknowledge the limitedness of our understanding: the possibility that we might be wrong, perhaps in particulars or even completely, and that the opponent sees something of the Truth that we do not. Hence Gandhi's name for nonviolent political action: *satyagraha*. This term is usually translated as "truth-force," or sometimes "soulforce," but its root meaning is "holding to the Truth." At first blush, this might seem like an arrogant and intransigent insistence upon one's own righteousness and infallibility, but while Gandhi does insist that we must not flinch from the duty of confronting injustice and falsehood as we see it, he understands the *satya-* of *satyagraha* in his particular way: as a Truth to which we have only partial access. Once again: his constructive skepticism. This means engaging the opponent resolutely but also openly, with the hope of genuine reconciliation at the resolution of the conflict. For Gandhi, this limitedness of ours can also be the source of the unity of religion, if only we will let it be:

> I believe that all the great religions of the world are true more or less. I say "more or less" because I believe that everything that the human hand touches, by reason of the very fact

---

[17] See Gandhi (1982, 54 and passim).

that human beings are imperfect, becomes imperfect. Perfection is the exclusive attribute of God and it is indescribable, untranslatable.... It is necessary for us all to aspire after perfection, but when that blessed state is attained, it becomes indescribable, indefinable.[18]

Gandhi's seemingly contradictory embrace of skepticism and idealism makes him what I would call a partisan of *asymptotic perfectibility*: that we may continuously approach but not decisively arrive at the Truth and absolute justice, because we are mortal and time-bound; still, we can make *progress towards* that endpoint, but only if we seek out constructive conflict as the necessary engine of that progression, and do so in the spirit of *satyagraha*. This is another way of understanding Gandhi's desire to reduce himself to zero, for that is what pushing ourselves to that limit-approaching-infinity means.

For Heidegger, too, conflict is essential to what it means to be human. As I have argued,[19] Heidegger takes his bearings from his interpretations of the one of the sayings of pre-Socratic philosopher, Heraclitus: "*Polemos* is the father of all things, and the king of all, and it reveals some as gods, others as human beings; it makes some slaves, others free."[20] The Greek *polemos*, from which we get the English *polemical*, means war, conflict, confrontation. Heidegger holds that *polemos* defines what it means to *be* human precisely because of our finitude and because there is no Absolute, no Truth existing in an ideal realm, by which we might reconcile our divergent ways of understanding the world. It is worth quoting at length one of the most chilling passages in Heidegger's work, from the same lecture of 1933–1934 discussed before, where he declares:

> One word stands great and simple at the beginning of [Heraclitus'] saying: *polemos*, war. This does not mean the outward occurrence of war and the celebration of what is "military," but rather what is decisive: standing against the enemy. We have translated this word with "struggle" to hold on to what is essential; but on the other hand, it is important to think over that it does not mean *agon* [Greek: contest], a competition in which two friendly opponents measure their strengths, but rather the struggle of *polemos*, war. This means that the struggle is in earnest; the opponent is not a partner but an enemy. Struggle as standing against the enemy, or more plainly: standing firm in confrontation.
>
> An enemy is each and every person who poses an essential threat to the Dasein of the people and its individual members. The enemy does not have to be external, and the external enemy is not even always the more dangerous one. And it can seem as if there were no enemy. Then it is a fundamental requirement to find the enemy, to expose the enemy to the light, or even first to make the enemy, so that this standing against the enemy may happen and so that Dasein may not lose its edge.
>
> The enemy can have attached itself to the innermost roots of the Dasein of a people and can set itself against this people's own essence and act against it. The struggle is all the fiercer and harder and tougher, for the least of it consists in coming to blows with one another; it is often far more difficult and wearisome to catch sight of the enemy as such, to bring the enemy into the open, to harbor no illusions about the enemy, to keep oneself ready

---

[18] Gandhi (1982, 56).

[19] See Fried (2000), chapter 1.

[20] I take responsibility for this rendering of Heraclitus' fragment 53, although I gratefully acknowledge advice from Martin Black. The Greek, transliterated, is: *pólemos pántôn men patêr esti, pántôn de basileús, kai tous men theoùs édeixe tous de anthrôpous, tous men doúlous epoíêse tous de eleuthérous.*

for attack, to cultivate and intensify a constant readiness and to prepare the attack looking far ahead with the goal of total annihilation.[21]

The contrast with Gandhi could not be more extreme: rather than reconciliation, the expected end of conflict is "total annihilation" (and it must not be forgotten that at this time in Germany, the paramount internal and hidden enemy was supposedly the Jew); the opponent is a true enemy in the most extreme sense of that word: someone whose very existence constitutes a threat to one's own existence. Conflict is then not a step to self-purification in reconciliation with the opponent on the pathway to a Truth that both parties could, in principle, share. This means that violence, both in spirit and in deed, is inevitable. Indeed, Heidegger seems to imply that violence is desirable, because a people's sense of itself as a unity may even require that it "*make* the enemy."

At issue between Heidegger and Gandhi is the ontology of politics. We do not have to accept Gandhi's entire ethic of nonviolence or his views on religion to agree that something like his conception of finite understandings of the truth is a necessary public epistemology for a democratic, pluralistic society, and even for relatively peaceful international relations. Heidegger forces us to confront the idealism inherent to a universalistic pluralism. For Gandhi, recognition and acceptance of our finitude is what keeps hubris at bay; we may be radically incomplete beings, doomed to the cycle of birth, living, and death, but this fundamental limitation may also redeem us if we strive, in a kind of resolute modesty, to catch the glimmerings of Truth in the contingency of our existence. For Heidegger, though, there is no transcendence, no release in *moksha*, no escape from Plato's cave, and therefore we must cleave to what is ours, here and now, as our only fleeting foundation. Peace would then at best only be a transitory truce between otherwise incompatible worlds, something possible only temporarily between nations, for a nation, to be a nation, must live through a people's finite but shared self-understanding.

4.2 Self-rule and Pluralism

The contrast between Heidegger and Gandhi now seems at its starkest. But there is a surprising point on which they seem to agree, one indicated above: both hold that human beings must draw upon their own traditions in order to own up to what faces them in any particular time, and both insist upon a form of national autonomy in doing this. Although militant nationalism has found little support in contemporary theory, since the publication of the now-classic essay, "National Self-Determination" (1990) by Avishai Margolit and Joseph Raz, the question of the right to a national identity has received wide attention.[22] The controversies that have erupted since the publication of Samuel Huntington's "clash of civilizations" thesis in *Foreign Affair*

[21] Heidegger (2010, 90–91); translation amended.

[22] See Margalit and Raz (1990). For an example of how this question has played out, see Bachman (1997).

(1993)[23]—and, in particular, the question of whether we should understand the so-called War on Terror as such an existential clash—show that the problem of national and cultural difference remains very much alive. The comparison between Heidegger and Gandhi may cast these issues in a productive new light by showing what is at stake. Gandhi famously struggled for India's *swaraj*, its independence from the British Empire. When Heidegger assumed the role of rector, or president, of Freiburg University in 1933, he entitled his inaugural speech "The Self-Assertion of the German University."[24] For Heidegger then, *Selbstbehauptung*, self-assertion, was the path to both university reform and national resurgence. For both Heidegger and Gandhi, the key again is *human finitude*: we necessarily find ourselves as members of an existing, historical community whose horizons are bounded by its own historical understanding, and we can only come to understand ourselves individually through a confrontation with our own community's history, both backwards into the past and forwards into the future. But this needs unpacking.

Swaraj literally means self-rule, which usually was understood to mean political independence for India, but Gandhi also took this word in the most expansive sense. He wrote once to a friend: "For me, even the effort for attaining *swaraj* is a part of the effort for *moksha* [ultimate liberation]. Writing this to you is also part of the same effort."[25] Self-rule, then, involves all aspects of both a person's and a people's striving for self-realization. Political emancipation is only one part of that; self-rule as governing the self ranges from economic independence and accountability for all classes in society to each individual's final self-realization in the liberation (*moksha*) from a time-bound existence. But the key for Gandhi is that each such path to self-realization begins within an embeddedness in a particular place, community, and tradition. When he proclaims that "all religions are true," this emphatically does not mean that they are simply identical and therefore indifferent as to content. Gandhi believed that conversion from one religion to another, while possible, is often ill-advised: one should work from the tradition in which one has one's roots, or else the very idea that all religions share a unity past their differences is belied.[26]

---

[23] Huntington (1993). See also Huntington (1996), which removes the question mark and expands upon the thesis. It is worth noting, given the argument later in this essay, that Huntington's final sentence in the original articles was this: "For the relevant future, there will be no universal civilization, but instead a world of different civilizations, each of which will have to learn to coexist with the others." On this point, Huntington and I agree that we cannot address reality by simply imposing ideal theory upon it. The question remains, of course, what the ideal should be, and to what extent we can realize it in the messy present of the real and not allow that reality to overwhelm what improvements might be possible. Once again, Gandhi's pragmatic idealism seems to me to strike the right balance, even if one might not agree with his particular policies or his method of nonviolence.

[24] See Heidegger (1991).

[25] Gandhi (2003, 29).

[26] For example, see Gandhi (1962, 60–85). "I would no more think of asking a Christian or a Musalman or a Parsi or a Jew to change his faith than I would of changing my own" (1962, 66). Gandhi allows that true conversions may occur, but he is suspicious of missionaries of any faith, particularly those who prey on the poor, depriving them of their indigenous faith and thereby "destroying their social superstructure, which notwithstanding its many defects has stood now from time immemorial the onslaughts upon it from within and from without" (1962, 67).

In this sense, Gandhi shares with Heidegger an emphasis on historical authenticity. Heidegger's *Being and Time* (1962 [1927]) emphasized *authenticity* (*Eigentlichkeit*) as an essential potentiality of human existence, one in which an individual, or perhaps a community, might self-consciously take on the burdens and opportunities of its own history rather than letting that history simply carry one along unthinkingly. Although Gandhi's notion of *swaraj* is no simple equivalent to Heidegger's *Eigentlichkeit*, both concepts share the sense that human beings are indebted to the historical situations within which they simply happen to find themselves, and that therefore authentically being a self must mean confronting that tradition in a constructive way, not avoiding it or passively allowing it to define one's existence. Self-rule for both individuals and communities, then, means a genuine engagement with the self, making sense of this individual and communal self both within a tradition and as having a future that is open to new possibilities that must always be drawn from that historical inheritance. It means confronting the history that has been granted, not running away from it into the exotic other. Gandhi understood national independence as *swaraj* in this way: not as a rejection of the unity of humanity, but rather as a recognition that distinct peoples must be free to make sense of their own histories and futures for themselves, without imperial or colonial interference.[27]

Heidegger used the term *Selbstbehauptung*, self-assertion, in the early 1930s when he was an open and dedicated National Socialist. It is closely related to a family of words, such as *Selbstverantwortung* (self-accountability), that he employed to address how a community may take possession of its own destiny. In November of 1933, Hitler presented a plebiscite to the German people, asking them to approve or reject his national and international policies, including his plan to withdraw Germany from the League of Nations as part of the effort to overcome the effects of the treaty of Versailles. Heidegger made impassioned speeches in favor of a Yes vote on the plebiscite:

> Neither ambition nor thirst for glory nor blind obstinacy nor lust for dominion, but solely the clear will to an unconditioned self-accountability in the bearing and mastering of the fate of our people demanded from the Führer the withdrawal from the "League of Nations." This is not a turning away from the community of peoples, but on the contrary: Our people, with this step, sets itself under that essential law of human Being to which every people must render allegiance, if it wishes to remain a people.
>
> Precisely from this allegiance, equally observed, to the unconditional demand of self-accountability does the possibility of taking one another seriously arise, and so then of affirming a community. The will to a true community of the people holds itself as much aloof from an untenable, bondless reduction to world brotherhood as from a blind domination by violence. This will operates beyond these two opposing poles; it creates the open and manly standing by and up to one another of peoples and states. What happens in such willing? Is this descent into barbarism? No![28]

---

[27] It is worth comparing Gandhi on this point with a contemporary political theorist such as David Miller, who argues in Miller (1997) that liberal-minded people should not be afraid to embrace the idea of *nationality*, which can subsist in the context of respect for other national identities without leading to crude *nationalism*.

[28] Schneeberger (1962, 148–149); my translation.

What distinguishes Gandhi's struggle for *swaraj* as self-rule from Heidegger's insistence on self-accountability here? On the surface, it would *seem* not much. Heidegger says that the withdrawal from the League of Nations is predicated on a desire for genuine national independence and the rejection of a phony appeal to "world brotherhood." He wants to argue that a *true* community of peoples is based on each national community first standing on its own and for itself, for otherwise there can be no self-respect or mutual respect among nations. In an essay of 1937, "Paths to Discussion," aimed at a French audience, Heidegger claims that in facing up to its own historical tasks, a nation needs its neighbors to sharpen and bring into focus what is at stake:

> Understanding one another here is also—and here above all—a struggle [*Kampf*] of putting oneself into question that is reciprocal between the participants. Only confrontation [*Auseinandersetzung*] impels each participant into what is most his own. This happens only if confrontation gathers up and endures in another way, in the face of the threatening uprooting of the West, an uprooting whose overturning demands the initiative of every people capable of creativity. The grounding form of confrontation is the actual conversational exchange of the creative in a neighborly encounter.[29]

Once again, it seems as if both Heidegger and Gandhi locate the necessity of conflict in the finitude from which each historical person and community takes its bearings. It certainly sounds like Heidegger means that each community comes to greater self-understanding only through a "struggle" and "confrontation" that takes the form of a "conversational exchange" and "neighborly encounter" that does not seek to repress the other in its distinct finitude, but rather to allow that other to help one's own community to discern and confront what are its own historical tasks and burdens. Then it might seem as if both Heidegger and Gandhi advocate a similar view of national self-assertion: that each people must not surrender to a crude universalism that eradicates historical difference, but rather embrace its own traditions, in resolute but open "conversation" with other traditions.

And yet we must not ignore that "struggle" (*Kampf*) and "confrontation" (*Auseinandersetzung*) are two of Heidegger's preferred renderings for the Greek *polemos*, and it then becomes impossible to forget that passage in which he says that *polemos* is war in earnest with the enemy—an enemy that poses an existential threat to the people (even if that enemy must first be *made*!), an enemy that must be attacked to the point of "complete annihilation." Then his evocation of the "neighborly encounter" and his repudiation of "barbarism" ring hollow—especially in the light of what happened to France and the rest of Europe, not to mention the "hidden" enemies of the German people: the Jews, the Roma, and others.

At the root of what separates Heidegger and Gandhi, even in their evocation of national independence, is again their differing understanding of human finitude. In Gandhi's case, because our finitude is informed and guided by what transcends finitude, even if we can at best only grasp it fleetingly, then the differences of tradition—while real and deserving of respect—are not ultimate and need not irrevocably divide us. Gandhi's is a soft finitude. By contrast, Heidegger's finitude is a hard

---

[29] Quoted in Fried (2000, 180); translation amended.

one: because there is no universal, no Idea, no transcendence beckoning us from beyond our limited historical situatedness, communal difference may be (and often must be) an unbridgeable divide. The worlds that peoples inhabit, as what give them meaning, are simply incommensurable, and difference then may (or must) become implacable enmity—even as that enmity, through the inevitable confrontation, helps each group understand itself better in its own necessary and defining historical limitations.

4.3   Action and Ideal

Some might argue that even if this antagonistic sense of human identity might be true of the Heidegger of the 1930s, it is not true of the Heidegger after the war, the Heidegger who emphasized not *polemos* as the way for human beings to engage Being, but rather *Gelassenheit*: letting-be, or releasement.[30] With *Gelassenheit*, so goes the argument, Heidegger sought to counter the rampaging human will, and especially the will to power in the era of total war and the global reign of technology, with an unobtrusive openness and an attitude of simply letting what is *be*, and to be thankful for it.

But even if it were true that Heidegger made such a turn in his thinking, this turn can itself be criticized from a Gandhian point of view: *ahimsa*, or nonviolence is precisely a kind of *acting*, not a form of passivity. Must any assertion of the will be condemned as form of Nietzschean hubris now? Heidegger appears to have lurched to the opposite extreme from the 1930s and given up on action altogether. Gandhi insists on a justice that is not limited by human finitude, even if we can only imperfectly grasp what justice demands; but even that imperfect understanding demands that we engage the world in the light of ideas and ideals that transcend the imperfections of what merely happens to be.[31]

Where does this leave us? Readers who balk at Gandhi's religious language and nonviolence, or at Heidegger's opaque ontology, might wonder what any of this has to teach us about coping with enmity in the modern (or post-modern) age of terrorism, the diffusion of weapons of mass destruction, and rapid globalization, with all the environmental and human disasters that attend this break-neck pace of change.[32]

But the key to addressing human enmity in such a world lies in what we think about the question of human finitude. We face the question of whether the diverse civilizations of this planet are fated to implacable conflict, rooted in their attachment

---

[30] The central text is Heidegger (1959, 1969). For an exemplary reading of the later Heidegger, in the spirit indicated here, see Richard Capabianco (2010).

[31] I am grateful to Richard Polt for suggesting this point.

[32] Another fruitful topic for comparison between Heidegger and Gandhi would be the question of technology and globalization, but there is no space for that here. Both are deeply suspicious of the modernist project for the conquest of nature, and both believe that technology uproots human beings from their attachments to tradition and to nature.

to incommensurable traditions, or whether we can find sufficient grounds for common understanding, even agreement—as temporary as it may be—while not sacrificing our sense of historical belonging to particular communities. As Nir Eisikovits suggests in his essay for this volume, "Truce!", the Western emphasis on an absolute dichotomy between war and peace may have the paradoxical effect of making war all the more inevitable and intractable as an attempt to produce a permanent peace. Instead, we need to reconsider less ambitious peacemaking ventures, such as the truce, which acknowledge the limitations of human action to eliminating disagreement and conflict all at once.[33] What we need now are ways that we can avoid the absolutist "friend and foe" divisions of the world while neither ignoring our serious differences nor depending on dangerously utopian expectations for resolving those differences at one fell swoop. These more modest measures may give us the breathing room in which enmity may fade and lasting peace slowly and organically evolve in the absence of outright and intransigent confrontation. This does not mean relinquishing our ideals. Nevertheless, we must not make the mistake of missing opportunities for an imperfect peace in the present for the sake of a perfect peace imagined in the future.

Heidegger and Gandhi force us to confront these questions about the response to human divisions. For my money, Gandhi's pragmatic idealism provides a far more compelling model for the kinds of epistemology and civic habits that are necessary for a diverse, democratic community that is sensitive to cultural difference while still upholding universal principles. This practical epistemology may be extended to international relations, too, with reservations granted for the lack of stable, democratic forms for global governance. Gandhi teaches us not to fear a *soft* enmity (rather than a hard, or utterly incommensurable enmity, as in Heidegger or Schmitt), for in the confrontation with the opponent, we presume the possibility of reconciliation, as well as the possibility that we ourselves might be proven wrong—and that we too may have something to learn. A community that embodies these virtues of resolute openness to constructive conflict must necessarily be an evolving balancing act. Quite the contrary to being nihilistic, Gandhi's skeptical idealism points the way to making sense of conflict as an opportunity for enlarging human life and understanding.

Gandhi's justifications for his political practice exemplify what I have elsewhere called a *situated transcendence*:[34] namely, the recognition that human beings must necessarily start out as members of the distinct historical communities to which they are attached, but also that fully understanding that attachment and refining it in the light of the struggles over justice that define all communities, forces us to evaluate our convictions in the light of ideals that transcend them. In turn, that confrontation between our convictions and our ideals forces us to understand more fully what those ideals really imply, and what they really are. Without this dialogue between

---

[33] See also Eisikovits (2010), where he has argued that openness understood as *sympathy* may be the royal road to forms of peace-making that are all the more successful because they don't presume to settle all the sources of a given conflict at once.

[34] See Fried (2006).

our rootedness and our aspiration to something beyond it, we surely will lapse into the barbarism of self-idolatry and intransigent enmity. That is the true nihilism: a world without light at the end of the tunnel.

Acknowledgments I gratefully acknowledge the comments and critiques of Richard Polt and Joseph Prabhu, who read early drafts of this essay.

References

Arendt H (1978) Martin Heidegger at eighty. In: Murray M (ed) Heidegger and modern philosophy. Yale University Press, New Haven, pp 293–303

Bachman A (1997) Theories of succession. Philos Public Aff 26(1):31–61

Bondurant J (1965) Conquest of violence: the Gandhian philosophy of conflict. University of California Press, Berkeley

Capobianco R (2010) Engaging Heidegger. University of Toronto Press, Toronto

Eisikovits N (2010) Sympathizing with the enemy: reconciliation, transitional justice, negotiation. Martinus Nijhoff Publishers, Dordrecht

Fried G (2000) Heidegger's polemos: from being to politics. Yale University Press, New Haven CT

Fried G (2006) Back to the cave: a platonic rejoinder to Heidegger. In: Hyland D, Manoussakis JP (eds) Heidegger and the Greeks. Indiana University Press, Bloomington

Gandhi MK (1957) An autobiography: the story of my experiments with truth. Beacon, Boston

Gandhi MK (1962) In search of the supreme, vol II. Navajivan Publishing House, Ahmedabad

Gandhi K (1982) All men are brothers: autobiographical reflections. Continuum, New York

Gandhi R (2003) Essential writings of Mahatma Gandhi. Oxford University Press, Oxford

Heidegger M (1959) Gelassenheit. Verlag Günther Neske, Tübingen

Heidegger M (1962) Being and time. Harper, New York

Heidegger M (1969) Discourse on thinking, 1st edn. Harper Torchbooks, New York

Heidegger M (1989) In: von Herrmann F-W (ed) Beiträge zur Philosophy, Gesamtausgabe, vol 65. Frankfurt am Main, Vittorio Klostermann

Heidegger M (1991) The self-assertion of the German University. In: Wolin R (ed) The Heidegger controversy: a critical reader. Columbia University Press, New York

Heidegger M (2010) Being and truth. Indiana University Press, Bloomington

Huntington S (1993) The clash of civilizations? Foreign Aff 72(3):22–49

Huntington S (1996) The clash of civilizations and the remaking of world order. Simon & Schuster, New York

Hyland D (2006) Heidegger and the Greeks: interpretive essays. Indiana University Press, Bloomington

Margalit A, Raz J (1990) National self-determination. J Philos 87(9):439–461

Miller D (1997) On nationality. Oxford University Press, Oxford

Murray M (1978) Heidegger and modern philosophy: critical essays. Yale University Press, New Haven

Parkes G (1987) Heidegger and Asian thought. University of Hawaii Press, Honolulu

Polt R (2006) The emergency of being: on Heidegger's contributions to philosophy. Cornell University Press, Ithaca

Schneeberger G (1962) Nachlese zu Heidegger. Suhr, Bern

Watkins C (1985) The American heritage dictionary of Indo-European roots. Houghton Mifflin, Boston

Chapter 5
Basic Challenges for Governance in Emergencies

François Tanguay-Renaud

Abstract What are emergencies and why do they matter? In this chapter, I seek to outline the morally significant features of emergencies, and demonstrate how these features generate corresponding first- and second-order challenges and responsibilities for those in a position to do something about them. In the first section, I contend that emergencies are situations in which there is a risk of serious harm and a need to react urgently if that harm is to be averted or minimized. These conceptual features matter morally, since it is precisely to them that those who invoke emergencies to justify otherwise impermissible actions tend to appeal. The basic first-order challenge facing emergency responders is two-fold. It is, first, to identify how these features shape circumstances of action in ways that affect (or do not affect) which reasons for action and which corresponding courses of conduct are justifiably available to them. In situations when emergency responders are compelled to make authoritative determinations due to significant contestability and indeterminacies in the contours or materialization of the said features, their challenge is then also to make these determinations legitimately. In the second section, I argue that second-order challenges having to do with the foreseeability of emergencies, the value of exposure to them, and their preventability further compound the predicament of emergency responders. I conclude by saying a few words about one last morally salient feature shared by many, though not all, emergencies considered in the chapter—namely, their public dimension.

F. Tanguay-Renaud (✉)
Department of Philosophy, Osgoode Hall Law School, York University,
4700 Keele Street, Toronto, ON M3J 1P3, Canada
e-mail: ftanguay-renaud@osgoode.yorku.ca

A. MacLachlan and A. Speight (eds.), *Justice, Responsibility and Reconciliation in the Wake of Conflict*, Boston Studies in Philosophy, Religion and Public Life 1, DOI 10.1007/978-94-007-5201-6_5, © Springer Science+Business Media Dordrecht 2013

5.1   Setting the Stage and Two Sets of Basic Challenges

"Everyone's troubles make a crisis," writes Michael Walzer. "'Emergency' and 'crisis' are cant words, used to prepare our minds for acts of brutality" (Walzer 1977, 251). In light of provocative assertions of this sort, one cannot help but wonder: is "emergency" really such a cant and malleable concept? History gives us numerous reasons to think it may be. How many times in the last century alone have heads of state invoked looming or ongoing emergencies as grounds for imposing harsh "emergency measures" on their populations? How frequently have state-governments sought to account for attacking, invading, or occupying foreign territories by pointing to urgent threats to the interests of their constituency or to those of others?[1] Indeed, for some leading emergency theorists, it is the very manipulability of the idea of emergency that accounts for its practical salience. According to Carl Schmitt, for example, while it is not *everyone's* troubles that make an emergency, the existence of an emergency is still contingent on *someone's* say-so. It is the mark of a society's "sovereign," Schmitt famously writes, that he decides whether there is an emergency as well as what must be done to eliminate it (Schmitt 2005, 12).

In this chapter, I want to dispute this way of thinking about emergencies and their moral importance. I intend to do so, first, by outlining the specific features of the concept that I take to be both definitive and morally significant and, second, demonstrating how these features generate corresponding first- and second-order challenges and responsibilities for those in a position to do something about them. To borrow language from the European Convention on Human Rights,[2] my focus will primarily be on "war" and "other public emergencies" and the basic, emergency-specific challenges they pose for those—notably, governments and their agents—who strive to handle them appropriately, that is, in a morally justified way. I speak of "basic" challenges to reflect the fact that the challenges with which I will be concerned here are not inherently public. In other words, except for some remarks made in conclusion, my focus will not be on the public dimension of the emergencies in question and its distinctive moral implications, but on their character as emergencies *simpliciter* and the challenges they may pose as such. Thus, the scope of my argument will sometimes extend beyond cases of war, civil conflicts, and the like, and so will some of my illustrations. Still, I intend to concentrate my attention on these emergencies in particular, since they typically feature additional complexities of scale, which a focus on more discrete or individual emergencies would risk eliding. Note also that, to reflect contemporary reality and for the sake of simplicity, I will tend to assume that governments and their agents are those who are best placed to address these emergencies appropriately. In doing so, I do not mean to rule out the possibility that other (domestic or international) entities or individuals may sometimes be in as good a position, or even be better placed, to address them.

---

[1] Amongst the many existing studies, useful starting points include Ramraj and Thiruvengadam (2010), Scheppele (2006), and Loveman (1993).

[2] Convention for the Protection of Human Rights and Fundamental Freedoms (European Convention on Human Rights, as amended) s 15(1).

So it is untrue that whatever someone—sovereign or anyone else—declares to be an emergency is in fact an emergency (accounting, of course, for the possibility that anyone may, through their behaviour, create emergencies for themselves and others). All, including those in relevant positions of authority, can be wrong about the existence of emergencies. The concept of emergency is a normative concept and has contours that impose at least some limits on what situations can properly be described as such. Emergencies, I will contend, are situations in which there is a risk of serious harm and a need to react urgently if that harm is to be averted or minimized. These features—i.e. urgency, the potential for serious harm, needed response for harm avoidance or minimization—matter conceptually since not all situations encompass them, or encompass them in the same way. Only emergencies do. When one of these features is missing, an event is not an emergency. Thus, as I discuss at greater length later, a fast unfolding risk of serious harm whose materialization cannot realistically be averted or minimized does not constitute an emergency. If anything, it is a tragedy, a disaster. Consider also an urgent risk of a mere inconvenience or trifling harm. Such risk can at best be metaphorically analogized to an emergency. A fresh ketchup stain on my white shirt may be akin to an emergency in that I am urgently required to soak it in water if I want to avoid it becoming indelible. All else being equal, though, it is not *really* an emergency.

The identified features also matter morally, since those who invoke emergencies to justify otherwise impermissible actions tend to appeal precisely to them in doing so. For Schmitt, who assumes that the "sovereign" is only ever constrained in his actions by the limits of his power and whatever social and political forces he deems prudent to take into account, the moral importance of these features is largely irrelevant.[3] Yet, one would be ill-advised to follow him down this nihilistic path. Although an anarchist attitude vis-à-vis the law and social conventions is—irrespective of its rightness or wrongness—intelligible, amoralism is not. Morality, as I understand it here, refers to the true, or valid, reasons that people have—reasons that apply to whomever they address and whose scope is determined by their content.[4] Thus understood, morality is often described as the art of life. In virtue of its very nature, it applies to all agents capable of understanding it, irrespective of their interest in it, of who they are, of what they feel about it, and of the predicaments in which they find themselves. Of course, reasons for action that differ in strength or type from those ordinarily at play may sometimes prevail in emergency situations. This is why some emergencies are thought to have special moral salience and warrant certain departures from 'normality.' In other words, morality is not inflexible. What it demands and permits can differ depending on the circumstances, such as in some emergency contexts. Thus, morality does not simply cease to apply in such situations. To put the point more concretely, if we take morality to be the true or

---

[3] Although Schmitt contends that his methodological ambitions are purely descriptive, many passages of his relevant work—such as his assertion that states have a right of self-preservation (Schmitt 2005, 12)—sit awkwardly with this contention.

[4] On this broad understanding of morality, see e.g. Raz (2004, 2–3).

valid reasons that people have for acting, we may, in ordinary or non-emergency contexts, be capable of recognizing and codifying these reasons into moral precepts—such as, *arguendo*, the Golden Rule, the categorical imperative, justice as fairness, respect for basic human rights, and the rule of law. It can appear that emergencies are exactly those situations in which morality, understood merely as those precepts, ceases to apply. However, while emergencies may well depart from normality, morality—that is, true or valid reasons—is not also left behind. Different reasons, or reasons of different force, may be at play in emergencies, but reasons nonetheless.[5]

So, one of the very real challenges of emergencies—such as wars or other violent conflicts—for those who have to contend with them is to identify and assess their salient features and craft responses that give them their due (some may prefer the term 'proportionate') moral importance, in light of all relevant circumstances, without going overboard and abusing the label. At this point, the following objection is somewhat predictable: aren't the features of emergencies listed above so vague that, in most situations, at least some human determinations will be required about the extent to which they obtain in fact and are morally salient? The answer to this question must admittedly be a qualified one. As I suggested, the concept of emergency refers to needs for action (to be understood as including both acts and omissions). More specifically, emergencies involve a specific kind of need for action: a need to act to avoid or minimize serious harm. The idea of need in question has some definite objective contours. For example, soldiers who lie on the battlefield bleeding to death clearly need emergency treatment. Their need is entrenched in the sense that treatment is categorically necessary, in any realistic possible future we can devise, if they are to survive. Some pressing needs are also non-substitutable in the sense that nothing else than φ would fulfil them as well or nearly as well—e.g. intake of some sufficiently hydrating substance is necessary, in a non-substitutable way, to avoid dehydration.[6] Then again, it is true that the claim that there are no alternatives to φ will sometimes, depending how specifically φ is defined, be debatable. Likewise, what constitutes serious harm—which the concept of emergency assumes we have a

---

[5] I defend this claim in Tanguay-Renaud (2012, 30–36). It is true that certain doomsday scenarios threatening the annihilation of human civilization and the subversion of the very foundations of morality may challenge its applicability. The point is that these supreme moral emergencies are the rarest of the rare, the unlikely exception to the exception, and that it is clearly inadvisable to take them as paradigms for the understanding of the relationship between emergencies, morality, and appropriate responses. On this point, see further Tanguay-Renaud (2009, 47–50).

[6] On categorical needs—elaborated in terms of the necessity to avoid serious harm and understood in contrast to mere instrumental needs—and the entrenched and non-substitutable character of many such needs, see Wiggins (1987, 1–57). Wiggins's account of needs remains one of the most insightful to date, despite being lacking in nuance in some notable respects. For example, while he sometimes seems to assume that needs to avoid serious harm must, as a conceptual requirement, be morally compelling, we can easily think of cases where this is not the case. A moral monster like Hitler, afflicted by a fatal though easily curable disease, may well need treatment, while saving him is not a morally compelling goal. Something similar may also be said of the need to rescue the individual in poor health who, after careful and measured deliberation, has decided to end his life.

forceful reason to avoid—is itself somewhat indeterminate and, thus, may at times be contestable. Some cases of serious harm are quite uncontroversial, and provide clear examples of the moral content of the concept. Consider the case of the person being violently tortured to the point that she will undoubtedly be left in a permanent vegetative state if no action is taken. Think also of cases where it is obvious that one thing would be significantly more harmful than another—*ceteris paribus*, for the political institutions of a decent state to collapse, as opposed to being temporarily inhibited. At bottom, though, the assessment of harm and its seriousness requires at least some judgment and, therefore, may on occasion leave room for reasonable disagreement. If, as a matter of ordinary meaning, harm to people is what makes them worse-off than they were, or are entitled to be, in a way that affects their future well-being or flourishing, then we must appeal to a value-based explanation of what makes it so whenever we use the concept of harm. Detailed accounts of the content of that value-based explanation may be disputable, and lead to conflicting claims about the harm potential of a particular emergency. Consider, for example, the various plausible answers that could be given to the question of how harmful—as well as to whom, and in what ways—the Taliban's destruction of the Buddhas of Bamian actually was.

The existence of such areas of contestability may lead some to think that responses to given events should only be treated as responses to *emergencies* when the urgent necessity of these responses, and the seriousness of the harm they seek to avoid, are unambiguous. There is perhaps a grain of truth in this thought, to which I will eventually return in the last section of the chapter. At this stage, however, it is important to realize that emergencies will also exist in situations where it is debatable how serious the harm at issue really is and whether a given response is strictly necessary to avert it. In such situations, authoritative determinations may have to be made by those who are in a position to make them. Yet, *pace* Schmitt, such determinations must themselves be justified since, like all other forms of human conduct, they are themselves subject to moral appraisal. Here, I do not wish to revisit the deep and extensive literature on what makes exercises of practical authority justified, inside or outside the political context.[7] Suffice it to say that whatever the correct grounds for their justification—be they voluntarist or non-voluntarist—authorities cannot escape evaluation in such terms.

Thus, the basic challenge facing authorities in emergencies is two-fold. It is, first, to identify how emergencies shape (or do not shape) circumstances of action in ways that affect which reasons for action and which corresponding courses of conduct are justifiably available, in the sense of not being morally defeated by other, more compelling ones. For example, does the fact that a rogue regime possesses a few weapons of mass destruction, and threatens to use them unjustly, justify a defensive yet pre-emptive military campaign, as opposed to a trade embargo or other such robust diplomatic manoeuvres? Insofar as it does justify a military campaign, what

---

[7] For a remarkably succinct and cogent survey of the theoretical literature on the question of legitimate practical authority, see generally Green (2010).

kind of campaign, given, *inter alia*, the number of innocent civilians who may be killed in the process? Does the fact that a country transitioning out of a bloody civil war is on the brink of reverting to that state justify targeted killings of agitators or, say, their exemplary and retroactive punishment in defiance of the rule of law? The second basic challenge is that, when authoritative determinations are required due to significant indeterminacies and contestability, those who make them must ensure that their exercises of authority are themselves justified. Depending on one's theory of legitimate authority, one may ask, for example, whether such decision-makers are better placed than others to assess that a military campaign or targeted killings would be just, necessary, and proportionate. On might also ask whether, in the circumstances, they have been appropriately authorized by those in whose names they purport to make decisions. Of course, while all emergency-related determinations have to be morally justified, not all of them have to be justified *qua* exercises of authority. This is because, conceptually speaking, authority is exercised over *others*, as a means of altering their normative position.[8] It is my focus on governmental responses to emergencies—which characteristically involve authoritative determinations—that leads me to emphasize this additional, yet important, layer of complexity.

At this juncture, one may rightly point out that an inquiry into the moral salience of emergencies that restricted its focus to the need to avoid serious harm would overlook one crucial feature. Emergencies are not only important but also *urgent* needs. Assuming that serious harm would ensue in the absence of a certain reaction, an emergency's urgency is a function of how rapidly this reaction must occur. Urgency and harm operate on different axes of salience. While these axes may coalesce in the most exigent emergencies, they may also diverge. Meeting a need may be urgent, but a matter of moderately harmful consequences. Conversely, a need may be a matter of little urgency, yet be otherwise very important, as measured by the amount of harm that would be occasioned if it were not met. Assuming, though, that we hold the harm variable constant, it becomes easy to see how various needs to avoid harm may be assessed in terms of what Thomas Scanlon calls a "hierarchy of relative urgency" (Scanlon 1975, 660–661). Of course, in some large-scale scenarios—such as wars, civil conflicts, and the like—emergency responders may simultaneously be confronted to many perils with differing levels of harm potential. In such cases, further variations on the axis of urgency can generate exceedingly complex moral dilemmas. Accordingly, it is important always to bear in mind the compounding effect of these two types of variations when assessing the overall challenges posed by large-scale, multifaceted emergencies such as international or civil wars. For the moment, however, I will continue to assume the simpler picture for the sake of clarity.

The concept of emergency implies a high degree of urgency, i.e. immediacy or near immediacy. This feature tends to limit the opportunities that emergency responders have to act if they are to avert harm. In other words, urgency tends to make some reactions less substitutable—or, so to speak, more necessary—for the

---

[8] On this point, see Gardner (2010, 83–89).

purpose of harm avoidance. Therein lies the specific moral salience of the urgency dimension: urgency may make some courses of conduct related to harm avoidance more rationally eligible than they would otherwise be. Thus, even if, ideally, it would be better for a government to take the path of diplomacy and multilateralism in lieu of attacking another state in self-defense, it may not have the opportunity to do so if it faces an ongoing neo-colonial invasion. When serious harm is threatened and there is no time to engage in otherwise-favorable courses of action, it may become justifiable to take less ideal paths.

Urgency as a moral feature also has its loose ends. It is true that some emergencies are so urgent that, when faced with them, one should not ask oneself what to do, but react to the situation as one sees it. Otherwise, both thought and action may simply come too little, too late. Think, for example, of a soldier who jumps swiftly out of the way of a bullet shot in her direction. However, most emergencies are not so urgent as to preclude all deliberation. While in some cases, deliberation, although possible, only amplifies the emergency—think of endless deliberations about how best to address ongoing global warming—in many others, a necessarily limited amount of deliberation is critical to an appropriate response.[9] Consider the case of the military surgeon who (to some extent at least) must weigh pros and cons before proceeding to an emergency surgery, or the squad leader who ought to assess (at least minimally) risks to her soldiers as well as chances of success before launching a rescue operation of an endangered captured squad member. Before attacking other territories in self-defense and risking the killing of innocents, one would also hope that state-governments deliberate at least minimally. With a traditional separation of powers model, a full legislative debate may not be possible given time constraints. The executive branch of government might be the only organ in a position to devise and implement a quick enough response. Yet some deliberation still ought to take place. Thus, in all these cases, an important question for emergency responders will no doubt be how urgent the emergency really is. And here again, when the degree of urgency is significantly unclear, authoritative determinations may be needed. However, this additional level of complexity must not detract us from the basic moral salience that an urgency-constrained set of opportunities for the avoidance of serious harm will often have in fact.

5.2   Second-Order Basic Emergency Challenges

5.2.1   Emergencies, Foreseeability, and the Importance of Prevention

The account just given of the moral significance of emergencies, and the challenge of assessing it correctly, may seem intuitively accurate—at least when considered in the context of emergencies that could not reasonably be expected. In such situations,

---

[9] This point is eloquently articulated in Scarry (2011).

one typically needs to take action swiftly while the stakes are high. Available opportunities for thought and action are fixed by immediate circumstances, and emergency responders have no relevant influence over them given the suddenness of the situation. They are often confronted with the emergency due to no unreasonableness of their own, and are constrained to act on reasons as they encounter them at the time. But what about emergencies that are intentionally provoked or are somehow predictable, and whose occurrence may have been avoided, or characteristics mitigated, by preventive measures or altogether different choices of prior conduct? Confronting an emergency may be an urgent necessity at time t_2, in the sense of being impossible to evade, but what if one could have ensured at antecedent time t_1 that the emergency would not occur, or would occur in a mitigated form? Although they have no direct bearing on what constitutes an emergency from a conceptual standpoint, such challenging questions seem to speak to the moral salience of emergencies. In fact, some theorists even assume that the only genuinely significant emergencies are those "such that people are not likely to plan to be in that kind of situation" (Gert 2004, 72–73).[10] What should one make of such assertions?

Early deliberations, advanced planning, and anticipatory decisions are central features of rational activity. However, to be able to plan ahead appropriately and behave accordingly, one must often have some idea of the circumstances for which to plan. It might be objected that one can always insure or save money so as to be better able to deal with whatever situation may arise, without knowing anything about it in advance. However, the strength of this objection is relatively limited with regard to emergencies. There are many cases of emergencies in which no amount of money could make up for the serious harm incurred due to lack of planning and preparation—e.g. (from the standpoint of an individual) violated sexuality and associated psychological trauma, ruined reputation, unremediable physical handicap, death or (from a more collective perspective such as that of a state) collapsed institutions and mass casualties. Furthermore, the fact that money *could* have been saved or insurance bought in anticipation of any possible emergency does not itself entail that these precautions are the most reasonable or morally appropriate, compared to others. Foreseeability matters because it tends to affect the ways in which we can respond to emergencies by shaping our opportunities to prepare for them appropriately or avert them altogether.

As I suggested earlier, the idea of emergency implies a lack of real alternatives if serious harm is to be avoided. It implies necessity or, in Harry Frankfurt's words, "something that [one] cannot help needing" (Frankfurt 1984, 6). In cases in which one could have planned ahead, but in which one did not want or care to plan, it seems more problematic than in reasonably unexpected cases to characterize the situation as one in which there were no alternatives, no opportunity to "help needing." Although such characterization might be possible at time t_2 immediately preceding the emergency, if it was not at earlier time t_1 or t_0, the fact that the predicament

---

[10] Note that Gert recognizes that emergencies that are unlikely to be foreseen are only a "kind of emergency situations" and, thus, that emergencies can very well be foreseeable.

was somewhat foreseeable may give a related claim of emergency an aura of bad faith. The necessity of harm avoidance at time t_2, although indisputable, may be felt to be, as it were, less genuine or less authentic. One way of articulating this thought in rational terms is to note that in some situations the first-order reasons supplied by an emergency—linked primarily to its urgency and gravity—may be excluded, either fully or partially, by second-order considerations related to the emergency's foreseeability. Commentators sometimes seek to put this point across by arguing that those who embark on a course of action that foreseeably leads them to confront a preventable emergency implicitly consent to, or assume, inherent risks. Others speak of forfeiture, either full or partial, of the ability to invoke the emergency as a justification for otherwise impermissible behaviour.

This is not to say that foreseeability always changes emergency responders' moral position in this way. Surely, emergency responders ought not anticipate and seek to prevent every single emergency that could conceivably be foreseen. If this were the salient threshold, all circumstances in which what I have termed "unexpected emergencies" could arise would have to be pre-emptively managed or averted, leading to a constant worry that everything that goes up may one day come down and generate an emergency! Regress in foreseeability would be infinite and make life and attempts at societal governance very daunting indeed. Therefore, to understand the relevance of foreseeability to the moral salience of emergencies, we must consider when the first-order reasons supplied by these emergencies—that is, the urgent needs to avert or mitigate serious harms—may lose some of their rational standing due to foreseeability-related concerns. In the following sections, I consider some key issues that are either directly or indirectly relevant to such a challenging and crucial assessment.

5.2.2 When Emergency Prevention Matters

The answer to the general second-order puzzle about emergency prevention introduced in the last section depends, I think, on a multivariable case-by-case evaluation of: the risk of emergency—that is, the probability that serious harm will urgently need to be avoided or minimized, and its discoverability; the gravity of the harm at risk; the value of the course of action that would expose agents to the emergency; and the burdens and costs associated with emergency prevention or avoidance. As a rule of thumb, the higher the risk of emergency, the more serious the harm at risk, the lower the value of the course of action leading to exposure, and the lighter the burden of emergency prevention, the more one ought to seek to pre-empt, avoid, or minimize an emergency (and vice-versa). Thus, the significance of foreseeability may be a matter of degree. I have already spoken about the question of harm, but more must now be said about the other variables just introduced, as well as about their interrelations. I discuss them in turn.

5.2.2.1 Risk and Risk Assessment

That the notion of risk is intrinsically connected to the concept of emergency should come as no surprise. It is only when there is a risk of serious harm that a need to react urgently to avert or minimize its materialization can arise. The risk of harm primarily at issue is the actual risk of harm in the physical world, as opposed to the epistemic risk as it may be estimated by emergency responders. This is because they are susceptible to making mistakes as well as neglecting probabilities, and morally significant risks are facts that exist irrespective of neglect and mistakes. For example, in emergency settings, ignorance of relevant facts, unaccustomed thinking, and emotions like fear may cause rational judgment to go awry. This is not to say that emotions cannot be rationally helpful in emergencies, as in the case of the soldier driven by raw fear to jump out of the path of a rocket fired in his direction. I am also not denying that moral agents may be trained to assess and handle risks better, or that epistemic aids such as safety standards may be fixed *ex ante*. However, even with all the precautions in the world, errors in judgment may still happen: excusable errors that do not ultimately reflect badly on their makers perhaps, but errors nonetheless.

Here, one should not make the mistake of discounting too readily the significance of the knowableness, or discoverability, of a risk, and the challenges it may pose to potential emergency responders. Indeed, it seems reasonable to think that, in order to weigh for or against prevention, risks must be epistemically available as grounds for action. This conclusion seems to flow from the fact that an agent cannot take steps to avoid harm unless he or she is able to foresee it, based on the evidence available. Of course, even for those who seek to know a risk, knowledge may be elusive for reasons such as lack of resources, concealment (think of military strategy), scientific uncertainty (think of complex risks of pandemics), or absence of time between the creation of the risk and its materialization. However, even if a risk is not fully cognizable, it must at least partially be in order to be capable of grounding avoiding action. Knowableness seems to matter to a risk's moral significance, and this means that even partial knowableness might sometimes affect it (or, at least, affect our evaluation of what responses are morally acceptable in the circumstances).[11]

Another important feature of the risk *problématique* that has captured the attention of emergency theorists is its temporal scope. Just as the risks of emergencies may be ephemeral, they may also persist over time. Some speak of long or chronic emergencies, even of permanent ones.[12] There is some truth to such accounts, but

---

[11] In fact, as Victor Tadros (2011, 217–240) points out, evidence-relative risks, as opposed to genuine fact-relative or merely belief-relative risks, may sometimes play an even more morally significant role than I allow here.

[12] Cf. Rubenstein (2007) on chronic challenges linked to underdevelopment and lack of access to basic resources in some parts of the world. Another oft-cited example is the so-called ever present threat of terrorism. Given the pervasive nature of the phenomenon (however defined), it is often argued that the fight against it is urgent, although likely to be very long and unlikely to be won like a traditional war. Some even argue that it cannot terminate definitively.

various qualifications are in order. Let us consider a paradigmatic example of what could be described as a "prolonged emergency": a protracted all-out war. From the perspective of a state, the risk of harm may be continuously high, calling for relentlessly urgent planning and vigilance. The same might be said from the point of view of soldiers and civilians in or near combat zones. However, instead of focusing on the general risk of harm, the emphasis could also be placed on the multiple risks of emergenc*ies* that constitute the so-called prolonged emergency. If, from the perspective of soldiers and civilians, their life is constantly at risk, it is at least partly because of a succession of more discrete emergencies in the form of ground attacks, air raids, and so forth. In the case of states, combined attacks may heighten the risk of harm, but a war in the traditional, perhaps non-nuclear, sense is also constituted by successive campaigns, missions, and offensives, each of which may be more or less probable, urgent, and harmful to the recipient. Therefore, all-out wars may be said to be "states of emergency" for both individuals and states—in the sense of periods in which the occurrence of many specific and successive emergencies is highly probable. This way of thinking about prolonged emergencies permits the breaking up of overall risks into manageable units that rational agents may seek to address based on each unit's distinctive characteristics. This approach also accounts for the possibility that some emergencies may lead to further emergencies, in the sense of causally increasing their probability. For example, a series of attempted political killings may set a civil war in motion.

Such thinking about wars, civil conflicts, and other so-called prolonged emergencies presents them as situations that are significantly more morally complex than many of the moral and political theorists who write about them assume.[13] This complexity should not be avoided. Understanding the plethora of discrete moral dilemmas with which prolonged emergencies are typically rife is essential to making complete sense of them, and the challenges they pose. Different individuated emergencies, with different urgency and harm components, may justify different individuated responses than those for which the overall character of the war is otherwise thought to account. Of course, the converse is also possible. Various individuated risks will sometimes conflict in ways that make certain emergency responses—that would be justified if taken on their own—unjustified, all things considered. Indeed, emergencies will sometimes conflict with each other. With such moral assessments, the devil tends to be in the details, and we must not shy away from addressing these details, as well as the compounded complexities they entail for emergency prevention. The flipside of this argument is that situations involving long-term risks that, from the relevant standpoints, are devoid of such discrete and successive urgent moments should likely not bear the label "emergency" at all. As one social commentator notes in respect to such situations: "How long might the Long Emergency last? A generation? Ten generations? A millennium? Ten millennia?

---

[13] More recent engagements with just war theory, such as McMahan (2009), go some way towards remedying this methodological defect by focusing on the responsibility of various individual players in wars. Yet, the background unit of evaluation tends to remain whether one is fighting in a just or unjust *war*, as opposed to more discrete campaigns or missions.

Take your choice. Of course, after a while, an emergency becomes the norm and is no longer an emergency" (Kunstler 2005, 8).[14]

Is this account of prolonged emergencies too cut and dry? What about enduring second-order risks of first-order risks of emergencies? Here, I am referring to the possibility of meta-emergencies, at times also dubbed states of emergency, about the incidence of emergencies—that is, emergencies that might be grounded in second-order risks that currently unknown and unascertainable first-order risks of emergencies may come into being (or secretly already are). The portrait of protracted warfare that I painted earlier assumed the existence of more or less ascertainable first-order risks that could be addressed at face value. Although it is true that some risks may be ascertainable in this way, it is the nature of war that not all will be. Part of the art of warfare are tactics like strategizing in secret, coming up with unprecedented maneuvers, taking one's enemy by surprise, demoralizing it through shock and awe, and infiltrating it on all conceivable fronts. Sometimes, all that is known (and knowable) from an attacked party's perspective are the generic types of risks that could possibly arise in times of war, such as food shortages, civil disorder, treason, bombings, and so forth. It may be uncertain whether these or other potential threats will ever come into being and, in the eventuality that they do (or already secretly are), it might be impossible to anticipate where, when, and how. Yet, it might also be the case that if preventive action were not taken immediately, it would be too late to react if and when those threats materialize. Therefore, to avert or minimize harm, states may need to make decisive and immediate provisions for such uncertain possibilities, as rough and approximate as these provisions may be, given the information at hand.[15] Governments may need to impose rules seeking to tie up possible loose-ends while there is still time, and instruct immediate preventive food rationing, tighter checks on people with access to sensitive information, public order policies like curfews, if nothing more drastic. They may also need to establish in advance who would be responsible for evaluating and responding to different kinds of potential urgent needs, and develop coping routines and mechanisms. Such pre-emptive approaches to uncertainty are often grouped under the headings of "contingency planning" or "emergency preparedness."

---

[14] A similar type of criticism could be directed at states such as Brunei Darussalam, Swaziland, Israel, Egypt and Syria that claimed for many decades—and in many cases still claim—to be facing perpetual emergencies justifying resort to harsh "emergency powers" to control their populations. See e.g. Reza (2007). The further point to be made, of course, is that unjust regimes treating insurgent movements as emergency threats to their subsistence generally fail to acknowledge that they themselves—*qua* unjust regimes—can generate prolonged emergencies that may, or should, be resisted (given their more harmful character overall). No doubt, the "Arab Spring" uprisings of 2011 against oppressive dictatorships ruling through "emergency measures" are a sobering reminder of this possibility.

[15] Such cases are distinguishable from emergencies characterised by temporally distant, though highly probable harm, in which we *know* that if we do not act now, harm will likely result at a later point. Consider for example the case of early Canadian settlers who needed to store food in the summer to be able to survive the winter. In so-called meta-emergency cases, it is uncertainty as to the very existence of serious risks that is the operative variable. Note, however, the reservations expressed in the next paragraph.

Earlier, I suggested that, all else being equal, the lower the risk of emergency, the less reason one has to bother with it. Could we not argue that second-order risks are too hazy and remote ever to warrant special attention? As I tried to show in my discussion of warfare, such a general conclusion would seem counter-intuitive. Although, at a given point in time, first-order risks of emergencies may be unknown and unascertainable, the likelihood (or second-order risks) of such risks ever coming into being (or already secretly existing) may be somewhat foreseeable given the context. Once we accept this line of reasoning, it becomes easier to see how probabilities about the very incidence of risks of emergencies may point to a need for immediate contingency planning, and have moral implications. What is debatable here is not whether so-called second-order risks matter, but whether we are in fact dealing with a different, or "meta," kind of emergency. Arguably, a first-order risk and a second-order risk of the incidence of this risk are merely facets of the same overall risk. The overall risk may be very low or hazy but, as I observed earlier, to the extent that it is at least partially knowable, even if only through experience, it may matter morally. In the same way as a virtual certainty, a mere possibility of emergency may be balanced with other variables—such as the gravity of the harm risked, the value of the activity exposing one to the risk, and the burdens of prevention—to assess the reasonableness of prevention. Therefore, so-called second-order risks of emergencies can also contribute to shaping the landscape of reasons for action applicable to emergency responders (including counter-emergency planners) and, in the same breath, the morally justified courses of action available to them.

5.2.2.2   The Value of Risky Behaviour

Some courses of action are clearly better or worse than others. Contrast the declaration of an unjust war of aggression with an innocent state's wholly proportionate and necessary self-defensive response to a threat or, perhaps even more revealing, with a humanitarian intervention aimed at rescuing a foreign minority group from genocide. In fact, activities are sometimes so valuable that the value of engaging in them outweighs associated risks. The risks incurred while driving at 140 km/h through a 100 km/h zone may not be outweighed by the value of arriving at a party on time, but they may well be by that of getting one's pregnant wife in painful labor to the maternity ward in due course. Accordingly, the value of a risky activity may influence which associated risks, including risks of emergencies, ought to be proactively avoided and which may reasonably be discounted.

The value of an activity does not necessarily depend on the good consequences of its performance. Risk taking may itself form part of what makes an activity worth pursuing. Just as virtually any human activity involves some risk, intrinsically valuable risk-taking is a pervasive feature of human life. Think, for example, of the value of love affairs, business ventures, extreme sports or, in the international realm, the value of standing up for a friendly nation in the face of adversity. Many such activities have their intrinsic value enhanced by their inherent riskiness. Their riskiness counts against them consequentially, but in favour of them non-consequentially.

Of course, I am not hereby denying that riskiness may also count *against* an activity non-consequentially (*i.e.* irrespective of deleterious consequences). Criminally prohibited inchoate wrongs, such as attempted arson or murder, or conspiracies, reflect this fact, and there is little doubt that the moral position of perpetrators may be affected accordingly.[16] International inchoate wrongs, such as attempted aggressions, fall in the same category. My aim here is to emphasize that the intrinsic value (and, to a lesser extent, intrinsic disvalue) of some risks is an oft-neglected second-order factor in practical thinking about emergencies—a factor that may have significant ramifications for the reasonableness of different ways of planning for and responding to them.

Now, it is noteworthy that the (positive) value to be derived from risk-taking on both consequential and intrinsic accounts might only justify disregarding risks beyond some minimal level of care and restraint. A purported war hero ought to use appropriate and reliable equipment, and ensure levels of fitness and skill sufficient to allow her to carry out her heroic acts. A state-government ought to do at least some basic risk assessment before standing up for another nation in a way that could trigger a bloody international conflict that would significantly harm its members. Such minimal thresholds of care pertain to the domain of value to the extent that they represent a balance between valuable and non-valuable aspects of activities—risks, consequences, and others—in a way that makes the realization of value possible through the activity. The tension inherent in these thresholds comes out perhaps most clearly in cases of valuable activities for which it is unclear whether any amount of precaution could even minimally bring the inherent risks of emergencies under control. An incurable coronary patient, who also happens to be an army doctor, may increase her life expectancy by living a life of contemplation and quiet inactivity. However, what if she wants to continue working hard at her stressful career in order to serve her country and fellow soldiers, even at the risk of a sudden and fatal heart attack? What about the members of a persecuted minority group who insist on going out in the open to work, shop and, perhaps also, try to influence general public opinion, despite the presence of a dangerously racist and militarized majority?

In both cases, it may be reasonable to proceed with the more dangerous path, despite the deep loss of control over related risks that such a decision would entail. With respect to the coronary patient, there is no easy answer, and her options may well be incommensurable. Each may have its costs and benefits both consequentially and intrinsically speaking, resulting in two very different, yet rationally undefeated, life paths. With respect to the minority group members exposing

---

[16] As noted by Suzanne Uniacke (1994, 83–84), "in the case of a hijacker holding hostages who kills in self-defence in a shoot-out with police, it very clearly makes a difference to the normative background that the hijacker has foreseeably and *wrongfully* created the circumstances in which he is endangered."

themselves to the dangerously racist majority, prudence may recommend restraint. However, many may also share Tom Sorell's intuition that the risks of emergencies at issue are risks for which the relevant "preventive treatment is whatever cures racism, rather than avoiding action on the part of [those who may be victims of it]" (Sorell 2002, 24).[17] Since it is unlikely that individual minority group members would be in a position to cure racism by themselves, could they not reasonably disregard related risks and continue with their activities in the morally tainted environment? Some may anticipate the prudent mother's objection, imploring her daughter to avoid all contacts with the oppressive majority if she has the opportunity to do so, perhaps adding that if she goes ahead and gets into trouble, she will have courted it. This is where the question of value comes into play. One way of rationalizing Sorell's intuition in the face of the mother's objection is to posit that the value of being able to go out in the open freely to work, shop, and carry on with life is so important as to make it reasonable to discount racism-related risks. Here again, it might be a matter of incommensurable choices for those involved, assuming that they indeed have safer alternatives. They might reasonably choose to be prudent and avoid confrontation, or be courageous, affirm their beliefs, and face the potential consequences. In such cases, then, it may be that the moral salience of foreseeable risks of emergencies must not only be assessed in terms of their consequential and intrinsic (dis)value. The reasonableness of responses to such risks may also need to take into account the value for potential emergency responders of deciding for themselves how to respond.

At this point, it bears emphasizing that, unlike the minority group members taken individually, their political leadership or the government of the state in which they reside may be in a position to do something about the occurrence of the unwelcome incommensurable dilemmas they face. When this is the case, they may have a correspondingly strong reason, if not a duty, to do so. Other states may also have strong reasons to demand change and, sometimes, even to intervene in more direct ways. Thus, the preventability of emergencies, assessed in light of the burdens associated with it, also seems to matter a great deal to how emergencies should feature in our practical thinking and behavior, as well as in that of our governments.

5.2.2.3 Burden of Emergency Prevention and Emergency Preventability

The relevance of foreseeability to the moral salience of emergencies depends largely on their preventability, because foreseeability is a precondition for purported harm prevention and, as such, loses much of its significance when prevention is impossible. To put the matter crudely, what is unavoidable remains unavoidable whether it is foreseeable or not. That being said, the preventability of an emergency is rarely

---

[17] This intuition applies to a much broader array of daily situations, such as threats of terrorism for air travelers or risks of rape for women who interact with men. Should airplane users stop flying, and women seek to seclude themselves from men?

an all-or-nothing issue. Thus, it is often possible to inquire whether one should try to take preventive action, or if it would be reasonable to refrain from doing so. We have seen that, generally speaking, considerations of harm seriousness, risk, and value of emergency exposure are relevant to such assessments. Yet, the picture would not be complete without adding that emergency prevention can be more or less burdensome and costly, and that this feature also has a direct bearing on its reasonableness.

One way of framing the issue might be to say that, all else being equal, the more a foreseeable emergency is preventable, the less reasonable it is to carry on without seeking to prevent or minimize it (and vice-versa). This rule of thumb warrants some important qualifications. First, the nature of the precautions that would be necessary to prevent the emergency must be taken into account. According to Tom Sorell, one should consider whether the requisite precautions would be "morally harmless and undaunting."[18] This formulation, perhaps too lacking in nuance, begs for an explanation that Sorell does not explicitly provide. Presumably, what he has in mind is that if the burden or cost of emergency prevention is onerous, it may entail unreasonable trade-offs. For example, if steps necessary for emergency avoidance are all-things-considered more harmful than the harm to be avoided, and more risky than the risks already incurred, the case for prevention will likely be defeated. Consider the case of soldiers in the field who would need to kill their prisoners of war to eliminate limited risks of mutiny, or the controversial example of resort to torture as—allegedly—the only means of ascertaining some remote risks of emergency. Consider also a situation in which the amount of scarce resources that would need to be diverted to prevent a localized emergency would endanger a larger segment of population even more seriously. The complexity of preventive measures, their chance of success, their side-effects, their costs to the actor, as well as other related situation-specific factors may further compound the equation, weighing either for or against prevention.

Given these intricacies, it helps to think in terms of degrees of preventability. One may conceive of situations in which harmless and relatively straightforward preventive measures could significantly *reduce* the probabilities of emergencies and the amount of harm risked. However, within the same parameters, measures that would virtually *eradicate* those risks may require excessively onerous trade-offs. In such circumstances, taking preventive steps with a view to mitigating emergencies, short of preventing them completely, may be a reasonable option. For example, conducting thorough searches of every commuter using the London Tube, as well as their every piece of luggage, might virtually eliminate risks of bombings inside stations and trains. However, such an approach could be deeply invasive and likely cause massive congestion, if not cause the entire city to grind to a halt. Sweeping schemes of this kind may be contrasted with more moderate and practicable mitigation strategies such as CCTV surveillance, regular police patrols, clearly marked and accessible emergency exits, public reminders not to leave belongings unattended,

---

[18] Sorell "Morality and Emergency" (n 28) 23.

and the removal of strategically located litter bins and other concealed spaces. As an author fittingly remarks, it is clear that "safety [*i.e.* the prevention of risks] has a price, in terms of its impact on other things we want or value, and there are limits to what we are prepared to pay" (Wolff 2006, 415). So not only might there be minimal thresholds of reasonable care, as I postulated in the last section, there may also be maximal ones. Insofar as this is the case, reasonableness will likely lie somewhere within that range, unless additional considerations such as specific duties of care further complicate the appraisal.

Of course, the possibility of wholly unavoidable and unmitigable emergencies cannot be excluded. However, one should not make the mistake of confusing them with emergencies that are inescapable by specific agents, but preventable by others. In 2005, Mumbai endured a record monsoon season that saw almost a litre of rainfall within 1 day. More than a thousand people were estimated killed, and, as is often the case, the poor were hardest hit, with the highest concentration of deaths found in the city's slums. Could slum dwellers not have minimized the devastating impact of the monsoon, especially since it is a predictable yearly occurrence (albeit usually in a weaker form)? It is possible that, at a rudimentary level, they could have better prepared themselves and their immediate environment. However, given their negligible financial means and lack of access to expertise and material resources, it is nearly certain that they were unable to do anything significant on their own, including relocating. Thus, for scores of urban poor, a flood emergency could well seem unavoidable. Yet, just as in the case of the member of a minority group confronting endemic racism, this is a perspectival observation which does not imply that, all things considered, nothing could be done to prevent the emergency.

The Indian government at all levels, in tandem with local corporations and NGOs, could contribute to the design and construction of infrastructures capable of absorbing and draining heavier rainfalls. If the Indian state was too poor to build sufficiently effective infrastructures, other states, as well as foreign corporations and individuals, were undoubtedly in a position to aid in providing the necessary funds, resources, expertise and skills. When individuals, collectivities and institutions face emergencies that they are unable to prevent on their own, it is often the case that third parties may assist in preventing or minimizing risks. The question then becomes who is in a better position to act preventively and who, if anybody, should bear the burden, or part of the burden, of doing so.[19] Unsurprisingly, this line of questioning tends to loom large in international debates about the legitimacy of United-Nations-led economic and military operations, as well as more state-driven humanitarian interventions aimed at pre-empting bloody conflicts in foreign lands.

What about situations in which harm cannot realistically be avoided at all?[20] Such cases warrant independent treatment. As I already suggested when discussing

---

[19] On task-efficacy as grounding a duty to govern (and, perhaps, a duty of assistance more generally), see Green (2007).

[20] I resort to the admittedly vague and general concept of "realistically unavoidable harm" to prevent any distracting digression into metaphysical debates about "can" and "could."

the concept of emergency, the existence of such a situation is conditional upon the existence of harm that can be averted or significantly minimized. This relation holds true because emergency is a category of practical thought and, as such, presupposes sufficiency of means to address it. Why? As Anthony Kenny remarked many years ago, "the purpose of practical reasoning is to get done what we want," so that a practical category presupposes a reachable goal (Kenny 1966, 73).[21] If no realistic means would be sufficient for the goal to be achieved, the situation falls outside the scope of the relevant practical category. In the cases that concern us, if nothing can realistically be done to prevent or minimize serious harm, then there is no necessity to take action, and thus no emergency.

One might seek to counter this point by appealing to hypothetical examples of unavoidable and unmitigable harm, like that of a giant asteroid about to collide with Earth. Do we not envisage such *in extremis* threats of (*ex hypothesi*) unavoidable harm as generalized emergencies? In my view, conflicting intuitions may come from the fact that when we imagine such extreme situations, we also tend to envision the social chaos that would likely accompany them. Amidst pre-Armageddon civil disorder, there might be countless threats of avoidable harm calling for urgent reactions, amounting to a general state of emergency. Yet, the imminent and all-encompassing destruction to be brought about by the giant asteroids does not per se constitute an emergency. In a counterfactual world in which such pervasive harm is avoidable or mitigable, its threat would no doubt constitute one. However, where it is realistically unavoidable, a would-be emergency turns out to be a tragedy. In fact, one does not need to think of such far-fetched examples to appreciate the tragic nature of inescapable threats of unavoidable harm. A tragedy arises whenever serious harm becomes unpreventable, as assessed from the standpoint of agents who cannot realistically do anything about it. Large earthquake scenarios involving rescuers too far-off to reach victims in time and a shortage of effective means of rescue, cases of slum dwellers trapped in flooding rooms with no help in sight, instances of non-deflectable missiles fired in error, are perhaps even more vivid illustrations due to their prior historical occurrence and possible recurrence. Of course, this is not to say that inescapable threats of unavoidable harm cannot constitute reasons for action for helpless agents. However, if they do constitute reasons, these reasons will at most be of an expressive nature—*e.g.* reasons for engaging in futile rescue attempts as a means of symbolically demonstrating how much one cares, reasons for telling others one last time what they mean to us, reasons for offering to sacrifice oneself first as a mark of solidarity.

To summarize, emergencies matter at a basic, first-order level and pose the practical challenges they do because of the potential for serious harm that they represent and the urgency of the responses needed to avert or minimized that harm. The contours and materialization of such broadly defined featured may require determinations, which relevant authorities may be in a position to provide legitimately.

---

[21] Of course, "what we want" should be read to refer to what we rationally want, as opposed to raw desire.

Even then, though, the justification of responses to emergencies will frequently also depend on second-order considerations, including how foreseeable, valuable, and preventable these emergencies were in the first place.

5.3   Some Concluding Remarks About Public Emergencies

Other features of emergencies may also be morally salient, and affect how they may be addressed. I want to conclude by saying a few words about one such feature—namely, the public dimension that many emergencies considered in this chapter happen to share. Bernard Williams once wrote that the "first political question" is "the securing of order, protection, safety, trust, and the conditions of cooperation," and that the modern state presents itself as its solution (Williams 2005, 3). State-governments, it is widely believed, exist primarily to provide these public goods. Depending on whom one asks, the list is sometimes more or less extended to also include a plethora of other goods and values that markets are thought ill-suited to fulfil. I have argued elsewhere that public emergencies are emergencies that interfere, or threaten to interfere, with the provision of public goods—with international and civil wars perhaps constituting paradigmatic examples (Tanguay-Renaud 2009). Thus, public emergencies are the emergencies towards which state-governments should first and foremost turn their attention, and which they should primarily seek to prevent.

However, in striving to address such emergencies, governments must be careful not to become part of the problems they exist to solve. In Williams's words, they must not resort to terror. So, while they may need to resort to coercion to achieve their legitimate ends, they should always strive to do so consistently with the harm principle, or some similar principle of toleration. That is, their invasions of personal autonomy for the suppression of public emergencies (themselves morally costly) should not be disproportionate to the moral gains on offer. Since governments tend to have significant *de facto* authority over the governed and to be in a position to modify their normative position in radical ways by altering their legal duties, rights, and permissions, they must also strive to do so in accordance with the ideal of the rule of law. In other words, governments must strive to exercise their authority in ways that are clear, prospective, open, stable, consistent, and general, so that the governed are able to conduct their lives in ways that avoid the stigma and disruption of the adverse consequences that can follow from the breach of governmental rules and directives. These moral constraints are *additional* to the ones considered earlier. They apply to state-governments in particular, in virtue of their social power, authority, and the means they employ to discharge their legitimate functions.

Admittedly, these additional constraints are not absolute. For example, governments may sometimes be justified in leaving behind the rule of law for the sake of other, weightier values that can only be vindicated through more flexible means.

Yet, if governments are to avoid becoming part of the central problems they exist to solve, such decisions must not be taken lightly. Thus, although some public emergencies will be unpredictable in their timing, such unpredictability does not mean that rules that are clear, prospective, etc., cannot be ready for when these emergencies occur. Countless jurisdictions possess a myriad of "stand-by" or "backup" emergency laws waiting to be used to deal with public emergencies.[22] These laws are not applicable in normal times because the factual situations to which they relate do not exist, but they remain available on the statute books. Similarly, in most legal systems, swift legislative action often makes it possible to introduce *ad hoc* measures that accord with the rule of law to deal with unforeseen emergencies that are not covered by stand-by legislation. These institutional facts may seem somewhat banal, but they are often ignored in discussions of the particular challenges posed by public emergencies and appropriate means of prevention. In fact, even when *ad hoc* legislation is impossible, governments are still often in a position to provide general notice to the governed that their normative position is about to be changed in unforeseen ways, by declaring a "state of emergency" publicly. Thus, they may at least be able to comply partially with the rule of law.

Although I can only discuss cursorily such additional considerations tied to public emergencies, I mention them in conclusion to contextualize my earlier discussion of *basic* challenges posed by emergencies. In other words, more work needs to be done if a complete picture of the governance challenges posed by *public* emergencies is to be provided.

Notice also that most of my discussion in this chapter has been about emergency justifications, as opposed to excuses that emergencies may provide for impermissible behaviour. However, as I remarked before, many emergencies demand that those who address them assess the parameters of their predicament hastily. Many emergencies also trigger strong emotions. Thus, emergency responders' interpretation of the situations they are facing can at times be distorted, and lead to unjustified wrongful responses on their part. Yet, if their unjustified wrongful responses are understandable in the circumstances, should they be excused in ways that allow them to avoid blame and cognate consequences? This is not the place for a discussion of standards of excuses. Note, however, that while it is often acknowledged that individual emergency responders may be entitled to emergency-related excuses, many theorists resist the ascription of such excuses to the state.[23] One important ground for this reluctance is the thought that excusing states for wrongs perpetrated in emergencies may send the wrong message, and invite an erroneous perception amongst governmental officials that no more is demanded of them in such situations. Given the high stakes typically involved in public emergencies and the importance of moral constraints like the ones just discussed, such "emergency thinking" slippages are not to be encouraged. This is not to say, of course, that state-governments may

---

[22] See e.g. Emergencies Act, R.S.C., 1985, c. 22 (4th Supp.) (Canada), online: http://laws-lois.justice.gc.ca/PDF/E-4.5.pdf.

[23] See e.g. Simester (2008, 299–304).

never be excused. Yet, it is at least a strong reason to think that appropriate standards for state excuses for wrongdoing in emergencies may be significantly higher than those applicable to ordinary individuals. This, I think, is the grain of truth in the assertions of those who would want us to restrict "emergency thinking" to the clearest cases of emergency, at least insofar as governmental responses are concerned.

Acknowledgments Special thanks are owed to Kimberley Brownlee, David Enoch, John Gardner, and Alice MacLachlan for comments and discussions.

References

Frankfurt HG (1984) Necessity and desire. Philos Phenomenol Res 45:1–13
Gardner J (2010) Justification under authority. Can J Law Jurisprud 23:71–98
Gert B (2004) Common morality: deciding what to do. Oxford University Press, Oxford
Green L (2007) The duty to govern. Legal Theory 13:165–185
Green L (2010). Legal obligation and authority. In: Zalta EN (ed.) The Stanford encyclopedia of philosophy (Spring 2010 edn). http://plato.stanford.edu/archives/spr2010/entries/legal-obligation/
Kenny AJ (1966) Practical inference. Analysis 26:64–75
Kunstler JH (2005) The long emergency: surviving the converging catastrophes of the twenty-first century. Atlantic Books, London
Loveman B (1993) The constitution of tyranny: regimes of exception in Spanish America. University of Pittsburg Press, Pittsburg
McMahan J (2009) Killing in war. Oxford University Press, Oxford
Ramraj VV, Thiruvengadam AK (eds) (2010) Emergency powers in Asia: exploring the limits of legality. Cambridge University Press, Cambridge
Raz J (2004) Incorporation by law. Legal Theory 10:1–17
Reza S (2007) Endless emergency: the case of Egypt. New Crim Law Rev 10:532–553
Rubenstein J (2007) Distribution and emergency. J Polit Philos 15:296–320
Scanlon TM (1975) Preference and urgency. J Philos 72:655–669
Scarry E (2011) Thinking in an emergency. W.W. Norton & Company, New York
Scheppele KL (2006) North American emergencies: the use of emergency powers in Canada and the United States. Int J Const Law 4:213–243
Schmitt C (2005) Political theology: four chapters on the concept of sovereignty. Chicago University Press, Chicago
Simester AP (2008) Necessity, torture and the rule of law. In: Ramraj VV (ed) Emergencies and the limits of legality. Cambridge University Press, Cambridge, pp 289–313
Sorell T (2002) Morality and emergency. Proc Aristot Soc 103:21–37
Tadros V (2011) The ends of harm: the moral foundations of criminal law. Oxford University Press, Oxford
Tanguay-Renaud F (2009) Making sense of "public" emergencies. Philos Manage 8:31–52
Tanguay-Renaud F (2012) Individual emergencies and the rule of criminal law. In: Tanguay-Renaud F, Stribopoulos J (eds) Rethinking criminal law theory: new Canadian perspectives in the philosophy of domestic, transnational, and international criminal law. Hart Publishing, Oxford, pp 19–54
Uniacke S (1994) Permissible killing: the self-defence justification of homicide. Cambridge University Press, Cambridge
Walzer M (1977) Just and unjust wars: a moral argument with historical illustrations. Basic Books, New York
Wiggins D (1987) Needs, values, truth, 3rd edn. Clarendon, Oxford

Williams B (2005) In the beginning was the deed. Princeton University Press, Princeton
Wolff J (2006) Risk, fear, blame, shame and the regulation of public safety. Econ Philos
    22:409–427

Part II
Framing Responsibilities

Chapter 6
At War's End: Clashing Visions and the Need for Reform

Brian Orend

Abstract The topic of post-war justice has only recently been getting the attention it deserves. Historically, it was assumed that, as the old saying goes, "to the victor go the spoils of war." This, however, is a sub-optimal state of affairs which needs very much to be changed. The goal of this essay, accordingly, is to construct a general set of plausible principles to guide communities seeking to resolve their armed conflicts fairly and decently. After that, quick application will be made of these principles to the on-going cases in Afghanistan and Iraq.

6.1 Introduction

The topic of post-war justice has only recently been getting the attention it deserves. Historically, it was assumed that, as the old saying goes, "to the victor go the spoils of war." As a result of this widespread belief, there is actually next to no clear international law regulating the termination phase of war (Buergenthal and Maier 1990; Orend 2000). This, however, is a sub-optimal state of affairs that needs very much to be changed. In fact, I would argue that there needs to be *a brand new Geneva Convention*—one devoted exclusively to the vital issues raised by the endings of wars. Why?

- *Completion.* There are many international laws regulating both the start of war and the middle (or conduct) of war. Moreover, many of these laws make sound strategic, and good moral, sense (Best 1994). Thus, to complete our analysis of war's many impacts on international life, we need to consider the ending phase

B. Orend (✉)
Department of Philosophy, University of Waterloo, Waterloo, ON N2L 3G1, Canada
e-mail: bdorend@uwaterloo.ca

A. MacLachlan and A. Speight (eds.), *Justice, Responsibility and Reconciliation in the Wake of Conflict*, Boston Studies in Philosophy, Religion and Public Life 1, DOI 10.1007/978-94-007-5201-6_6, © Springer Science+Business Media Dordrecht 2013

of war. Bottom line: if it's important to guide both *the start* and *the middle*, it's just as important to guide *the end*. Completion demands it.

- *Focus.* The practical task of drafting, and then ratifying, a binding legal document on this issue would focus international attention on doing something constructive and improving about war in general, and take "*jus post bellum*" (i.e., justice after war) out of abstract theory and into the concrete reality of global politics.

- *Guidance.* The function of any kind of law is to guide behaviour, hopefully in a way useful, advantageous, and improving for all. The laws of *jus ad bellum* (i.e., the justice of the start of war) and *jus in bello* (i.e., the justice of the conduct of war) are designed to guide the behaviour of all belligerents (Walzer 1977; Orend 2006). The rules of *jus post bellum* could likewise guide both the winner and the loser in the aftermath of armed conflict. (This is assuming there even *is* a clear-cut winner and loser, which sometimes *isn't* the case, such as with the Iran-Iraq War of 1979–1989, when the belligerents just stopped fighting after—eventually—realizing that neither of them could win.) Contrary to the old cliché mentioned at the start, *both winners and losers would gain* by there being clear post-war rules. The losers, of course, could be assured that they would not be subjected to cruel, vindictive treatment at the hands of a gloating, arrogant winner. And the winners could get a clear understanding of their rights and obligations during the aftermath of war. In particular, winners would appreciate being able to point to such rules and say: "Look, we've done what we're duty-bound to do, and now we are out of here." It seems to me that America, e.g., would have very much wanted to say this, and benefit from this, earlier on during its difficult, on-going occupation experiences in Afghanistan and Iraq. Rules provide assurances and expectations for everyone, plus clear ways of proceeding, and all parties benefit from such clarity and can put greater confidence in the process moving forward.

- *Ending the Fighting.* Failure to regulate war termination probably prolongs fighting on the ground. Since they have few assurances, or firm expectations, regarding the nature of the settlement, belligerents will be sorely tempted to keep using force to jockey for position. Since international law imposes very few constraints upon the winners of war, losers can conclude it is reasonable for them to refuse to surrender and, instead, to continue to fight. Perhaps, they think: "We might get lucky and the military tide will turn. Better that than just throw ourselves at the mercy of our enemy." Many observers felt this reality plagued the Bosnian civil war (1992–1995), which had many failed negotiations and a 3-year "slow burn" of continuous violence as the very negotiations took place (Rieff 1995).

- *Restraining the Winner.* Failure to construct principles of *jus post bellum* is to allow unconstrained war termination. And to allow unconstrained war termination is, indeed, to allow the winner to enjoy the spoils of war. This is dangerously permissive, since winners have been known to exact peace terms which are draconian and vengeful. The Treaty of Versailles, terminating World War I in 1918–1919, is often mentioned in this connection. It is commonly suggested that the sizable territorial concessions, and steep compensations payments, forced upon Germany created hatred and economic distress, opening a space for Hitler to capitalize on, saying in effect: "Let's vent our rage by recapturing our lost lands, and let's rebuild our economy by refusing to pay compensation, and by ramping up war-related manufacturing" (Boemeke 1998; Keegan 1994; Macmillian 2003).

- **Preventing Future Wars.** When wars are wrapped up badly, they sow the seeds for future bloodshed. Some people, e.g., think that America's failure to remove Saddam Hussein from power after they first beat him in 1991 prolonged a serious struggle and eventually necessitated the second war, of regime change, in 2003. *Would the second war have happened at all had the first been ended differently—* i.e., more properly and thoroughly, with a longer-range vision in mind? Many historians ask the exact same question of the two World Wars and the recent, related Serb wars, first in Bosnia and then over Kosovo (Dodge 2003; Mills 2008).

Peace treaties should still, of course, remain tightly tailored to the historical realities of the particular conflict in question. There is much nitty-gritty detail which is integral to each peace treaty. But admitting this is *not* to concede that the search for general guidelines, or universal standards, is futile or naïve. There is no inconsistency, or mystery, in holding particular actors, in complex local conflicts, up to more general, even universal, standards of conduct. Judges and juries do that on a daily basis, evaluating the factual complexities of a given case in light of general moral and legal principles. We should do the same regarding war termination. The goal of this essay, accordingly, is to construct a general set of plausible principles to guide communities seeking to resolve their armed conflicts fairly and decently. After that, quick application will be made of these principles to the ongoing cases in Afghanistan and Iraq.

6.2   Responding to Objections

Three strong objections are often mentioned to defeat, or at least challenge, this proposal for a brand new Geneva Convention devoted exclusively to post-war justice. The first is that the existing Geneva Conventions don't get perfectly adhered to anyway, and so what's the point, really, of adding another one to them? The weakness of this pessimistic challenge is shown by analogy. The challenge is like saying: "Look, because no one adheres to the speed limits on the road anyway, why should we have speed limits at all? Why not let everyone do whatever they want?" But the existence of law-breakers does not negate the point of having law: should we, e.g., get rid of the laws on property ownership because there will always be some thieves? And, as Alice MacLachan points out, even when rules are not perfectly followed, the standards they establish help increase at least partial compliance, and this partial compliance is still often much better than no standards at all.

The second challenge has to do with the power of the winner in the post-war moment. The winner is in the position of power: wouldn't it penalize the winner to restrict what it can do, perhaps leading to a less effective post-war experience for both winner and loser? In reply, the winner does occupy a powerful role, but this objection seems to confuse power (i.e., the factual ability to get what you want) with authority (i.e., the moral or legal right to use that power). Having won a war does not entitle the winner to do whatever it wants—there is never a moment of total moral vacuum—nor does placing some restrictions on its post-war conduct show disrespect to its power, or cause unhelpful interference. To the contrary, as explained above, it is in the selfish interests of war winners to have clear rules guiding everyone's conduct.

The final challenge has to do with how such a new piece of international law might get agreed upon and enforced, especially in the typical chaos and instability of the post-war moment. This is a practical challenge, one confronted by every new piece of international law. There is some reason to believe, though, that if states have already agreed on other, controversial rules of war—and controversial human rights treaties, and difficult trade deals—that they can also find common ground on rules of post-war conduct. Once drafted and agreed-upon, such a new treaty could be subjected to whichever tools of enforcement states would find useful. There are many such tools in international law, such as: fines; court cases and trials; the creation of a new international body or bureaucracy whose job it is to ensure compliance; and so on (Buergenthal and Maier 1990). But the better point is to ensure that the rules to begin with are—to the extent possible—in everyone's interests for, as the realist would tell us, that is the most effective enforcement mechanism of all.

6.3   Clashing Visions: Retribution vs. Rehabilitation

To guide the construction of a new post-war Geneva Convention, we can turn to two dominant, contrasting visions, or models, of post-war justice: that of *retribution* and that of *rehabilitation*. It seems fair to say that the retribution model is older, but that rehabilitation has made a strong showing for itself since the end of World War II. There are, perhaps, some grounds for detecting a pendulum swing between these models over time, and moving into the future.

According to the retribution model, the basic aspects of a decent post-war peace are these (and they assume—for the sake of both conceptual convenience, and of getting at the construction of some helpful principles—that "the good side" won, and that the aggressive side lost. This doesn't always happen, of course, but it seems reasonable to claim that imperfect war-endings can be modelled, to the extent possible, after the more idealized scenario) (Orend 2002b):

- **Public Peace Treaty.** While it does not need to be nit-picky in detail, the basic elements of a peace agreement should be written down, and publicly proclaimed, so that: everyone's expectations are clear; everyone knows the war is over; and everyone has an idea of what the general framework of the new post-war era will be. (Sometimes, by contrast, back in medieval Europe, the most crucial parts of a peace treaty were kept secret from the public.) (Buergenthal and Maier 1990; Orend 2000)

- *Exchange of Prisoners of War (POWs).* At war's end, all sides need to exchange all the POWs from the armed conflict.
- *Apology from the Aggressor.* The aggressor in war, like the criminal in domestic society, needs to admit fault and guilt for causing the war by committing aggression. (And aggression is understood to be the first use of force across an international border, thus violating the rights of political sovereignty and territorial integrity which all recognized countries enjoy.) This may seem quaint and elemental yet it can be quite controversial. For example, Germany has offered many, and profuse, official apologies for World War II, and especially for The Holocaust. (Germany to this day still pays an annual reparations fee to Israel for the latter.) By contrast, Japan has been nowhere near as forthcoming with a meaningful, official apology for World War II (perhaps as a result of suffering the atomic bombings of Hiroshima and Nagasaki?). This reticence enrages China, in particular, which suffered mightily from Japanese aggression and expansion in the 1930s (Buergenthal and Maier 1990; Walzer 1977).
- *War Crimes Trials for those Responsible.* The world's first post-war international war crimes trials were held after World War II, in 1945–1946, in both Nuremberg and Tokyo (Maya 2001; Orend 2009). The vast majority of those tried were soldiers and officers charged with *jus in bello* violations, like torturing POWs and targeting civilians. But a handful of senior Nazis were also charged with the *jus ad bellum* violation of "committing crimes against peace," i.e., of launching an aggressive war. In 1998, the international community passed the Treaty of Rome, creating the world's first *permanent* international war crimes tribunal. Situated mainly at The Hague, in Holland, its ambitious mandate is to prosecute *all* war crimes, committed by *all* sides in *all* wars, and to do so using lawyers and judges from countries which were *not* part of the war in question. Recently, this new court has heard many cases from the Bosnian civil war and from various African wars. It has even put on trial former heads-of-state, and not just ordinary soldiers: Slobodan Milosevic of Serbia (until his death in 2006); and Jean Kambanda, the former prime minister of Rwanda during the 1994 genocide (Schabas 2001).
- *Aggressor to give up any gains.* The thinking here is that the aggressor, as the wrongdoer, cannot be rewarded for its aggression and be allowed to keep any gains it may have won for itself during its aggression. For instance, during its initial campaign in 1992–1994, the Serb side of the Bosnian Civil War initially conquered 70% of Bosnia, way beyond the area traditionally occupied by ethnic Serbs. More dramatically, during the Blitzkrieg of 1939–1940, Hitler's Germany conquered Austria, Czechoslovakia, France, Poland and the Scandinavian countries. This principle requires that, at war's end, the aggressor give back all such unjust gains (Rieff 1995).
- *Aggressor must be demilitarized to avoid a repeat.* Since the aggressor broke international trust, so to speak, by committing aggression, it *cannot* be trusted *not* to commit aggression again (at least in the short-term and in the absence of regime change there). The international community is entitled to some added security. The tools the aggressor may use to commit aggression must thus be

taken away from it, in a process known as demilitarization. This is to say that, often, defeated aggressors lose many of their military assets and weapons capabilities, and have "caps" placed on their ability to re-build their armed forces over time.

- *Aggressor must suffer further losses.* What makes this model one of retribution is the conviction that it is not enough for the defeated aggressor merely to give up what it wrongly took, plus some weapons. *The aggressor must be made worse off than it was prior to the war.* Why? Several reasons. First, it is thought that justice demands retribution of this nature—the aggressor must be made to feel the wrongness and sting of the war which it unjustly began. Second, consider an analogy to an individual criminal: in domestic society, when a thief has stolen a diamond ring, we don't just make him give the ring back and take away his thieving tools. We also make him pay a fine or send him to jail, to impress upon him the wrongness of his conduct. And this ties into the third reason: by punishing the aggressor, we hope *to deter or prevent* future aggression, both by him (so to speak) and by any others who might be having similar ideas.

But what will make the aggressor worse off? Demilitarization, certainly. But two further things get heavily mentioned: *reparation payments* to the victims of the aggressor, plus *sanctions* slapped onto the aggressor as a whole. These are the post-war equivalent of fines, so to speak, on all of the aggressive society. Reparations payments are due, in the first instance, to the countries victimized and hurt by the aggressor's aggression and then, secondly, to the broader international community. The reparations payments are *backward-looking* in that sense, whereas the sanctions are more *forward-looking* in the sense that they are designed to hurt and curb the aggressor's future economic growth opportunities, at least for a period of time (a sort of probation) and especially in connection with any goods and services which might enable the aggressor to commit aggression again.

While there is no denying the coherent, internal logic of the retribution model—especially if one believes that justice requires retribution, in some sense—it does have significant drawbacks as well. A policy of retribution may, e.g., create new generations of enemies, as rough treatment is typically resented, even by those who objectively deserve it. In this sense, the retribution model can sow the seeds of future wars (see the two examples below in particular). And it's a bad model of post-war settlement if, *far from ending a war, it actually creates a new one.* As for sanctions, there is compelling historical evidence—say, from post-World War I Germany and post-1991 Iraq—that sweeping sanctions hurt the well-being of civilians, i.e., those innocent of the war and who have done nothing to deserve vengeful post-war treatment (Albert and Luck 1980; Simons 1996). This is to say that the retribution model can violate the *jus in bello* principle of discrimination and non-combatant immunity. Next, we might ask philosophically, whether justice actually does require retribution in analogy to the criminal justice system. Why not move on—forgiving, if not forgetting—and concentrate on bettering things for all in the future? Finally, the retribution model does not confront the continuing existence of the bad regime in aggressor, i.e., the regime which caused the war.

It merely seeks to punish that regime, and reduce the resources it has to cause future trouble. By contrast, the rehabilitation model attempts to dismantle and reconstruct bad regimes.

6.4 Two Examples of the Retribution Model

Two of the most obvious, and infamous, historical examples of the revenge model in action concern the settlements of World War I and the Persian Gulf War.

The Treaty of Versailles ended World War I (1914–1918), and is widely deemed to be a controversial failure which in a clear sense contributed to the conditions sparking World War II. The First World War had been a disaster for perhaps all belligerents except the USA. It cost way more, and lasted so much longer, than anyone had predicted and, indeed, it only came to an end, and with victory for the Allied side, when America intervened in 1917. Because of all the cost and misery, the European powers were determined to punish Germany for invading Belgium and sparking the war to begin with. So Germany was extensively demilitarized, had all its war gains taken away and, furthermore, lost some valuable territory of its own as one aspect of punishment. Crushing reparations payments were levied upon Germany, and they would have lasted into the 1980s (!) had the peace terms stuck. But they didn't, because essentially these fines bankrupted Germany within only a few years, causing massive economic dislocation, hard-ship and, eventually, civil unrest. The victorious powers also tried to force elections upon Germany, but the only result was that the people there came to associate democracy with the economic problems, and they began to turn to radical, non-democratic parties promising simple solutions in a time of complex crisis. Hitler was thus able to come to power; he stopped all reparations payments; he cancelled all elections and named himself the dictator; and he re-built the German war machine—growing the economy—and promised to get all the lost lands back. He did, or tried to, thus sparking World War II (Boemeke 1998; Keegan 1990; MacMillan 2003).

The 1991 Treaty ending the Persian Gulf War was similarly punitive and also paved the way for a second war. The treaty called upon Saddam's Iraq to give up any claims on Kuwait, officially apologize for the aggression, and surrender all POWs. Saddam was left in power, though, and no attempt was made either to change the regime or to bring anyone to trial on war crimes charges. But Iraq *was* to be extensively demilitarized. It lost many weapons, and had strict caps put on any re-building. Iraq had No-Fly-Zones (NFZs) imposed on it, both in the north (to protect the Kurds in Iraq from Saddam) and in the south (to protect the Shi'ites). Saddam also had to agree to a rigorous, and UN-sponsored, weapons inspections process. This process lasted from 1991 to 1998, and it found and destroyed literally tons of illegal weapons, including chemical and biological agents. After Saddam kicked out the inspectors in 1998, this issue grew into a major factor in favour of war in 2003, as the Americans suspected Saddam still had weapons of mass destruction (WMDs) and, moreover, was plotting to give some to al-Qaeda to enable another 9/11-style terrorist strike on America. Finally, and financially, Iraq had to pay reparations to Kuwait for the aggressive invasion in 1990 and, moreover, had to suffer continuing sweeping sanctions on its economy, especially on its ability to sell oil. These sanctions devastated Iraqi civilians and did very little to hurt Saddam. There is, in fact, evidence that the sanctions only cemented Saddam's grip on Iraq, as increasingly impoverished citizens grew more and more dependent on favours from Saddam's government in order to survive (Hampson 1996; Orend 2009; Simons 1996).

6.5   The Rehabilitation Alternative: Reconstructing Germany and Japan

As mentioned, there is no sharp split between the retribution and rehabilitation models. They share commitment to the following aspects of a decent post-war settlement: the need for a public peace treaty; official apologies; exchange of POWs; trials for criminals; some demilitarization; and the aggressor must give up any unjust gains. There is thus a substantial "overlapping consensus," in the Rawlsian sense, between them (Rawls 1999; Minow 1999; Walker 2006)—and so we should see the existence of a continuum, instead of an either/or split, in this regard. Where the models importantly differ is over three major issues. First, the rehabilitation model *rejects sanctions*, especially on grounds that they have been shown, historically, to harm civilians and thus to violate discrimination. Second, the rehabilitation model *rejects compensation payments*, for the same reason. In fact, the model favors *investing in* a defeated aggressor, to help it re-build and to help smooth over the wounds of war. Finally, the rehabilitation model *favors forcing regime change* whereas the retribution model views that as too risky and costly. That it may be, but those who favour the rehabilitative model suggest that it can be worth it over the long-term, leading to the creation of a new, better, non-aggressive, and even progressive, member of the international community. To those who scoff that such deep-rooted transformation simply can't be done, supporters of the rehabilitative model reply that, not only *can* it be done, it *has* been done. The two leading examples are West Germany and Japan after World War II.

World War II's settlement was not contained in a detailed, legalistic peace treaty. This was, partly, because Germany and Japan were so thoroughly crushed and had so little leverage. But World War II's settlement was sweeping and profound, with immense effects on world history. It was worked out, essentially, between America and the Soviet Union at meetings in Tehran and Yalta, but with participation from the U.K., France, China, and other of the "lesser" Allies. Both Britain and France kept control over their colonies, but everyone knew that powerful forces of anti-colonialism—abetted by the exhaustion of England and France—would soon cause those old empires to crumble. As for the new empires, it was understood that the USSR would hold sway in Eastern Europe, ostensibly to serve as a barrier between itself and Germany, preventing another Nazi-style invasion. (It also, though, provided for the export and spread of communism the other way.) The USA, by contrast, would get Hawaii, a number of Pacific Islands, and total sway over the reconstruction of Japan. As for Germany, it was agreed that America, Britain, France and Russia would split it, into Western and Eastern halves. Ditto for the German capital Berlin, which was otherwise entirely within the Eastern, Soviet territory. Within this Soviet sphere, police-state communism came to dominate as readily as it did in Russia. But within the West, there was a concerted effort to establish genuine free-market, rights-respecting democracies. In Japan, the same experiment was undertaken, but there the US military, under the firm leadership of Douglas MacArthur, held more direct control, for longer, than it did in West Germany.

The Allies, genuinely working with nationals in both countries—more so in Germany than Japan, perhaps—first undertook a purging process, which in Germany came to be known as "denazification." All signs, symbols, buildings, literature and things directly associated with the Nazis were destroyed utterly. The Nazi party itself was abolished and declared illegal. Surviving ex-Nazis—but not all of them— were put on trial, put in jail, or otherwise punished and prohibited from political participation (Thacker 2009). The militaries of both Germany and Japan were utterly disbanded, and for years the Allied military became *the* military, and the direct ruler, of both Germany and Japan.

After the negative purging process, the Allies in both countries established written constitutions or "Basic Law." These constitutions, after the period of direct military rule ended, provided for bills and charters of human rights, eventual democratic elections and, above all, the checks and balances so prominently featured in the American system. Since government had grown so huge and tyrannical in both Germany and Japan in the 1930s, it had to be shrunk down, and then broken into pieces, with each piece only authorized to handle its own business. Independent judiciaries and completely reconstituted police forces were an important part of this—and they went a long way to re-establishing the *impersonal* rule of law over the *personal* whims of former fascists. The executive branches, much more so than in the American system, were made more accountable to, and closely tied to, the legislative branch. The goal, of course, was to ensure that the executive couldn't grow into another dictator. By design, there were to be no strong presidents. So Germany and Japan became true *parliamentary* democracies, more in the European than in the American style.

Western-style liberal democracy was not the only change forcibly implemented. The education systems of both Germany and Japan were overhauled, since they played huge propaganda roles for both regimes and the content of their curricula had been filled with racism, ultra-nationalism and distorted ignorance of the outside world. Western experts re-designed these systems to impart concrete skills needed to participate in reconstruction, as well as to stress a more objective content favoring the basic cognitive functions ("the three Rs") as well as critical thinking and especially science and technology. The curricula were radically stripped of political content, though of course some lessons on the new social institutions and their principles were required.

The Americans quickly saw that their sweeping legal, constitutional, social and educational reforms would lack stability unless they could stimulate the German and Japanese economies. The people needed their vital needs met, as well as a sense of hope that, concretely, the future would get better. Otherwise, they might revolt, and the reforms fail. Instead of making the (World War I) mistake of *sucking money out* of these ruined countries through mandatory reparations payments, the Americans were the ones *who poured money into* Germany and Japan. America shunned the revenge paradigm and embraced the rehabilitative one. It was a staggering sum of money, too, channeled through the so-called "Marshall Plan" (Behrman 2008; Mills 2008). Money was needed to buy essentials, as well as to clear away all the rubble and ruined infrastructure. It was also just needed to circulate, to get the Germans and Japanese used to free market trading. Jobs were plentiful, as entire systems of infrastructure—transportation, water, sewage, electricity, agriculture, finance—had to be rebuilt. Since jobs paid wages, thanks to the Marshall Plan, the people's lives improved and the free market system deepened. But it wasn't just the money. American management experts poured into Germany and Japan, showing them the very latest, and most efficient, means of production. Within 30 years, Germany and Japan had not only rebounded economically, they had the two strongest economies in the world after America itself, based especially on quality high-tech manufacturing, for instance of automobiles.

The post-war reconstructions of Germany and Japan easily count as the most impressive post-war rehabilitations in modern history, rivaled perhaps only by America's re-building of its own South after The Civil War (1861–1865). [These processes weren't perfect—see Thacker 2009—yet clearly, over the long view, successful.] Germany and Japan, today, have massive free market economies, and politically remain peaceful, stable and decent democracies. They are both very good citizens on the global stage. In addition, these countries are by no means "clones" (much less colonies) of America: they each have gone their own way, adding local color, and pursuing political paths quite distinct from those that most interest the United States—consider especially Germany's formative role in the European Union (EU). So we have clear evidence that even massive and forcible post-war changes need *not* threaten "a nation's character," or what makes it unique and special to its people. But such success *did* come at a huge cost in terms of time and treasure: it cost trillions of dollars; took trillions of "man-hours" in work and expertise; it took decades of real time; it took the co-operation of most of the German and Japanese people; and, above all, it took the will of the United States to see it through. It was American money, American security, American know-how, American patience and American generosity which brought it all into being. Such is the magnitude of commitment needed by any party bent on successfully implementing substantial post-war rehabilitation (Davidson 1999; Dobbins et al. 2003; Orend 2006, 2009; Schonberger 1989; Segal 1989).

6.6 Suggested General Principles for the New Post-War Geneva Convention

Having considered some of the most relevant historical cases and lessons, I would now like to propose one general way in which any new *jus post bellum* Geneva Convention ought to be structured. (Again, not that these principles exhaust what a comprehensive treaty ought to include but, rather, that these principles ought at least to be part of such a body of law.) Any such Convention needs to have a sense of *the goal to be achieved* by the settlement, as well as an understanding of *the means needed* to secure that goal. I favour the rehabilitative model over the retributive model—for the reasons given above in Sect. 6.3—and I would thus like to suggest that the goal of post-war justice ought to be the construction of something we might call "a minimally just regime" in any defeated aggressor (Orend 2002a, 2009). A minimally just regime is *not* narrowly a Western one; rather, it is capable of existing and thriving in non-Western contexts as well, as shown by Japan. A minimally just society satisfies three general principles:

P1. It is peaceful, non-outlaw, and non-aggressive.

P2. It is run by a government seen as legitimate *both* in the eyes of its own people and in the eyes of the international community. The clearest way to prove political legitimacy—i.e., the right and authority to exercise power within a society—is by having the government be selected democratically, i.e., by a free and fair, public and regular, election, based on the principles of "one person, one vote" and majority rules. Such a process, more than any other, shows the consent of the people. Yet we might imagine more complex alternatives where there is widespread, uncoerced social peace in a society, and acknowledge that such may show consent and legitimacy, too. International recognition is shown by diplomatic recognition and by welcoming that society into membership in all the major international institutions, notably the UN (Rawls 1999).

P3. The society in question does what it can to satisfy the human rights of its people. The very point of government is to do its part to realize human rights. This is so because human rights are claims we all have to the most basic objects of vital human need, i.e., the things without which we cannot live a minimally good life in the modern world. I argue that, abstractly, there are five major objects of human rights claims: personal security; individual freedom; elemental equality; material subsistence; and social recognition as a person and rights-holder. I propose this as a general, abstract, first-level understanding of human rights objects, from which we can derive—based on combination and circumstance—particular, concrete, more detailed second-level lists of human rights objects, such as that contained within the UN's *Universal Declaration of Human Rights* (Orend 2002a, 2006).

6.7   The Process

If that is the kind of society to be sought after, when pursuing post-war reconstruction, what are the means needed to achieve it? I have structured what I call a ten-step recipe to take us from here to there, and it is based on what we have learned from the historical best cases, such as the reconstruction of Germany and Japan

(Dobbins et al. 2003; Dobbins and Jones 2007). A war winner, striving to achieve the goal of creating, in the defeated aggressor, a minimally just society, ought to do all of the following:

- *Adhere diligently to the laws of war during the regime takedown and occupation.*
- *Purge much of the old regime, and prosecute its war criminals.*
- *Disarm and demilitarize the society. (But then:)*
- *Provide effective military and police security for the whole country.*
- *Work with a cross-section of locals on a new, rights-respecting constitution that features checks and balances.*
- *Allow other, non-state associations, or "civil society," to flourish.*
- *Forego compensation and sanctions in favour of investing in and re-building the economy.*
- *If necessary, re-vamp educational curricula to purge past propaganda and cement new values.*
- *Ensure that the benefits of the new order will be: (1) concrete; and (2) widely, not narrowly, distributed.*
- *Follow an orderly, not-too-hasty exit strategy when the new regime can stand on its own two feet.*

This ten-point recipe for reconstruction is only a general blueprint; clearly, in particular cases, some things will need to be emphasized over others. The best recipes always allow for individual variance and input depending on time and the ingredients at hand. We should also note the heavy interconnectedness of many of these elements. U.S. Major-General William Nash is probably only exaggerating a bit when he declares: "The first rule of nation-building is that everything is related to everything, and it's all political" (Fukuyama 2005). Further, in spite of the variances among aggressive, rights-violating societies—different geography, history, language, economy, diet, ethnic composition—there has been striking similarity in the kind of regime here in view. Think of the major twentieth century aggressors and dictatorships: the USSR; Fascist Spain and Italy; Nazi Germany; Imperial Japan; North Korea; Communist China; Pol Pot's Cambodia; Idi Amin's Uganda; Saddam Hussein's Iraq; the Taliban's Afghanistan. In spite of all the differences among them, the regimes shared large affinities: a small group of ruthless fanatics uses force to come to power; it keeps power through the widespread use of violence, both internally and externally; it engages in massively invasive control over every major sphere of life, with no other associations allowed to rival the state's prestige; the rule of law is jettisoned; the military, or "in-party," becomes all-important; human rights are trampled upon, and so on. To a remarkable extent, in spite of all the other differences, *it's been the same kind of regime.* And this shouldn't, in the end, come as so much of a surprise: they all learned from each other and sought to emulate what worked elsewhere. The modern police state only has so many precedents to draw upon, and might in fact be located ultimately in such early examples as Napoleonic France, or most probably Robespierre's Reign of Terror during the

French Revolution (Fukuyama 2003). So, then, we shouldn't be all that shocked, surprised and skeptical if it turns out that one general recipe can, in fact, be found for transforming such regimes and societies away from rampant rights-violation into ones which are at least minimally just.

6.8   Application to Afghanistan and Iraq

Afghanistan has been in a period of post-war reconstruction since early 2002; Iraq since mid-2003. It seems true that the international community, as led by America, has—more or less—been trying to implement the above ten-step recipe in each instance. It has been a very difficult process, in both countries, and has seen a mixture of both successes and failures.

The major successes, in both nations, have been the replacement of aggressive, rogue or outlaw regimes with new governments. The old regimes have been purged; and these new governments enjoy democratic legitimacy—through multiple elections, in both countries (most recently in 2010)—and are based on written constitutions crafted by locals. Civil society—compared to what it was under Saddam, or the Taliban—has now blossomed. The gains in terms of personal freedom, in both societies, have been huge and must be noted. Also, in Afghanistan anyway, the gains in terms of gender equality have been very substantial with, e.g., the international community building and staffing many new schools for girls and women (Dodge 2003; Tanner 2009).

The problem, though, is that the evidence suggests that it is not abstract things, like individual liberty and gender equality, which matter most when it comes to the success and durability of post-war reconstruction. The historical data suggest, rather, that it is concrete things which are decisive, in particular security and the economy. Jim Dobbins, probably the leading scholar on the issue (Dobbins et al. 2003; Dobbins 2007), has distilled all this data into one crystal-clear rule-of-thumb regarding post-war success: **the war-winning occupier, and the new local regime, have about 10 years to form an effective partnership and to devote themselves in particular** *to making the average person in that society feel better off—more secure and more prosperous, especially—than they were prior to the outbreak of the war.* If they can do this, post-war reconstruction will probably succeed, in the sense that there will be a new country which is: (a) stable; (b) minimally just (in the three-fold sense described above); and (c) run entirely by locals. If not, there will be failure, and a serious risk of back-sliding into armed conflict. Using this rule of thumb, we note with concern that the approximate deadline for achieving this in Afghanistan would be 2012, and in Iraq, 2013. While the average person, in both nations, would, no doubt, report huge improvement in personal freedoms, what would they say about their security from violence, and their economic situation? They wouldn't all say the same thing, of course, but

I would suggest that, in both countries, five big obstacles stand in the way of timely and successful post-war reconstruction. They are:

1. *The Weight of History.* Psychologists have, as a maxim of treatment, the rule that the single greatest predictor of future behaviour is past behaviour. If this is true, and can be applied to societies as a whole, then the future does not bode well for these two countries. Both nations have been plagued by devastating, near-constant warfare since 1979, and their deeper histories have seen serious armed conflict and rivalries, inequality and instability, under-development and foreign power interference and meddling.

2. *Internal Divisions.* Though both countries have agreed upon new constitutions, and ratified them through elections, powerful internal group rivalries, and even bitter hatreds, exist. These call into question whether there is enough trust, and willingness to compromise, for these new regimes to work once occupying forces leave entirely. In Iraq, there is a powerful three-fold division between the Kurds in the north, the Sunnis in the middle, and the Shi'ites in the south. The Kurds want as much autonomy as possible and probably, one day, want their own new and separate country. The Shi'ites are the majority, and tend to be more religiously conservative in their interpretation of Islam whereas Sunnis are more moderate but, even though they are the minority, historically they are used to being in power. This has created resentment in the other groups. In Afghanistan, there are many more rival ethnic, religious and tribal groupings, compounding even further the issue of coming up with arrangements that can get everyone on board.

3. *External Interference.* With both these countries, there are neighbouring nations meddling with post-war reconstruction or, at least, making it difficult. With Iraq, each of the three groups has allies outside their borders who support them. With the Kurds, it is the Kurdish population in Turkey (which itself does *not* want to see Kurdish independence, lest it lose some of its own territory to an independent Kurdistan). With the Sunnis, it is Saudi Arabia and with the Shi'ites it is Iran. All these regional powers have tried to sway, or even sabotage, US-led reconstruction. Iran has also been involved in meddling with Afghanistan—giving support and sponsorship to terrorists and religious extremists, including al-Qaeda and the Taliban—but the real issue here is Pakistan. The border between Afghanistan and Pakistan is one of the most dangerous places in the world, and is the scene of multi-party scheming and conflict, very often still breaking out into open battles. The players include the Taliban, al-Qaeda, the Pakistan army (which contains internal divisions), the new Afghan army (ditto), and the international allies, especially the USA.

4. *Security.* The hot war along the Pakistan border means that Afghanistan is *not* secure. While the capital, Kabul, *is* quite secure, the same *cannot* be said for the rest of the nation: there is a deep urban-rural split in this regard. Afghanistan is a highly weaponized society, with nearly all men owning guns and with local tribal leaders protecting their families' farms and crops with their own armed militias. The Taliban—the former government of Afghanistan, overthrown by the USA during the post-9/11 invasion in November 2001—is making a comeback in rural

areas by clamping down on these local tribal "war lords" and promising a return to the very strict (religious) law-and-order state they feel they achieved when in power. So, would the average Afghani feel they are more secure now than back when the Taliban were in power? Probably not.

Things were so bad, security-wise, in Iraq during 2005–2006, that experts spoke openly of there being a civil war between the three groups. At the time, President George W. Bush ordered a big surge of more US troops into Iraq and, as led by General David Petraeus, they have succeeded beyond anyone's expectations in cutting down group-on-group violence and in keeping the peace. (This success is what inspired President Obama to order the same for Afghanistan, with Petraeus likewise in charge.) But is it enough? Dobbins would remind us that more security now than in 2006 is not the same thing as more security than back when Saddam was in power in 2003. Saddam was a brutal tyrant, but he did keep law-and-order. So would the average Iraqi say they feel safer and more secure than before the war? My sense is: not quite yet, in spite of real recent progress.

5. *Economy.* Would the average Afghani, and Iraqi, say they are more prosperous than prior to the war? Thankfully, the Americans did not implement the retributive model in either case, and instead have sent investment flowing into both countries. Iraq probably has a better shot here, as at least it has the oil and gas, as well as a large and reasonably educated workforce. Yet huge challenges remain. The near-constant war since 1979, plus the effects of the sanctions from 1991 to 2003, devastated Iraq's basic infrastructure and well-being. So much re-building needs to be done. Unemployment, estimated at *half* the workforce, remains a terrible problem. One solution would seem to be to pay the unemployed to perform all the re-building but the costs would be enormous—in the dozens of billions, or more—and the Americans have been reluctant to pay the bill all on their own (Dodge 2003).

Afghanistan is one of the world's poorest countries, where two-thirds of the population lives on $2 USD/day. The same proportion of the population is thought to be functionally illiterate, and unemployment is also thought to afflict half the workforce. Afghanistan faces the same issues of ruined infrastructure, and the brutal consequences which constant warfare has inflicted on the economy. (These consequences can be condensed as follows: would you open a business in a war zone?) Afghanistan's economy is a toxic mixture of war and drugs. Poppies grow well there, and farmers can earn much more growing them than legal crops like wheat or corn. It is estimated that one-third of Afghanistan's economy comes from poppy production, and the heroin and opium trade which comes out of it. Transforming Afghanistan's economy from one of war and drugs to a peaceful and legal economy rooted in broad-based, healthy economic growth is proving terribly hard. The local tribal war-lords sell drugs, and use the money to induce the farmers into growing poppies and not potatoes. They also use the money to pay officials to look the other way, creating widespread corruption in the Afghan government. Moreover, the war lords get into turf wars with each other, trying to capture each others' markets or to steal each others' drugs or crops. Thus, the drugs fuel the violence, and the violence perpetuates under-development. Afghanistan is dangerously close to being what political scientists call, in reference to societies like it and Colombia and even Mexico, a "narco-state." And this cycle of violence and under-development only deals with the drug side of the equation; the same cycle exists due to the religious and political instability and factionalism which sparks violence, which in turn hampers development. Somehow stopping these two terribly strong, and interlinked, vicious cycles is absolutely top-of-mind as the international community tries to prevent Afghanistan from becoming a failed state (Tanner 2009, UN Data 2012).

6.9   Conclusion

Thus, even though history shows that successful post-war reconstruction *has been*, and *can be*, done, it is a separate issue whether it will be done in Iraq and Afghanistan. Such are the problems there, that it may well produce a backlash effect against the rehabilitation model itself, causing the pendulum of public and elite opinion to sway back to the retribution model, which might be seen as simpler and less costly. That might be a shame, though, as we've seen the retribution model has substantial flaws of its own. Systematic debate and reflection on these difficult issues seems the only way out of this cycle, and such debate and reflection would be enhanced enormously by the creation of a brand new Geneva Convention, one devoted exclusively to justice after war. I do not pretend to have drafted a full list of possible and plausible principles of use in such a Convention, merely to advance reflection in this regard, with reference not merely to abstract philosophical concerns but also to real, empirical cases, both past and present.

References

Albert S, Luck EC (1980) On the endings of wars. Kennikat Press, London, p 1980
Behrman G (2008) The most noble adventure: the Marshall Plan and how America helped rebuild Europe. Free Press, New York
Best G (1994) War and law since 1945. Clarendon, Oxford
Boemeke M (1998) The Treaty of Versailles. Cambridge University Press, Cambridge
Buergenthal T, Maier HG (1990) Public international law. West, St. Paul
Davidson E (1999) The death and life of Germany: an account of the American occupation. University of Missouri Press, St. Louis
Dobbins J, Jones S (2007) The United Nations' role in nation-building. RAND, Washington, DC
Dobbins J et al (2003) America's role in nation-building: from Germany to Iraq. RAND, Washington, DC
Dodge T (2003) Inventing Iraq. Columbia University Press, New York
Fukuyama F (2003) State-building. Cornell University Press, Ithaca

Fukuyama F (2005) Nation-building: beyond Afghanistan and Iraq. Johns Hopkins University Press, Baltimore, MD

Hampson FO (1996) Nurturing peace: why peace settlements succeed or fail. U.S. Institute of Peace, Washington, DC

Keegan J (1990) The second world war. Vintage, New York

Keegan J (1994) The first world war. Vintage, New York

Macmillian M (2003) Paris 1919. Macmillan, New York

Maya T (2001) Judgment at Tokyo. University of Kentucky Press, Lexington

Mills N (2008) Winning the peace. Wiley, London

Minow M (1999) Between vengeance and forgiveness. Beacon, Boston

Orend B (2000) War and international justice: a Kantian perspective. Wilfrid Laurier University Press, Waterloo

Orend B (2002a) Human rights: concept and context. Broadview, Peterborough

Orend B (2002b) Justice after war. Ethics Int Aff 16(1):43–56

Orend B (2006) The morality of war. Broadview, Peterborough

Orend B (2009) On war: a dialogue. Rowman Littlefield, Lanham

Rawls J (1999) The law of peoples. Harvard University Press, Cambridge, MA

Rieff D (1995) Slaughterhouse: Bosnia and the failure of the west. Simon & Schuster, New York

Schabas W (2001) An introduction to the international criminal court. Cambridge University Press, Cambridge

Schonberger H (1989) Aftermath of war: Americans and the remaking of Japan. Kent State University Press, Ohio

Segal L (1989) Fighting to the finish: the politics of war termination in America and Japan. Cornell University Press, Ithaca

Simons G (1996) The scourging of Iraq, 2nd edn. Macmillan, New York

Tanner S (2009) Afghanistan: a military history. De Capo, New York

Thacker T (2009) The end of the Third Reich: Defeat, denazification & Nuremburg, January 1944–November 1946. The History Press, New York

UN Data (2012) www.data.un.org/Country/Profiles.aspx Search: Afghanistan

Walker M (2006) Moral repair: reconstructing moral relations after wrongdoing. Cambridge University Press, Cambridge

Walzer M (1977) Just and unjust wars. Basic Books, New York

Chapter 7
Is There an Obligation to Rebuild?

Paul Robinson

Abstract   In recent years, efforts have been made to create a new norm in international affairs stating that victorious states have an obligation to rebuild those whom
they have defeated in war. This chapter challenges the arguments put forward in favor
of this norm, showing that they rest on four false assumptions concerning: the alleged
post-bellum nature of the rebuilding process; the supposed justice of the wars waged
by liberal democratic states; the compatibility of the obligation to rebuild with the
Western just war tradition; and the ability of states to successfully rebuild their
defeated enemies. The chapter concludes that the practical application of the norm
would be counterproductive, as it would serve mainly to allow states which have
waged unjust wars to continue unjust occupations of conquered territories.

"That's all well and good in practice," an apocryphal French philosopher is supposed
to have said, "but does it work in theory?" This quip reminds us that when considering rules and norms we have to bear in mind not merely their theoretical merit but
how they will be applied in practice. In recent years efforts have been made to create
a new norm in international affairs stating that victorious states must rebuild those
whom they have defeated in war. This chapter challenges the arguments put forward
in favor of this norm. It does not dispute that states may have in some circumstances
a *right* to rebuild a defeated enemy or an *interest* in doing so. Instead it purely seeks
to challenge the idea that they are under an *obligation* to rebuild. Whatever the
intentions of its proponents, in practice the idea that states do have such an obligation
will serve not to reconstruct shattered societies but rather to justify liberal interven-
tionist policies manifested in prolonged wars of occupation.

P. Robinson (✉)
Graduate School of International and Public Affairs, University of Ottawa,
243 Augusta Street, Ottawa, ON K1N 8C6, Canada
e-mail: paul.robinson@uottawa.ca

A. MacLachlan and A. Speight (eds.), *Justice, Responsibility and Reconciliation
in the Wake of Conflict*, Boston Studies in Philosophy, Religion and Public Life 1,
DOI 10.1007/978-94-007-5201-6_7, © Springer Science+Business Media Dordrecht 2013

The reason for this is that the concept of an obligation to rebuild rests on four false assumptions. The first assumption concerns the alleged *post-bellum* nature of the rebuilding process. The assumption is that this process is taking place after war has ended, but in reality the principle of an obligation to rebuild tends to be applied in situations in which levels of violence remain high, and which are not really "post-conflict" at all.

The second assumption concerns the supposed justice of the wars waged by liberal democratic states. It is assumed that liberal democracies wage just wars, win them in a just way, and then justly occupy their defeated enemies. Proponents of the obligation to rebuild are in effect assuming an ideal situation, and proposing a norm to suit an ideally just war. But the reality in which the norm will be applied is far murkier and far from the ideal.

The third assumption concerns the compatibility of the obligation to rebuild with the Western just war tradition. As we shall see, the debate about this new obligation takes place within the confines of that tradition, but is in fact incompatible with it. Under normal interpretations of just war theory, the ideally just victor does not owe anything to his defeated enemies. Thus, the proposed norm lacks validity even in the ideal situation, at least if one stays within the traditional framework. A coherent argument can nevertheless be made for the obligation to rebuild, but only by jettisoning classical just war theory entirely and adopting a radically different viewpoint.

Finally, the fourth assumption concerns the ability of states to rebuild their defeated enemies. Proponents of the obligation to rebuild again assume an ideal situation, in which we know how to do such rebuilding and are able to carry it out successfully. Practice, once again, is very different.

Perhaps the most notable moment in the philosophical development of modern liberal military interventionism was the publication in 2001 of the International Commission on Intervention and State Sovereignty's report entitled *The Responsibility to Protect*. In laying out the case for the possible use of force in a humanitarian intervention, the commission argued that the responsibility to protect included a "responsibility to rebuild," which "will involve the commitment of sufficient funds and resources and close cooperation with local people, and may mean staying in the country for some period of time after the initial purposes of the intervention have been accomplished," and which will involve 'sustained daily efforts at repairing infrastructure, at rebuilding housing, at planting and harvesting, and cooperating in other productive activities.'(International Commission on Intervention and State Sovereignty 2001, p. 39) In this case, the responsibility to rebuild relates specifically to the aftermath of a humanitarian intervention, but other authors have extended the responsibility to *post bellum* situations more generally. US Admiral Louis Iasiello, for instance, states that, "Victors have a moral obligation to ensure the security and stabilization of a defeated nation … they must … repair and rebuild infrastructure essential to a vulnerable population's health and welfare" (Iasiello 2004). This duty to rebuild involves not merely economic reconstruction but also democratic reform, in order to create, if not liberal democracy, at least what Brian Orend terms "a minimally just political community" (Orend 2007, p. 581). Walking away before this is achieved would, according to Jean Bethke Elshtain, "be an act of moral dereliction of the most egregious kind" (Elshtain 2008).

Theoretically the obligation to rebuild could exist after any sort of war, but most discussions of the subject focus on situations in which the victor has occupied the territory of the vanquished. Because of this, the purported duty to rebuild serves to justify the continued occupation of the defeated (since without the occupation, rebuilding is obviously difficult if not impossible). Yet it is noticeable that while many in the West now argue in favour of the legitimacy of occupations by Western states and the efforts taken by the Western occupiers to reconstruct the occupied nations, in the past commentators in the Western world have consistently rejected occupations carried out by those of whom they disapprove.

Afghanistan provides an interesting contrast in this respect. The idea that, having invaded Afghanistan in 2001, NATO countries now have a moral obligation to rebuild that shattered country, is often used as a justification for the continued presence of NATO troops there. Yet, in the 1980s nobody in the West spoke of a Soviet "responsibility to rebuild" Afghanistan following the Soviet invasion of that country in December 1979. Indeed, Soviet efforts to carry out economic and state reconstruction were almost universally condemned. It is worth noting that the Soviet Union devoted very large resources to building and rebuilding efforts, providing humanitarian aid, and strengthening state institutions (For details, see Robinson and Dixon 2010). Yet Western commentators, rather than praising the Soviets for fulfilling their obligation to rebuild, denounced the economic and technical assistance they provided to Afghanistan as "the crudest and crassest colonial exploitation" (Shroder and Assifi 1990, p. 97), and the provision of education and training as an attempt to "indoctrinate" the Afghans and to destroy the existing culture and Sovietize the population (For instance, Amin 1990, pp. 301–333; Laber 1980, 18 December). In a similar manner, after the Vietnamese invaded Cambodia in December 1978 and overthrew the Pol Pot regime, the West did not call upon Vietnam to fulfil its responsibility to continue occupying and rebuild the country; rather it repeatedly insisted that Vietnam withdraw. And moving further forward in time, Western states have consistently rejected claims by Russia that its troops need to continue occupying Transdnestr, Abkhazia, and South Ossetia.

It is probably no coincidence that claims that there is an obligation to rebuild were largely absent when countries the West disapproved of were doing the occupying and rebuilding, and came to prominence once it was the West that was doing it. The *Responsibility to Protect*, for instance, followed NATO's occupation of Kosovo in 2001. Debate on the subject then really kicked off in the aftermath of the invasions of Afghanistan and Iraq. Suddenly, what had once been reprehensible when carried out by others became a moral obligation.

The fact that proponents of a given theory are hypocrites does not tell us anything about the validity of the theory, but it does tell us something about why they are propounding that theory and thus about how they are likely to put it into practice, which is, after all, what ultimately matters. In this case, it is clear, as Doug McCready says, that "the impetus for this development is the current Iraq war" (McCready 2009). Many believe, as Noah Feldman says, that "even after the occupation [of Iraq] formally ended, the Coalition was under a duty to guarantee that the country would not revert to anarchy" (Noah Feldman, cited in Gheciu and Welsh 2009), and that, "we cannot, and must not, walk away" (Elshtain 2007). Similar arguments are deployed to justify the continued Western presence in Afghanistan. Yet in reality the situations in Iraq and Afghanistan cannot genuinely be described as *post-bellum*. Fighting in parts of both countries (such as the battle for Fallujah in Iraq, and much of the war in Helmand province in Afghanistan) has often been, and in Afghanistan continues to be, so intense that even phrases such as "irregular warfare" do not adequately describe the scale of combat. So, when commentators speak of the obligation to rebuild they are not actually propounding a post-war duty as part of a theory of *jus post bellum*, rather they are arguing in favour of continued military operations.

In this regard, *jus post bellum* appears not as a moral argument but as a tool in the modern Western tactic of counter-insurgency. Some writers state this quite explicitly. Rebecca Johnson, for instance, argues that, "*jus post bellum* ... can inform military action in the hostile post-conflict settings found in contemporary counterinsurgency" (Johnson 2008). (Johnson's bewildering terminology "hostile post-conflict" is revealing.) Meanwhile, Brian Orend, possibly the most prominent scholar of *jus post bellum*, states that others "are hung up too much on the word 'post': I prefer to speak of the third phase of war as 'the termination phase' to capture more accurately this sense of process even amidst endings," and that one should not "give up entirely on the task of providing belligerents with guidance during the termination phase" (Orend 2007, pp. 573–574). Yet the "termination phase" in both Afghanistan and Iraq has lasted far longer than the original war and killed far more people; it is quite ridiculous to refer to it as a "termination phase" at all. Whatever the theory may say, as applied in practice, there has so far been nothing in the slightest *post bellum* about the obligation to rebuild.

Worse, the theory serves to provide retroactive justification to acts which would otherwise be acknowledged as unjustifiable. For instance, the supposed justice of British and American efforts to rebuild Iraq is used to obscure the injustice of the original invasion. And here we confront a serious problem with the theory of the obligation to rebuild; most of the arguments in its favour assume "just" victors in "just" wars, but in reality, as will be shown below, the obligation can only exist in the case of "unjust" victors in 'unjust' wars, while the whole category of "just" victors is suspect, especially in the context of invasions and occupations.

One can see the assumption of a just occupation following a just war in a number of writings on the subject. Gary Bass, for instance, writes that, "There may also be a case for a more limited kind of foreign reconstruction in cases where a just war has left a defeated country on the verge of anarchy" (Bass 2004), while Tony Coady argues that, "It may seem paradoxical that just victors should acquire obligations to restore the circumstances of the unjust, defeated enemy, but several considerations support this" (Coady 2011). Brian Orend is even more explicit, saying that [his emphasis]:

> It is only when the victorious regime has fought a *just and lawful war*, as defined by international law and just war theory, that we can speak meaningfully of rights and duties, of both victor vanquished, at the end of armed conflict. ... *if an aggressor wins a war, the peace terms will necessarily be unjust* ... once you are an aggressor in war, everything is lost to you morally. ... So, for the rest of this article, I shall assume that the winning side fought with *jus ad bellum* on its side. (Orend 2007, p. 578)

These just victors are, of course, liberal democracies. "Think of the major twentieth-century aggressors and dictatorships," Orend writes, "the USSR, fascist Spain and Italy, Nazi Germany, imperial Japan, North Korea, communist China, Pol Pot's Cambodia, Idi Amin's Uganda, Saddam Hussein's Iraq, the Taliban's Afghanistan. ... To a remarkable extent, in spite of all the other differences, *it has been the same kind of regime*" (Orend 2007, p. 587). The possibility that liberal democracies can also be aggressors and fight unjust wars appears not to occur to Orend, or at least he chooses to ignore it.

Indeed, "just and lawful wars" are few and far between; just and lawful wars won by the just side are even rarer (since one may assume that the just side does not always win); and just occupations after just victories in just wars are rarer still. As David Rodin points out, "under standard interpretations of *jus ad bellum*, it is not possible for a war to be just on both sides simultaneously, but it is possible (and indeed relatively common) for a war to be unjust on both sides. ... therefore ... at most 50 per cent of all wars can be just" (Rodin 2008, p. 58). But that is an optimal position. The reality is far worse. If taken seriously, the criteria of *jus ad bellum* are extremely difficult to satisfy, especially as most commentators take the position that *all* the criteria must be satisfied for a war to be considered just. An almost certain conclusion, therefore, is that in most cases both sides fail to meet the conditions of *jus ad bellum*, which means that the percentage of wars which are just is *less* than fifty percent. Put another way, it is a statistical certainty that most wars are unjust wars. And this is merely considering *jus ad bellum*; if one adds *jus in bello* to the equation, the number of just wars falls even further, since many of those which meet the criteria of *jus ad bellum* will not also meet the criteria of *jus in bello*.

It would also be rash to assume that the just side wins every time, so the number of just victors is necessarily smaller still. As for just occupations, while it is possible to imagine a scenario in which an occupation does not involve some form of regime change, either in the entire territory of the defeated nation or in part of it, the scenarios in which the obligation to rebuild are discussed generally do involve situations in which the previous government has been forcibly removed, such as in Iraq and Afghanistan. Yet this is problematic, because most commentators agree that, except in extreme circumstances, regime change is not a justifiable objective of war. Michael Walzer, for instance, argues that in World War II regime change was justifiable in the case of Nazi Germany but not in the case of Japan (Walzer 1992, p. 267). Only the genocidal nature of the former allowed the normal prohibition against regime change to be overcome. For this reason, we may conclude that it is particularly likely that occupations are the product of unjust wars, not just ones. We can see, therefore, that Orend is assuming something that almost never happens. He and others are creating a norm which applies only to a tiny percentage of wars, if any, but since most people will not accept that they have waged an unjust war, the norm will be applied in situations for which it was not designed, namely to justify unjust occupations. Furthermore, there is a danger that if we accept the legitimacy of occupations, we *de facto* render the idea of regime change more acceptable, both making war more likely and helping to push the conduct of war towards totality, since a regime threatened by destruction is going to be less restrained than one fighting a conflict for more limited aims.

The position is further complicated by what just war theorists call "simultaneous ostensible justice". As Francisco de Vitoria pointed out, while, in an objective sense, both sides in a war cannot have justice on their side, subjectively both sides can and do believe that they do, and can be excused for so believing given the inevitable veil of ignorance behind which humans operate. As Vitoria put it, "where there is provable ignorance either of fact or of law, the war itself may be just in itself for the side which has true justice on its side, and also just for the other side, because they wage war in good faith and are hence excused from sin. … In such situations the subjects on both sides are justified in fighting" (Reichberg et al. 2006, p. 322). To take a modern example, many would state that the cause of the Taliban in Afghanistan is unjust and that of NATO is just, but an Afghan peasant who sees his family killed by NATO troops, however accidentally, might be excused for having a different opinion and joining the Taliban, given his limited knowledge of the overall situation. We may conclude, therefore, that the justice of war is very likely to be disputed, and often for good reasons.

Furthermore, many wars will be just in part, and unjust in part also. For instance, many view the Allied struggle against Germany in World War II as the archetype of a just war. But even here there are complications. The Soviet Union was justified in defending itself against an unprovoked attack by Germany, but Moscow had previously joined Berlin in invading Poland, and had also invaded the Baltic States, Finland, and parts of Romania. The British and French governments thought that the Finnish cause was sufficiently just that they almost went to war with the Soviet Union in defence of Finland and permitted volunteers to join the Finnish army. Yet in December 1941, the British government declared war on Finland, because by then the Soviet Union was Britain's ally. So, parts of the Allied and Soviet wars were just, but other parts were not. And while the Soviet Union had *jus ad bellum* on its side in its war against Germany (if not against Finland and the Baltic states), it committed massive breaches of *jus in bello*. Declaring even this apparently clear example a "just" war is more problematic than it at first seems.

One of the problems with classic just war theory is that it tends to create a sharp distinction in people's minds between just wars and unjust wars, as if there are only two clear and separate categories of war. As the analysis above shows, the reality is far more complex, with many wars containing a mixture of justice and injustice on both sides. A theory resting on the assumption that just victors have won a just war rests on very shaky foundations. It is also potentially dangerous. As Alex Bellamy points out, the maximalist theory which includes the obligation to rebuild, "assumes that the justice of war is uncontested. … If the justice of an aggressive war (such as Iraq 2003) is contested, efforts to fulfil the maximalist peace might only compound the wrong in the minds of many (though not all) of those who disputed the grounds for war" (Bellamy 2008). Such efforts are therefore likely to encourage resistance producing prolonged violence. In this regard, it is interesting to note that a recent study suggests a very strong causal link between foreign occupations and the phenomenon of suicide terrorism (Pape 2005). Any norm that helps to legitimize occupations must be treated with great caution.

Let us assume, though, that we are faced by the rare case of a war which is just according to *jus ad bellum*, and which the just side has won, having fought at all times justly in accordance with the rules of *jus in bello*. It is not obvious why the victor in this case owes the defeated, unjust, enemy anything. The loser has brought his own destruction upon himself and the winner was justified in fighting him; if anything the loser has an obligation to repay the winner's costs. Indeed, it is noticeable that reparations are an important part of most theories of *jus post bellum*. As Brian Orend says, "in a classical context of interstate war, the aggressor nation owes some duty of compensation to the victim of aggression" (Orend 2002). Yet it would be absurd to insist that the defeated aggressor pay reparations to the victorious "victim," and at the same time insist that the victor pay to rebuild the aggressor.

In response, one might argue that in some circumstances the destruction caused by the war is so great as to create a need to rebuild which overrides the obligation of the defeated aggressor to compensate his victim. But, in the first place, this is a question relating to certain specific circumstances; it cannot be the basis for a general rule. And second, if we take just war theory seriously, we must consider the question of proportionality. If the destruction was so great as to place a country in a position of anarchy where it requires rebuilding, we must doubt whether the war abided by the rules of *jus in bello*, since it seems more than likely that the force used was disproportionate. In other words, although its supporters assume a just war, the obligation to rebuild almost certainly only applies in situations where the war was unjust. Alex Bellamy is therefore right to conclude that, "The problem is that maximalist ideas are almost utterly alien to classical Just War considerations" (Bellamy 2008, p. 621).

One could argue that imposing a responsibility to rebuild on states that wage war unjustly might serve some useful purpose. It is not impossible, after all, that a state will admit the injustice of its actions and choose to forego the fruits of its victory and instead reconstruct its defeated enemy. In 170 BC, for instance, the Senate of Rome admitted that the Roman general Lucius Hortensius had illegally attacked the city of Abdera. The Senate then freed all those he had enslaved and restored to Abdera its freedom and independence (Kern 1999, p. 329). This case is remarkable, however, precisely because it is so unique. A rule which says that unjust victors must rebuild their enemies is unlikely ever to persuade anybody to do any rebuilding, as very few will admit to acting unjustly. At the same time, it is not at all obvious how one could enforce such a rule. Precisely because the victors are victors they are in a position where others cannot easily force them to carry out such an obligation.

Still, this discussion provides a clue as to how an obligation to rebuild could theoretically be justified. Tony Coady argues that it is a question of "extrication morality": "We may well face situations where recognised immoralities of our own … face us with moral choices that require persistence for a time in the activities that fall under the blanket condemnation of injustice in order to most effectively and justly extricate from the immoral mess we have created" (Coady 2011). But, he cautions that, "such arguments nonetheless need to be treated with care since they are easily adapted to self-serving ends and the empirical judgements about likely chaos and bloodbaths tend to be elusive and fragile. … Frustrated invaders have a strong tendency to sustain the validity of their persistence by illusions that their presence is the only thing preventing disaster or promoting certain important goods, when often the reality is that their continuing occupation after an unjust war is a primary factor in an ongoing, deteriorating mess" (Coady 2011). In any case, "Whatever they do in this respect should, ideally at any rate, be informed by the fact that their war-making is indeed unjust in its beginnings and overall orientation" (Coady 2011).

In many cases, such as Iraq, the extrication scenarios which Coady refers to will involve violence. In such cases, under Coady's framework, in order to undo the mess one has made one must engage in "activities that fall under the blanket condemnation of injustice" while acknowledging the injustice of what one is doing. In other words, one must fight, even while knowing that fighting is unjust. This makes some sense, but it is not compatible with the just war tradition. It requires one to look at the morality of war in a very different way.

Mark Evans gets close to this in an article in which he argues that, "there should be considerable moral humility on the part even of just victors, which I think should be manifest in a commitment to do what they can, where appropriate, to repair the world that they will subsequently share with (some of) their former enemies. ... Just combatants should be sorry to have had to inflict pain and suffering on the enemy – a sorry of regret rather than admission of wrongdoing." The "commitment to post-conflict reconstruction" is thus "a manifestation of duty, derived from the original taking-up of arms" (Evans 2009). The reference to moral humility hits the mark, but Evans remains trapped in the assumption that just victors have won just wars. To make the argument for an obligation to rebuild work one has to jettison this assumption as well and consider the possibility that no war is truly just, even if some are necessary.

There is some support for this position from those who stand outside the Western just war tradition, such as Eastern Orthodox philosophers.[1] Stanley Harakas, for instance, argues that "Given the imperfect world in which we find ourselves ... wars of defense may sometimes have to be fought. ... But it appears to me that this acceptance cannot and should not be made into a virtue, into a moral good, and given the status of a moral good by being called a *just* war" (Harakas 1986, p. 259). According to this framework, it may be necessary to wage war to defeat a great evil, such as Nazi Germany or some other genocidal regime. But although wars without civilian casualties are theoretically possible, they are exceedingly rare. So in the process of defeating this evil, one will almost inevitably have to kill innocent people. This can in no way be called just. The war, therefore, is necessary but not just. Having unjustly harmed the innocent, one consequently has a moral obligation to help them once one has won the war.

This alternative framework thus provides a logical reason for a moral obligation to rebuild. Just war theory does not allow for this. Under the doctrine of double effect, which forms an important part of just war theory, one is not morally responsible for the innocent who are harmed by one's attacks, as long as one did not

---

[1] I have outlined this position in more detail in an analysis of the work of Russian philosopher Ivan Il'in: Robinson (2003).

intentionally harm them and as long as one took reasonable measures to avoid doing so. Adding an "obligation to compensate" to the doctrine of double effect could get around this problem, but would have enormous practical implications. Combatants would have to be much more cautious about what they targeted and much more generous with day-by-day reparations in the areas of fighting. This could well be a good thing, but it is very probable that combatants would consider the restrictions that such a change would place on their ability to wage war to be unacceptable. In any case, the obligation to compensate would only apply to individuals harmed unjustly, and would not constitute a general obligation to rebuild the society as a whole.

There is still one final problem facing the obligation to rebuild. This is the issue of whether it is possible to successfully fulfil such a duty in practice. The implicit assumption is that it is, for it is not, one cannot be obliged to do it. As Rory Stewart says with regards to Afghanistan, "we don't have a moral obligation to do what we cannot do" (Stewart 2009). One of the principles of *jus ad bellum* is that of a "reasonable chance of success." One should surely apply this principle equally to *jus post bellum*. There can only be an obligation to rebuild if one can reasonably expect that efforts to rebuild a war-shattered society will succeed and do more good than harm. There are, unfortunately, good grounds for doubting whether one can expect this.

The record of post-conflict reconstruction by states which have occupied other states is, to say the least, patchy. This is especially true in situations where the conflict has never fully ended, which, as we have seen, are often the situations in which interested parties claim an obligation to rebuild.

It is true that there have been some successes. Post-war Germany and Japan are the examples most often cited. According to Orend, these examples show that we can reconstruct post-war societies (Orend 2007, p. 590), which implies therefore that we should. He argues that there is a ten-point "historically grounded recipe" (Orend 2007, pp. 584–586), which we know produces positive results. The key factor determining success or failure is whether we commit sufficient time and resources to this recipe: "the commitment, presence, and investment of the *war winner* is the most necessary factor in the success of postwar reform" (Orend 2007, pp. 587–588). In short, it is merely a matter of will.

For Orend, the fact that rebuilding can work is enough to establish a moral obligation to rebuild. One might as well say that because playing roulette can sometimes be profitable, one should play roulette. The logic ignores all of the times when the proposed action does not work. It also ignores the peculiar contexts which may have produced the successes (such as, for instance, the fact that Germany and Japan were already advanced industrial states), and the possibility that the successes were in spite of the occupations rather than because of it. As Coady notes, citing Christopher J. Coyne's book *After War: the Political Economy of Exporting Democracy*, "The economic reforms in Germany that revived its economy and turned it eventually into an economic powerhouse were actually initiated by Ludwig Erhard, without the knowledge and against the authority of the occupying power" (Coady 2011).

Perhaps in an ideal world, where we really do know the formula for successful reconstruction and it truly is only a matter of will, Orend's argument might hold water, but the repeated failures of foreign aid projects over the past six decades have shown that we do not actually know the formula, or at least, that if we do, we are very bad at applying it. If we have learned one thing, it is probably that development is not a matter of capital investment; it is about a lot more than building things and training people and is largely a matter of governance and institutions. The problem is that aid "instils a culture of dependency, and facilitates rampant and systematic corruption" (Moyo 2009, p. 49), thereby undermining the institutions which are essential for development. As a result, although aid can produce positive results, very often (and perhaps even most often) it does not.

Alexandra Gheciu and Jennifer Welsh correctly note that, "*any* form of trusteeship … sets up a dangerously paternalistic relationship," (Gheciu and Welsh 2009, p. 137) with the "potential for dependency and distortion" (Gheciu and Welsh 2009, p. 138). And as Tony Coady says in response to Brian Orend, "The commercial rip-offs and staggering corruption unleashed by the invasion [of Iraq] and exploited by foreign security firms cum mercenaries, building contractors, and oil interests seem simply to have passed him [Orend] by. … If this is what the provision of 'minimum justice' looks like then the country is probably better off without it" (Coady 2011). The corrupting influence of foreign rebuilding efforts is even more visible in Afghanistan. Matthieu Aikins comments in a recent article that:

> With the surge, thousands of additional soldiers and billions of dollars in aid money have begun pouring into southern Afghanistan. Yet everything that's wrong with Kandahar – the violence, the corruption, the lawlessness – has gotten worse. … The inflow of cash has outpaced other economic activity in Afghanistan by an order of magnitude … as the volume of contracts increased, oversight decreased … It was irrational to be a member of the government or the army – an honest one at least. … Given the perverse incentive system ISAF has created, powerful Afghans now have a strong interest in perpetuating the conflict. … Under ISAF, international money has eaten through Afghan government and society like a universal solvent. … Nation building, as practised by the military in Afghanistan, has become self-defeating. (Aikins 2010)

It would appear, therefore, that even if we do know the recipe (which is debatable), we are not very good at turning the ingredients into a tasty dish. Furthermore, it is worth noting that multilateral entities which were not party to the original conflict are very often more successful at carrying out reconstruction than states which were involved in the conflict, as seen by a comparison between the relatively productive United Nations efforts in Cambodia and El Salvador and the less productive American and NATO campaigns in Iraq and Afghanistan. Indeed, in general United Nations interventions have a better track record than those undertaken by individual Western countries (Peceny and Pickering 2006, pp. 141–142). As Gheciu and Welsh write, "the actor who caused another actor to be in danger is not always best placed to rectify the situation. … it is not obvious that the responsibility for the aftermath should fall to those who caused the disruption" (Gheciu and Welsh 2009, p. 134).

In sum, the idea that there is an obligation to rebuild rests on a liberal fantasy in which democratic states wage just wars, win them, and then apply a sound formula guaranteed to produce a better peace. Since we are good, and moreover since we actually know how to make the world a better place, says this script, we have an obligation to combine our good intentions with our skills and resources to rebuild our defeated enemies and turn them into something at least a little bit closer to ourselves. Of course, if others wage wars and win them, they must immediately leave the countries they have occupied. The rules that apply to us do not apply to them, because, unlike ours, their wars are unjust. This fantasy bears little resemblance to the real world, in which liberal democracies are just as likely to be aggressors as anybody else, in which the just side does not always win, in which more often there is no just side, and in which attempts to rebuild shattered nations end in failure as often as in success. In this world, a norm which claims that states have an obligation to rebuild their defeated enemies will most likely be exploited by states which have waged unjust wars to continue unjust occupations, and as such will act to justify war rather than to limit it. Whatever the theoretical merits of the norm, its practical application will be counterproductive.

In any case, there are few theoretical merits. The concept of the obligation to rebuild rests on false assumptions, and is incompatible with the just war tradition as normally understood. It is possible to form a coherent argument in its favour, but only by abandoning the concept of a just war entirely and adopting a position which accepts that wars inevitably involve injustice. Even then, however, the idea runs into the practical difficulty that we do not actually know how to reconstruct states successfully, or if we do know how, we are not very good at actually doing it. As Tony Coady concludes, "we may do better to be less utopian, less lofty, and less consumed by our own righteousness, in prescriptions and principles for reconstructing conquered nations" (Coady 2011). This is absolutely right. Perhaps we should focus on not conquering others in the first place rather than focusing on what to do with them once we have.

References

Aikins M (2010) Last stand in Kandahar. In: The Walrus, December 2010. http://www.walrusmagazine.com/articles/2010.12-international-affairs-last-stand-in-kandahar/. Accessed 22 Nov 2010

Amin AR (1990) The sovietization of Afghanistan. In: Klass R (ed) Afghanistan: the great game revisited. Freedom House, New York

Bass GJ (2004) Jus post bellum. Philos Public Aff 32(4):403

Bellamy A (2008) The responsibilities of victory: *Jus post bellum* and the just war. Rev Int Stud 34(4):620

Coady CAJ(T) (2011) The just post bellum. In: Tripodi P, Wolfendale J (eds) New wars and new soldiers: military ethics in the contemporary world. Ashgate, Farnham

Elshtain JB (2007) Exit or no exit? Jean Bethke Elshtain's response. In: Dissent, 2 May. http://www.dissentmagazine.org/online. Accessed 22 Nov 2010

Elshtain JB (2008) The ethics of fleeing: what America still owes Iraq. World Aff 170(4):96

Evans M (2009) Moral responsibilities and the conflicting demands of *Jus post bellum*. Ethics Int Aff 23(2):154

Gheciu A, Welsh J (2009) The imperative to rebuild: assessing the normative case for postconflict reconstruction. Ethics Int Aff 23(2):124

Harakas S (1986) The N.C.C.B. Pastoral letter, the challenge of peace: an eastern orthodox response. In: Reid CJ Jr (ed) Peace in a nuclear age: the Bishops' pastoral letter in perspective. Catholic University of America Press, Washington, DC

Iasiello LV (2004) The moral responsibilities of victors in war. Naval War College Rev 57(3/4):42

International Commission on Intervention and State Sovereignty (2001) The responsibility to protect. ICISS, Ottawa

Johnson R (2008) *Jus post bellum* and counterinsurgency. J Military Ethics 7(3):216

Kern PB (1999) Ancient siege warfare. Indiana University Press, Bloomington/Indianapolis

Laber J (1980) Afghanistan's other war. New York Rev Books 33(2)

McCready D (2009) Ending the war right: *Jus post bellum* and the just war tradition. J Military Ethics 8(1):68

Moyo D (2009) Dead aid: why aid is not working and how there is a better way for Africa. Farrar, Straus and Giroux, New York

Orend B (2002) Justice after war. Ethics Int Aff 16(1):47

Orend B (2007) *Jus post bellum*: the perspective of a just war theorist. Leiden J Int Law 20(3):581

Pape R (2005) Dying to win: the strategic logic of suicide terrorism. Random House, New York

Peceny M, Pickering J (2006) Can liberal intervention build liberal democracy. In: Mason T, Meernik J (eds) Conflict prevention and peacebuilding in post-war societies. Routledge, London

Reichberg GM, Syse H, Begby E (2006) The ethics of war: classic and contemporary readings. Blackwell, Oxford

Robinson P (2003) On resistance to evil by force: Ivan Il'in and the necessity of war. J Military Ethics 2(2):145–159

Robinson P, Dixon J (2010) Soviet development theory and economic and technical assistance to Afghanistan. Historian 72(3):620–623

Rodin D (2008) The moral inequality of soldiers: why *jus in Bello* asymmetry is half right. In: Rodin D, Shue H (eds) Just and unjust warriors: the moral and legal status of soldiers. Oxford University Press, Oxford

Shroder JF Jr, Assifi AT (1990) Afghan resources and soviet exploitation. In: Klass R (ed) Afghanistan: the great game revisited. Freedom House, Lanham

Stewart R (2009) Afghanistan: what could work. In: The New York review of books, 17 Dec. http://www.nybooks.com/articles/archives/2010/jan/14/afghanistan-what-could-work/. Accessed 10 Nov 2010

Walzer M (1992) Just and unjust wars: a moral argument with historical illustrations, 2nd edn. Basic Books, New York

Chapter 8
Political Reconciliation, Punishment, and Grudge Informers

Colleen Murphy

Abstract In this paper I focus on a fundamental legal dilemma that the legacy of systematic injustice characteristically creates following periods of civil conflict and repressive rule. In the aftermath of injustice there is often a strong urge to punish those who committed morally egregious acts of injustice, but it is challenging to find legal grounds for such punishment. To explain this dilemma I summarize the case of the grudge informer. I then survey the different justifications for punishment found in the literature, concentrating on the idea that it is important to (re-)build a just order and sense of justice within transitional communities. To provide resources for understanding what constitutes a just order and for evaluating punishment's contribution to this order, I articulate a conception of just political relationships, which are realized in a just order. I then return to the case of the grudge informer and explain how punishment may facilitate the creation of a just order by fostering some of the social and moral conditions that underpin it.

8.1 Introduction

Dealing with a legacy of injustice following periods of war or repression and at the same time attempting to transition to peace raises complicated moral questions for transitional societies. In this paper I focus on a fundamental legal dilemma that the legacy of systematic injustice characteristically creates following periods of civil conflict and repressive rule.

C. Murphy (✉)
University of Illinois at Urbana-Champaign, Urbana, IL, USA

Department of Philosophy, University of Illinois,
105 Gregory Hall, 801S. Wright Street, Urbana, IL 61801, USA
e-mail: colleenm@illinois.edu

A. MacLachlan and A. Speight (eds.), *Justice, Responsibility and Reconciliation
in the Wake of Conflict*, Boston Studies in Philosophy, Religion and Public Life 1,
DOI 10.1007/978-94-007-5201-6_8, © Springer Science+Business Media Dordrecht 2013

Law represents a distinctive form of social ordering whereby officials govern conduct on the basis of rules. As Lon Fuller (1964) argues, this kind of social order is possible only when there is mutual respect for the requirements of the rule of law on the part of citizens and officials. For their part, officials must pass rules that are capable of figuring in the practical deliberation of citizens. This entails that laws must be, for example, prospective, possible to obey, non-contradictory, and general. These conditions ensure that citizens can take legal rules into consideration when deliberating about how to act. For law to govern it must furthermore be the case that officials in practice enforce declared rules. Insofar as officials respect these requirements, citizens are treated as agents; officials respond to their conduct on the basis of a standard that citizens are aware of and have a genuine opportunity to obey.

The dilemma is this: within transitional communities, in the aftermath of injustice there is often a strong conviction that individuals who committed morally egregious acts of injustice should be punished. However, there must be good grounds for punishment and it is difficult in transitional contexts to identify such grounds. In particular, it is difficult to demonstrate that such punishment is consistent with core principles of the rule of law, especially the requirement that laws be prospective. If such punishment violates principles of the rule of law it is difficult to establish that such violations are permissible, given that the rule of law is precisely what transitional communities are trying to establish and/or strengthen.

In the first section I summarize the case of the grudge informer, which was made famous by legal scholar Lon Fuller and which vividly illustrates the central legal dilemma just described. After presenting the dilemma I survey the different justifications for punishment found in the literature. I focus in particular on appeals to the importance of (re-)building a just order and sense of justice within transitional communities. My discussion highlights the general theoretical questions that remain unanswered by, but that are central to the success of, this idea. In particular, it remains unclear what constitutes a just order and whether punishment, especially if retroactive, contributes to its achievement. To provide resources for addressing these issues, in the second section I summarize the conception of just relationships that I have developed in prior work on political reconciliation. The third section then returns to the case of the grudge informer and explains how punishment may facilitate the creation of a just order, and what dimensions of that order punishment is in a position to affect.

8.2 Legal Dilemmas in Transitional Contexts

The term "grudge informers" refers to individuals who, during periods of conflict or repression, report personal enemies to authorities in order to get rid of them. Some German grudge informers from the Nazi period were prosecuted following World War II and became the subject of intense legal debate. One particular grudge informer, cited by Fuller, was a woman who alerted authorities to negative remarks about Hitler and the Nazi party that her husband, a German soldier, had made to her in their home during his visit in 1944. She reportedly noted to authorities that "a man who would say a thing like that does not deserve to live" (Fuller 1958, 653). The grudge informer was allegedly having an affair at the time her husband returned home and was motivated by a desire to free herself from him. Two statutes had been passed by the Nazis in 1934 and 1938 that prohibited any public comments against government leaders, the Nazi party, or government policies that would undermine the military defense of the German people or the government. Her husband was convicted by a military tribunal and sentenced to death. After the trial he was imprisoned and later sent to the front line. In 1949, following the war, the wife was charged by a West German court with illegally depriving her husband of his liberty. This was a criminal offense under the German Code of 1871, which remained in effect during the Nazi period. In her defense, the wife argued that she had acted legally and in accordance with the law and so could not justifiably be punished.

German courts as well as legal scholars have advanced a range of arguments justifying the punishment of grudge informers like the wife described above (Fuller 1958; Hart 1957; Dyzenhaus 2008). Here are five different kinds of justification that have been presented to support the conviction of the particular grudge informer Fuller considers:

- **Justification 1:** *Retroactive invalidation of Nazi statutes* This argument does not challenge the validity of Nazi statutes at the time of her actions to which the grudge informer appealed in her defense. However, it claims that the laws that justified the informer's action should be rendered invalid retroactively, either via court judgment or legislation. This would undermine the legal basis of the grudge informer's defense and open the door to punishing her for a despicably immoral act. The grudge informer could be legally charged with illegally depriving her husband of his liberty by reporting him to authorities and securing his imprisonment.

- **Justification 2:** *Improper use of valid Nazi statutes by grudge informer* This argument, like the first, assumes that the Nazi statutes to which the grudge informer appealed constituted valid law. However, it raises objections to the grudge informer's reliance on these statutes. In particular, it was not legally obligatory for the grudge informer to report her husband to authorities. Furthermore, the statutes only sanctioned public remarks; on no interpretation of "public" would the remarks made among spouses in the privacy of their own home be included. The grudge informer illegally deprived her husband of his liberty, then, because she reported him to the authorities on personal, not legal, grounds. The grudge informer knew that she could get rid of her husband by reporting his remarks, given that the court-martial took itself to be duty-bound to investigate any reports and that it was widely known that the purpose of the statutes in question was to terrorize the German population into submission. Thus the informer used the courts for criminal ends and was guilty of illegally depriving her husband of his liberty.

- **Justification 3:** *Improper interpretation and application of Nazi statutes by courts* Like justification 2, this argument assumes that the grudge informer was well aware of the probable consequences of reporting her husband to the authorities. However, unlike justification 2, this justification also finds fault with the actions of the court itself. As noted above, the statutes appealed to by the informer in her defense claimed that individuals would be guilty of undermining the effort to defend the German people militarily if they "publicly" tried to crush the morale of the German people. The court erred in finding the husband guilty because his remarks were not public and handed him a disproportionate sentence. These failings by the court were unsurprising because it was widely known that the courts based their judgments not on the law, but in response to administrative pressure to suppress dissenting voices and terrorize the population. The grudge informer knew this as well, and was thus complicit in illegally depriving her husband of his liberty insofar as she used the court's flawed procedure to rid herself of her husband.
- **Justification 4:** *Nazi statutes always invalid* This argument challenges on natural law grounds the validity of the Nazi statutes to which the grudge informer appealed. According to this argument, those Nazi statutes were never legally valid because they were "contrary to the sound conscience and sense of justice of all decent people" (Dyzenhaus 2008, 1004). Thus those laws are irrelevant in determining whether the grudge informer illegally deprived her husband of his liberty. The relevant law to consider in this case is the provision from 1871.
- **Justification 5:** *Symbolic retroactive invalidation of Nazi statutes* According to this argument, the legal status of the Nazi statutes to which the grudge informer appealed is unclear. The rule of law, or the governance of conduct on the basis of declared rules, declined to such a degree during the Nazi period that it is difficult to speak of *law* during this period. This was reflected in officials' widespread and systematic use of secret laws, retroactive legislation, and lack of congruence between declared rules and their enforcement. Furthermore, there was an erosion in the commitment to and sense of justice among officials and citizens, as reflected in the principles and statutes characteristic of the Nazi period, including the flawed principles of interpretation noted in justification 3 used by the court martial to convict the husband of the grudge informer. It was impossible for courts to declare invalid all Nazi statutes or completely overhaul the legal system at once; this would have created a radical uncertainty for citizens. However, it was possible to achieve reform piecemeal. Thus, though not obviously legally valid to begin with, the courts should have explicitly declared the Nazi statutes in question invalid retroactively. This would have allowed a clean break from some aspects of the Nazi legal past. Such a declaration would have opened the door to prosecuting the grudge informer for illegally depriving her husband of his liberty.

There are a number of theoretical questions to which these various justifications give rise. One question is a question of law, namely: what was the legal status of the Nazi statutes at issue in the case of the grudge informer? We see among these justifications fundamental differences in the criteria that need to be satisfied for a statute to be legally valid. In particular, the relevance of morality for questions of legal validity varies.[1] In justification 4 and justification 5 moral considerations, either stemming from precepts of natural law or the internal morality of law, influence the legal status of statutes. By contrast, justifications 1–3 separate questions of legal validity and morality.

In some justifications the answer to the question of the legal status of the statutes or actions of the grudge informer settles the question of why punishment is permissible. Justification 4 rejects the claim that the Nazi statutes were ever legally valid, given their substantive content. Justifications 2 and 3 draw attention to the way that individuals may use the law instrumentally to achieve morally reprehensible, indeed criminal, ends. Such manipulation of the law may be punished. However, interestingly, other justifications of punishment do not see the answer to the first theoretical question as implying an answer to the question of what treatment the grudge informer should receive. Implicit in justification 1 is the claim that there are good reasons to punish the grudge informer, regardless of the legal status of the Nazi statutes. Indeed, these reasons are so important they permit the violation of a fundamental principle of the rule of law. Justification 5 suggests that there can be important reasons to treat statutes as legally valid because of a concern for maintaining order, and then retroactively declare them invalid in order to allow for the punishment of individuals who committed morally egregious actions. Here too we see the idea that there are important reasons to punish the grudge informer, even if the legal status of the Nazi statutes and of the actions of the grudge informer is complicated to establish.

Appeals to the importance of punishment, irrespective of the legal status of actions or the requirements of the rule of law, raise the question: why exactly is punishment so important in this case, and other similar cases? The reasons that explain the importance of the punishment of the grudge informer are often not explicitly articulated. One idea we find is that punishment is the lesser of two evils; not punishing this immoral act would be a greater evil than punishing retroactively. Why punishment should be seen as the lesser of two evils is not articulated. However, another idea we do find, most explicitly expressed in justification 5, is that there is a need to reform and overhaul the conception of justice that is ordering transitional communities, and law plays a pivotal role in this process.

It is this second idea and its subsequent implications for the justifiability of punishment that I pursue in the rest of this paper, in part because the notion that there is a need to restore a sense of justice and a just order within transitional communities is widely held in the multidisciplinary literature on transitional justice.

---

[1] One of the central questions in the philosophy of law concerns the relationship between law and morality. Legal positivists maintain that there is no necessary connection between a rule's morality and its legality; legal status is a separate issue from moral status. By contrast, natural law theorists and advocates of the internal morality of law link the status of a rule as a legal rule with moral criteria.

This literature deals with general questions about how prior injustice should be confronted when societies are in transition from conflict or repression to peace and democracy. As expressed in the literature, there is a fundamental "normative shift" that must take place in transitional communities.[2] This is a shift in the conception of justice, as reflected in part in legal institutions and practices. Transitional societies thus are in an important sense normatively unstable; what counts as a good moral or legal reason for conduct is in flux and unsettled. When such societies are responding to wrongdoing, the very norms for wrongdoing, as reflected in law and other conventions, are in the process of change.

Interestingly, the particular debate about the punishment of the grudge informer to which legal scholars have devoted extensive attention is rarely referenced in general debates about transitional justice. Thus the case of the grudge informer provides a framework for examining the plausibility of the idea that punishment in fact contributes to the consolidation of a normative shift, and for considering what weight should be given to the presence or absence of available legal grounds for punishment.

To evaluate the claim that punishment is justified because it contributes to this shift the following questions must be answered. The first is: how does punishment facilitate a normative shift within transitional communities? Justifications 1 and 5 suggest that punishment expresses a break with the past, whereby legal statutes and principles are explicitly rejected. One reason for concern about this explanation is that punishment constitutes a rejection of past law only by violating a principle of the rule of law. Such violation seems to bear similarity with strategies used by repressive governments, thus it is unclear what makes punishment different in this case. That is, why does punishment strike a blow for justice when fundamental principles are being violated? Justifications 2 and 3 suggest that punishment may contribute to a shift by highlighting flawed applications of the law and misuses of the law by citizens and officials in the past. Punishment is based on a correct legal decision based on sound legal reasoning in the case at hand. This explanation avoids the problem of the violation of the rule of law. However, it is unclear how or why such correction will have a dramatic impact and facilitate a wholesale normative shift. Courts in many contexts overturn the opinions of lower courts and draw attention to flawed interpretations, yet such actions are rarely taken to constitute a radical repudiation of the past or current order.

A second question this explanation of the significance of punishment raises is the following: is punishment, or the turn to legal mechanisms, the only way for a community to symbolically break with the past? It is important to understand the grounds for taking seriously the justification for punishment of the grudge informer offered by legal theorists not only to assess the soundness of that particular argument, but also because there are a number of alternative ways in which societies may try to respond to the dilemma of law outlined above, not all of which involve punishment. Indeed, legal scholar Ruti Teitel (2000) advocates the use of the limited criminal

---

[2] The term "normative shift" comes from Teitel (2000).

sanction, which provides a pragmatic compromise to the rule of law dilemma. With this sanction prosecution processes do not automatically result in full punishment since it deals with the establishment and punishment of wrongdoing separately. In this way transitional punishment can achieve punishment's overarching goals while responding to the dilemmas inherent in transitional contexts. Other scholars have advocated nonpunitive legal responses or nonlegal responses, such as truth commissions, amnesty, or the establishment of memorials. The justification of the punishment of the grudge informer forces us to ask whether this particular way of responding must be the only way in which societies respond to injustice or whether alternative strategies are equally viable. More generally, there are questions about how we delimit the range of possible options that societies may adopt in order to transform the conception of justice and sense of justice within a community, and what factors should influence which option is in fact selected.

Answering the first and second questions depends in part on answering a third, more fundamental question: How exactly does the prior regime's conception of justice, reflected in law as well as the actions of the grudge informer and/or courts and legal professionals, need to be changed? Before we can explain the urgency of punishing the grudge informer we need to first have a more detailed understanding of the kind of just order, and commitment to that order among citizens and officials, that societies in transition are aspiring to cultivate and, similarly, what the prior conception of injustice was and how that conception was reflected in the legal order. Such understanding will provide a more specific sense of what precisely is missing in transitional contexts, both in terms of the norms and rules that regulate behavior and in the commitments among citizens and officials. In addition, a conception of the kind of just order that societies are striving to build will suggest criteria for evaluating punishment and other kind(s) of responses to wrongdoing.

I suggest that the conception of justice, reflected in a just order, that responses like the retroactive punishment of the grudge informer are designed to achieve can be best understood through the lens of political reconciliation. Political reconciliation broadly refers to the process of repairing political relationships damaged by civil war and repression. A conception of political reconciliation provides an account of how civil war and repression damage political relationships, articulates a view of the characteristics of repaired political relationships, and offers guidelines for assessing the effectiveness of putative processes of political reconciliation. The conception of political reconciliation I summarize in the next section and that is developed in my book *A Moral Theory of Political Reconciliation* (2010) provides important theoretical resources for specifying the just order envisioned by advocates of punishment.

Before turning to political reconciliation, let me offer some initial reflections on why it is plausible to think about justice as instantiated in a just order through political reconciliation. An account of political reconciliation has fundamentally normative dimensions. It does not simply provide a descriptive characterization of interaction during conflict and, conversely, repaired interaction in stable regimes. Rather, it offers a normative analysis, providing insight into normative reasons that make certain relationships morally valuable and assisting in identifying the damage done to those relationships. This normative dimension is necessary if an account is to speak to the pressing debates about political reconciliation, especially debates about the value of political reconciliation itself. Political reconciliation thus provides an account of the normative dimensions of relationships that are structured by a just order. Furthermore, as I discuss in detail below, a constitutive component of the pursuit of political reconciliation is the establishment or restoration of respect for the rule of law. Reconciliation is fundamentally concerned with law and appreciation of the kind of formal ordering of relationships that a system of law provides, and has substantive implications for the kinds of laws that should regulate relations.

In the next section I spell out the central ways in which political relationships are damaged during conflict and the characteristics of repaired relationships. The third section then describes what processes of political reconciliation must do, given the damage afflicting political relationships and the kind of relationships these processes hope to foster. It is in thinking about what processes of reconciliation must do that we find resources for responding to the general theoretical questions raise by the central justification for punishment of the grudge informer. Thus, after providing an overview of the conception of political reconciliation with which I am working, I return to the question of the grounds for taking seriously the justifications for punishment offered above and of the basis on which we can delimit justifiable versus unjustifiable sacrifices of rule of law principles, articulating the answers that the account of political reconciliation would suggest.

8.3 Political Reconciliation

At the core of my account is a realistically ideal conception of political relationships. My conception is realistic insofar as it does not depend on exceptional virtue, or selflessness, or solidarity among citizens or officials. It is ideal insofar as it characterizes a way of ordering political relations that is absent, remaining an aspiration, in transitional contexts. The realistic ideal serves two purposes. It enriches our understanding of the moral significance of the characteristic interaction among citizens and officials during conflict and repression, and in particular what dimensions of interaction are appropriately regarded as being of moral concern. Conversely, it provides a framework for understanding the characteristics and moral value of repaired political relationships.

In my view, at the most general level political relationships should be premised on reciprocity and respect for moral agency. Reciprocity captures the idea that the bindingness and justifiability of the claims we make on others to treat us in certain ways is grounded in a willingness to recognize and respect the claims that others make on us. Relationships premised on reciprocity reflect a mutual willingness to satisfy the terms of the relationship and recognition that one is answerable to the other party in a relationship for one's actions. Moral agency denotes the idea that citizens and officials have the capacity to be self-directed in their lives, that is, are capable of formulating and pursuing their own purposes, and are appropriately held accountable for their actions. Reciprocity and respect for agency are realized in political relationships, I argue, when such relationships are characterized by mutual respect for the rule of law, mutual reasonable trust and trust-responsiveness, and the mutual enjoyment of central relational capabilities.

As noted in the introduction, law represents a distinctive form of social ordering whereby officials govern conduct on the basis of rules by satisfying the requirements of the rule of law. Insofar as officials respect these requirements citizens are treated as agents; officials respond to their conduct on the basis of a standard that citizens are aware of and have a genuine opportunity to obey. Governance by law also depends on the actions of citizens. In particular, for law to be a form of social order that governs conduct citizens must on the whole obey the law. Widespread disobedience on the part of citizens renders futile the actions of officials; the rules that officials pass will not in any meaningful sense govern conduct. When law governs conduct, political relationships express to some degree reciprocity and respect for agency. Relationships express reciprocity because the social order of law is possible only when there is reciprocal and systematic fulfillment of the requirements of the rule of law on the part of citizens and officials. Relationships express respect for agency because law, and governance by law, is a social order that makes possible self-directed action and interaction. Law provides a framework for interaction in which our expectations of how others will behave are based on what law permits and prohibits and, furthermore, that these expectations are satisfied in practice. This allows individuals to formulate plans and actions to realize their goals on the basis of reliable and stable assumptions about others. Furthermore, law treats individuals as agents by holding them accountable to a standard of conduct that they are in a real position to satisfy.

Important as law is in structuring action and interaction among citizens and officials, it is not the only way in which reciprocity and respect for agency are realized in political relationships. Equally significant is the default attitude that citizens and officials take toward others. Political relationships premised on reciprocity and respect for agency are characterized by a default attitude of trust and trust-responsiveness on the part of citizens and officials. In other words, citizens and officials presume that others are competent, that is, they are able to fulfill their role-related responsibilities and that they lack ill will, and so are willing to engage in cooperative action with others. When they trust, citizens and officials also expect that fellow citizens and officials will prove trust-responsive, or will give significant weight to the fact that they are being relied on by others when determining what to do. Similarly, in relationships citizens and officials are willing not only to trust but also to prove trust-responsive when trust is placed in them. When reasonable, default trust and trust-responsiveness can express reciprocity and respect for agency. They express reciprocity insofar as individuals take a presumptive view of others that they desire others to take of themselves. Insofar as they respond to the trust placed in them by others, they expect others will respond to their trust. Default trust and trust-responsiveness express respect for agency because they acknowledge that others are agents. A precondition for being competent in the manner trust presumes is the capacity for agency. Responding to the trust of others is one way to acknowledge that such others have the standing as agents to make demands on us, and are not simply objects to be treated in whatever manner we desire.

The concept of capability refers to the genuine opportunity, or effective freedom, that individuals have to achieve valuable doings and beings (Sen 2000; Nussbaum 2001). Capabilities are a function of both what an individual has (e.g., her internal resources such as talents and skills, and external resources such as income and family support) and what an individual can do with what she has (e.g., given laws, social norms, and the physical infrastructure within a community). As a form of positive freedom, capabilities provide information about the extent to which an individual is able to exercise her agency, determining the goals she will pursue and the kind of interaction she will have with others. In the context of political relationships, certain fundamental relational capabilities, or capabilities necessarily achieved in relationships with others, are of special concern. These include being recognized as a member of the community; being respected; and participating in the economic, political, and social life of the community. All of these relational capabilities are impacted by a general capability to avoid poverty. The key insight of the capability framework is that the exercise of agency and the enjoyment of central relational capabilities depends on what an individual has as well as the general context in which an individual acts. Thus the framework focuses attention on the importance of the character of the general social context and the distribution of resources among individuals within a community.

In addition to specifying the defining characteristics of political relationships premised on reciprocity and respect for agency, the realistic ideal for political relationships articulated above provides resources for understanding why and how patterns of interaction during civil conflict and repression undermine defining features of a just order. In particular, as justification 5 in the previous section correctly highlighted, transitional societies characteristically emerge from a period in which there is a steady erosion of the rule of law. The congruence between official action and declared rules frequently breaks down. Official conduct may not be not guided by what declared rules prohibit or permit, and official response to the conduct of citizens may not be not based on whether citizens have violated declared rules. For example, torture, though legally proscribed, may become common. In some contexts, disregard of declared rules by citizens may be widespread. Declared rules may become increasingly unclear, so vague and broad as to provide little practical guidance in terms of the conduct being prohibited. The impact of the erosion of the rule of law is that citizens act in an increasingly uncertain environment, unclear as to what official treatment their actions are likely to receive. Insofar as they can form reasonable expectations about how officials will respond, the basis of these expectations is non-legal, stemming from widely known practices instead of what declared rules prohibit or allow. In either case, the kind of exercise of agency that law helps to make possible breaks down.

Additionally, the erosion of the rule of law is of special concern in the context of a discussion about the establishment of a just order because the form of order that law provides acts as an important constraint on the pursuit of injustice. Governance by law produces a transparency in official policy and action. Thus law makes denial about the injustice of policies being pursued more difficult and opens up a community to critical scrutiny by its members and others. In practice, this constrains the pursuit of unjust practices and policies by officials.

The erosion of the rule of law diminishes the capability of individuals to participate in the social, economic, and political life of a community. The violence constitutive of conflict and repression further undermines the exercise of their agency. Violence plays a central role in terrorizing a population into submission, a frequent goal of either a campaign of repression or of various parties to a conflict. Such violence is frequently extralegal in character, not officially sanctioned, and indeed often prohibited by declared rules. Violence constrains the capability of individuals to be respected, be recognized as a member of a community, and participate in the life of a community. As a consequence of being a victim of violence, individuals may refuse to engage in the life of a community so as to avoid becoming a victim again in the future. Violence may lead to a rift in relationships, especially if being a victim of violence is grounds for social stigmatization and ostracization. Members of a targeted group may constrain their actions and withdraw into their private life, understanding that they suffer from the threat of violence. Finally, violence affects the general social and material infrastructure of a community. Buildings, including hospitals and schools, are destroyed. Professionals in business, medicine, and education may emigrate. The ability of a community to tend to the educational, material, and health needs of its members subsequently diminishes. In some contexts group identity can exacerbate the vulnerability of individuals to forms of capability diminishment. When violence is driven by identity cleavages, then having a certain identity can make one vulnerable to certain forms of violence. Insofar as membership is tied to a specific ethnic or religious identity, this can undermine the capability of members of a different ethnic or religious group to be recognized and respected as members of the community. Finally, being a member of a marginalized group or community may limit an individual's ability to participate in the economic, political, and social life of a community insofar as social norms or laws informally or formally discourage interaction.

Unsurprisingly, the erosion of the rule of law and violence characteristic of conflict and repression are important sources of the breakdown of trust among citizens and officials, and, equally importantly, the conditions that make trust and trust-responsiveness reasonable. Indeed, deep and pervasive distrust, often reasonable, is a feature of transitional communities. Given an environment in which declared rules provide little guidance as to the actual conduct of other officials and citizens, and given the violence and wrongdoing that conflict and repression leave in their wake, it is foreseeable that citizens and officials presume that others are neither willing nor capable of fulfilling their role-related responsibilities and, moreover, will not prove responsive if trust is placed in them.

From the perspective of political reconciliation, the central task in rebuilding the kind of political relationships characteristic of a just political order is to promote reciprocity and respect for agency by cultivating respect for the rule of law and the kind of order law provides; default attitudes of trust and trust-responsiveness as well as the conditions that make such default attitudes reasonable; and central relational capabilities. Importantly, the framework of political reconciliation highlights that each of these characteristics depends on the presence of certain social and moral conditions. I concentrate on these conditions in the next section because they provide the key to understanding how and why to respond to the dilemma of legality that the case of the grudge informer highlights.

8.4 Responding to Legal Dilemmas

In Sect. 8.1 I discussed a set of theoretical questions to which justifications of the punishment of the grudge informer following World War II give rise. In this section I return to these questions, highlighting how the framework of reconciliation presented above provides resources for answering them, and so for understanding why punishment may be justified in transitional contexts and what alternative kinds of responses may be justifiable as well.

The first question evoked by the case of the grudge informer concerned the legal status of the statutes to which the grudge informer appealed in her defense, as well as the status of the Nazi legal system more broadly. Based on the conception of the rule of law at the heart of my account of political reconciliation, Justification 5, i.e. the symbolic retroactive invalidation of Nazi statutes, most accurately articulates the appropriate view to take with respect to these issues. Because of systematic violations of the principles of the rule of law by government officials, including requirements that laws be prospective, clear, and enforced in practice, law was systematically undermined throughout the period of Nazi rule. This makes unclear the legal status of statutes such as the one appealed to by the grudge informer. The particular case of the grudge informer also highlights flaws in the application of laws specifically by courts.

As was noted earlier, the legal status of the Nazi statutes to which the grudge informer appealed does not settle the question of how she, and others in a similar situation, should be treated. Indeed, as the range of justifications surveyed in the first section demonstrate, there are different explanations that may be given as to why it is appropriate to respond to the immoral actions of citizens with legal punishment and how much weight should be given to the legal status of particular statutes. One explanation I concentrated on in particular is the idea that punishment is important because of its role in consolidating a normative shift in the conception of justice endorsed by and reflected in the practices of a community. There are, I suggested, three questions about this idea that remain in need of answer. The first concerns the grounds for granting that punishment will in fact consolidate a normative shift. The second focuses on whether punishment is unique in fostering a normative shift. Both of these questions, I suggested, could be answered only if we understood more clearly in what the normative shift consists, and in particular the kind of order that punishment seeks to cultivate. In the previous section I summarized part of the conception of political reconciliation I develop in previous work, which fleshes out central dimensions of political relationships structured by a just legal order.

I now want to show how this conception helps us understand the role of punishment and other responses in cultivating the normative conditions that underpin that order.

It is important to be able to evaluate whether punishment can plausibly be claimed to break with the past and consolidate a new order. The key to such an evaluation is an appreciation for the conditions that underpin political relationships and a political order premised on mutual respect for the rule of law, trust, and relational capabilities. One especially important condition in the current context is a general respect for the values that underpin these relationships and this order, namely, reciprocity and respect for agency. However, as each of the justifications for punishment implicitly acknowledges, there was an erosion of the concern for promoting the agency of citizens during the Nazi period, either through the erosion of respect for the requirements of the rule of law or through the content and substance of the laws that were passed. An erosion of such concern is common during conflict and repression.[3] For a new conception of justice to animate the legal order and political relationships structured by that order, the absence of reciprocity and respect for agency in political interaction and the legal order that structures that interaction must be acknowledged. It must also be recognized that this absence is morally troubling. In many cases, such acknowledgment requires the overcoming or countering of common forms of denial. There may be denial about the moral significance of certain wrongful actions, stemming from indifference toward members of the targeted group; rationalizations for the necessity of certain actions; or a rejection of the thought that wrongful actions implicate one personally. Appreciating why respect for agency and reciprocity matter in political relationships and acknowledging their absence will motivate citizens and officials to promote and realize these values in interaction.

In addition to a general respect for the values of reciprocity and respect for agency, there are specific conditions that underpin the rule of law, trust, and capabilities. For purposes of responding to the dilemmas of legality, the social and moral conditions underpinning the rule of law are especially pertinent. As Fuller recognized, for mutual respect for the requirements of the rule of law to be sustained, citizens must have faith in the law and officials must have legal decency and exercise good judgment.[4] Faith in law refers to a confidence that citizens must have that officials are in fact respecting the requirements of the rule of law. There are two general reasons why such faith matters. First, the willingness of citizens to fulfill the expectations of officials, namely, that they will obey laws and so govern their conduct on the basis of legal rules, is affected by the actions of officials. Citizens' willingness to constrain their conduct by law will diminish insofar as they lose faith in law, taking it to be futile to follow legal rules because officials fail to take into account whether citizens followed declared rules when responding to their conduct or becoming unwilling to utilize legal procedures because they are not followed by officials. Second, faith matters because the agency of citizens is inhibited if

---

[3] On this point see Murphy (2010), especially chapter 1.

[4] An extensive discussion of the social conditions of law is in Murphy (2010) chapter 6.

there is not some faith in law. If citizens need to constantly monitor the actions of officials because they cannot presume that officials are acting in accordance with proscribed procedures, then this will undermine their ability to pursue their goals and objectives on the basis of the expectations that the framework of law sets forth.

Officials must exercise legal decency and good judgment if the rule of law is to be maintained. The various rule-of-law requirements for officials cannot all be maximally respected, and so judgment is required to determine how best to satisfy the requirements of the rule of law such that self-directed action and interaction is facilitated. In Fuller's words (1964, 45–46), a utopia "of legality cannot be viewed as a situation in which each desideratum of the law's special morality is realized to perfection. There is no special quality – and certainly no peculiar defect – of the internal morality of law. In very human pursuit we shall always encounter the problem of balance." In addition, to maintain the fundamental purpose of law it may at times be necessary for officials to violate one of the general requirements. To illustrate, Fuller describes a situation in which the legal requirements for marriage include a special stamp being placed on a marriage certificate by the celebrant of the ceremony. The requisite stamp was not obtainable when the statute went into effect because of problems with the printing press producing the stamp. A retroactive statute would certify the marriages of those who, by the terms of the previous statute, were void. This illustrates the fact that "situations can arise in which granting retroactive effect to legal rules not only becomes tolerable, but may actually be essential to advance the cause of legality" (Fuller 1964, 53). Thus there is judgment inherently involved in determining whether a violation of a principle of the rule of law is inimical to or supportive of law's overall function. Legal decency can influence whether such judgment is used for good or ill, or in support of law or to undermine law. Furthermore, law constrains the exercise of political power; officials are not free to wield power in whatever would be the most efficient or effective manner to achieve their goals, control citizens, or eliminate rivals. Decency is also needed by officials to ensure that they are willing to abide by the constraints and processes law sets and so that they are committed to formulating rules that facilitate the capabilities of citizens and the exercise of agency more generally.

Legal decency and good judgment on the part of officials and faith in law on the part of citizens are characteristically absent in transitional contexts. The erosion of the rule of law itself systematically points to the absence of legal decency on the part of government officials. The justifications for punishment also vividly illustrate an absence of faith in law on the part of citizens. Citizens living in a context where actions like those of the grudge informer are possible recognize that any procedural guarantees of the rights of citizens will not be respected in practice. Furthermore, they recognize that laws will not be applied or interpreted in a manner that is congruent with the declared rules and, moreover, that the purpose of rules is often to terrorize a population into submission instead of to create a framework for sound and stable interaction. This is part of what enables law to be used successfully as an instrument to achieve criminal ends.

Punishment of individuals like the grudge informer can contribute to the development of a just order, I want to suggest, because of how such punishment generates a recognition of the degeneration of law and of respect for agency, and the subsequent moral flaws plaguing interaction. As the various justifications for the punishment of the grudge informer highlight, the punishment of individuals who engaged in actions that were common and formally or informally sanctioned is unnerving. It demonstrates that individuals cannot be complacent regarding the permissibility of what they do because the society in which they live permits or even encourages such actions. It also communicates that actions that were sanctioned in the past, formally or informally, should not have been tolerated and will not in fact be tolerated in the future.

In my view, whether such unnerving punishment will cultivate legal decency on the part of officials and faith in law on the part of citizens importantly depends on the rationale for punishment offered by courts and on that rationale being communicated to the public generally. Framing the justification for punishment in terms of the correction of the misuse of law on the part of citizens or officials in the past, as justification 2 (improper use of valid Nazi statutes by grudge informer) and justification 3 (improper interpretation and application of Nazi statutes by courts) do, may focus attention on the particular errors of particular individuals. It may even highlight that these particular errors were common. However, because of the continuity that remains with laws and procedures from the past, it does not powerfully communicate that there were pervasive problems in law stemming from widespread violations of the rule of law on the part of officials, or systematic absence of legal decency and good judgment, which in turn produced an erosion of faith in law as a system of government that facilitates self-directed interaction on the part of citizens.

By contrast, the retroactive repudiation of central statutes has a greater possibility of focusing attention on systematic problems in law and the erosion of the social conditions that are needed to maintain law. Retroactive legislation communicates a repudiation of statutes in the past, and so a repudiation of particular injustices it sanctioned. When coupled with an explanation that the legal status of these statutes themselves is unclear because of the pervasive violation of requirements of the rule of law, retroactive legislation draws attention to broader deteriorations stemming from systematic actions on the part of officials and of citizens who took advantage of officials' abuse. The dramatic character of retroactive punishment can generate reflection on the part of officials to the extent that their actions and practices are being rejected. It can also give citizens some hope for the possibility of future faith in law, insofar as it suggests the beginning of a new era and a new way of ordering relations. Retroactive punishment does involve a violation of a central principle of the rule of law. However, as we noted above, maintaining law as a form of social ordering that facilitates agency and self-directed interaction may require the periodic violation of one of the rule of law requirements. Any single violation of a principle of the rule of law is not necessarily inimical to law's purpose. Distinguishing this violation from violations inimical to the legal order depends on the purpose under-pinning this violation. Inasmuch as punishment in this case is designed to facilitate agency by highlighting the absence of important conditions required for its possibility, such a violation may be defensible. The sincerity of this purpose will be demonstrated or undermined by the additional actions governments take, or fail to take, in transforming the conception of justice that structures the community.

Finally, the justification for punishment in cases like the grudge informer provides insight into the other kinds of practices or responses to wrongdoing that may also contribute to the cultivation of a just order. Practices that draw attention to the absence of the social conditions required for relationships premised on reciprocity and respect for agency to flourish, and help a community acknowledge the detrimental consequences that this breakdown has all have the potential to contribute to the normative shift and establish the just order that societies in transition have as one of their central goals.

Acknowledgments This paper was written during my period as a Laurance S. Rockefeller Visiting Faculty Fellow at the Princeton University Center for Human Values (UCHV), an opportunity for which I remain grateful. Opinions and findings presented are mine and do not necessarily reflect the views of the UCHV.

References

Dyzenhaus D (2008) The grudge informer case revisited. New York Univ Law Rev 83:1000–1034
Fuller L (1958) Positivism and fidelity to law – a reply to professor Hart. Harv Law Rev 71:630–672
Fuller L (1964) The morality of law. Yale University Press, New Haven
Hart HLA (1957) Positivism and the separation of law and morals. Harv Law Rev 71:593–629
Murphy C (2010) A moral theory of political reconciliation. Cambridge University Press, New York
Nussbaum M (2001) Women and human development. Cambridge University Press, New York
Sen A (2000) Development as freedom. Anchor Books, New York
Teitel R (2000) Transitional justice. Oxford University Press, New York

Part III
The Shape of Reconciliation

Chapter 9
Freedom in the Grounding of Transitional Justice

Ajume Wingo

Abstract The South African truth and reconciliation commission ("TRC") during the post-apartheid era has made such commissions a staple of efforts to heal societies torn by conflict and internal strife. In this paper, I analyze the means by which TRCs help remedy such internal conflict. In particular, I focus on the tensions often noted between the role of TRCs as a means of creating population-level outcomes (such as a general reduction of conflict or violence) with the demands of justice for victims of past abuses for recompense or retribution. Such a tension is, I argue, a genuine one that cannot easily be resolved. This tension is analogous to a similar tension between what I refer to as "relational freedom" operating in many communalistic societies, and an alternative notion of freedom I refer to as "nyang." As I present these two conceptions of freedom, the former is characterized by the ability of individuals to develop connections and relationships with others in their community, and puts a premium on the forging of consensus and the avoidance of conflict. The latter is a more individualistic notion that, among other things, stresses the importance of accommodating conflict and constructing a modus Vivendi that allows individuals with conflicting beliefs and desires to live in peace without consensus.

Drawing on this analogy, I argue that TRCs should be seen not as some all-purpose approach to conflict resolution, but as a means of bridging the gap between genuinely conflict-torn states and structures capable of channeling conflicts through political institutions rather than having those conflict erupt into violence. TRCs thus emerge as a more than just a process for airing grievances, but as an important part of a strategy for moving developing societies away from their traditional (and often quite fragile) communalistic, consensus-based organization and toward a more individualistic and robust system built on the ideal of nyang.

A. Wingo (✉)
Department of Philosophy, University of Colorado at Boulder,
2300 Arapahoe Ave., 150, Boulder, CO 80302, USA
e-mail: ajume.wingo@colorado.edu

A. MacLachlan and A. Speight (eds.), *Justice, Responsibility and Reconciliation in the Wake of Conflict*, Boston Studies in Philosophy, Religion and Public Life 1, DOI 10.1007/978-94-007-5201-6_9, © Springer Science+Business Media Dordrecht 2013

South Africa's Truth and Reconciliation Commission (TRC) has played a key role in helping that country avoid what many feared would be a bloody period of recrimination after the end of apartheid. The South African success has been particularly significant in giving TRCs a reputation as a useful method for helping heal societies torn apart by internal conflicts. As a result, TRCs have sprung up in trouble spots the world over and for a variety of different kinds of conflicts.[1] At a London Conference held in January 2010, for instance, Afghan President Hamid Karzai presented a plan for reconciliation and reintegration of the Taliban,[2] and Palestinian factions in the West Bank and Gaza have reportedly considered TRCs in order to reconcile their differences.[3]

But the appeal of TRCs is not limited to societies torn by internal armed conflict. The promise of TRC has led some in the United States to propose TRCs as the remedy for all kinds of ills. For example, over the protests of their own city government, residents of Greensboro, North Carolina, organized a TRC to investigate a 1979 massacre of five protestors killed by members of the Ku Klux Klan and the American Nazi Party.[4] In 2009, the Senate Judiciary Committee Chairman Patrick Leahy proposed a TRC to address various acts of the Bush Administration, such as the firing of the U.S. attorneys in the Justice Department, the use of torture, the creation of secret prisons, the illegal detention of American citizens, the warrantless wiretapping of U.S. citizens, and the alleged misleading of Congress to authorize a disastrous war in Iraq.[5] Less ambitious examples include a proposal for a TRC to deal with the use of steroids in baseball.[6]

TRCs thus appear to be a highly adaptable tool for resolving a wide variety of kinds of conflict in very different societies and circumstances. But can TRCs really be an effective method of dealing with conflict and injustice in so many different situations? Put another way, does the effectiveness of TRCs presume any particular facts about the populations involved, and, if so, what are those facts?

---

[1] For instance, the *Comisión Nacional sobre la Desaparición de Personas* (National Commission for Forced Disappearances) was created in Argentina in the aftermath of the 'Dirty War' of the 1970s and early 1980s, the Indian Residential Schools Truth and Reconciliation Commission in Canada dealt with issues involving indigenous peoples, and the *Comisión para el Esclarecimiento Histórico* (Historical Clarification Commission) in Guatemala investigated abuses during four decades of military governments. Several other TRCs have been established in Africa, including Rwanda's *gacaca*, Ghana's National Reconciliation Commission, Liberia's TRC, Morocco's Equity and Reconciliation Commission, and Sierra Leone's TRC. For an extensive list of TRCs (and their associated documents and reports), see the United States Institute of Peace website at http://www.usip.org/publications-tools/latest?filter1=**ALL**&filter0=**ALL**&filter2=2222&filter3=**ALL**&filter4=**ALL**.

[2] "Is Negotiating with the Taliban the Solution for Afghanistan?" ASDHA Conference, 25, 26 and 27 January 2011.

[3] See, for example, Wing (2008).

[4] See Greensboro Truth & Reconciliation Commission, at http://www.greensborotrc.org/, Magarrell and Wesley (2008), Cunningham et al. (2010).

[5] Stein (2009) and Cavallaro (2009).

[6] Abrams (2009).

In this paper, I examine the relationship between TRCs and two types of facts about the populations involved in those TRCs: the dominant views of those population regarding personal freedom, and the basis for political cooperation within those populations. I argue that TRCs are not neutral with respect to either the particular conception of personal freedom a population generally holds or to that population's general view of what is required to ground political cooperation. As a consequence, TRCs should be expected to be more successful when applied to those populations that have a compatible understanding of freedom and cooperation, than to other populations.

I do not claim, of course, that the "fit" between TRCs and particular populations is determined solely by how those populations generally conceive of freedom and cooperation, for there are bound to be several other respects in which TRCs promote certain values at the expense of others. But I believe that appreciating the relationship between TRCs and the concepts of freedom and cooperation gives us both a more nuanced understanding of how TRCs function, as well as an interesting and fruitful way to understand the likely effects and the potential limits of TRCs.

In Sect. 9.1, I present a general characterization of TRCs, and draw on Emile Durkheim's notion of anomie to account for the broad appeal of TRCs as a means of dealing with the aftermath of conflict. In Sect. 9.2 I discuss the commonly recognized limits on the ability of TRCs to deliver justice to the victims of conflict. I argue that instead of regarding those limits as a general objection to the use of TRCs, we should take those limits to show instead that using TRCs requires trading off one good for another, e.g., while it may not deliver justice with respect to certain goods, it may do so with respect to other goods. The appropriateness of using a TRC in any particular case, then, depends on whether it delivers what is needed or valued in that particular case. As a consequence, assessing the utility or appropriateness of TRCs demands looking closely at the circumstances in which they are used and the particular values of the populations involved.

In that sense, TRCs are just like other particular institutions we associate with a system of justice in that in particular cases, they may produce certain outcomes we value, but do not purport to deliver everything we might want. By recognizing that TRCs promote certain kinds of outcomes but not others, we can begin to identify general circumstances in which TRCs are more likely to be appropriate than in others. In Sect. 9.3, I examine the relationship between TRCs and personal liberty or freedom. I present two different conceptions of freedom; the first of which is what Isaiah Berlin called "negative liberty," and the second is what I refer to as "relational freedom," a conception of freedom exemplified in certain highly communal traditional cultures of Africa (in particular, the Nso, an ethnic group in the North West of Cameroon). I argue that as a means of restoring personal connections and relationships in post-conflict societies, TRCs are particularly appropriate for use in those populations that prize relational freedom over negative liberty.

In Sect. 9.4, I discuss the relationship between TRCs and a population's general understanding of how to secure the bases for cooperation. I contrast the approach employed in the United States and other liberal democracies that is predicated on constitutional protections for minorities and for the orderly transition of power from one group to another, with the consensus-based approach of many traditional African cultures. I argue that TRCs can be seen as particularly well suited for dealing with problems of transitional justice in those communities that prize consensus as a basis for cooperation.

Section 9.5 concludes with some suggestions as to how the more fine-grained analysis of the effects of TRCs should influence our views both of the nature of TRCs and of how we might more effectively respond to conflict in the future.

9.1   TRCs and Anomie

Any general discussion of TRCs requires formulating a concept of "the TRC method" that captures the salient properties of particular instances. While even a quick survey of particular TRCs shows that while there is no obvious set of necessary and sufficient conditions for being a TRC, there are certain general characteristics that most examples share.

One commonly used definition of TRCs characterizes them as focusing on past injustice, rather than on preventing future ones; as investigating patterns of abuse over time, rather than a specific event; as being established for a limited time, rather than being a permanent institution; and as being supported by the state.[7] In addition, TRCs have developed so as to serve principally as a forum for publicly airing grievances and creating a shared account that the facts underlying injustices, rather than prosecuting those who perpetrated those injustices.[8]

With this general concept of "the TRC process" in mind, let's consider what makes the TRC process so attractive. From a normative perspective, they are desirable because they hold out the promise of a fair and nonviolent means of responding to mass injustice. That is, they provide a deliberative and dispassionate venue for those most closely affected by injustices to voice their opinions. This is a way to pay respect to those individuals and their suffering, while at the same time tempering any anger or demand for vengeance by those individuals. Further, TRCs have a rehabilitative effect, since by participating in the process, former oppressors acknowledge their vulnerability by expressing repentance, while their victims have the opportunity to demonstrate strength by being magnanimous.

Apart from their attractive normative features, TRCs also have significant practical virtues. For instance, in conflict-ridden societies or states in transition between regimes, there may simply be no institutions with the credibility or authority to hold wrongdoers

---

[7] Hayner (2001).

[8] In this capacity, the TRC process aims to produce an "official story" as to what happened: "Their goal is to create a rigorously-constructed 'truth,' thereby 'redu[cing] the number of lies that may be circulated unchallenged in public discourse.'" Cunningham et al. (2010) (quoting Ignatieff 1996).

accountable; in such cases, a TRC could be a useful mechanism for resolving issues without having to submit them to discredited institutions of the former regime. TRCs may also allow decision-makers to delegate judgments on divisive and controversial issues to some other body, much as "blue-ribbon commissions" and expert advisory boards are sometimes used to make particularly hard decisions.[9] Finally – and most tragically – the TRC process may make it the only practical means of addressing injustices when a society has been devastated by conflict or its more conventional methods of investigation and prosecution are overwhelmed by mass atrocities.[10]

So how exactly do TRCs achieve these various ends? One way to think of how TRCs works is to think of the state and the effects of internal conflict along the lines suggested by Emile Durkheim, who introduced the concept of *anomie* to refer to a disequilibrium brought about by crises such as war, internal conflict, or economic collapse. According to Durkheim, anomie arises when an individual either lacks a purpose or pursues aims that are unattainable:

> [O]ne does not advance when one proceeds toward no goal, or – which is the same thing – when the goal is infinity. To pursue a goal which is by definition unattainable is to condemn oneself to a state of perpetual unhappiness.[11]

Social institutions such as religion and marriage serve both to give individuals a purpose and – more significantly – to constrain the scope of individuals' aims and desires to match their capacities and resources. These institutions do this by making individuals aware of others and their relationship to those others, since "[m]an is the more vulnerable to self-destruction the more he is detached from any collectivity, that is to say, the more he lives as an egoist."[12]

The happiness of individuals thus requires that they be aware of others and the way that their relationships to others limit what they should desire or pursue. In that sense, a properly functioning society is similar to a healthy body that maintains a proper balance among its component organs:

> The state of anomie is impossible whenever interdependent organs are sufficiently in contact and sufficiently extensive. If they are close to each other, they are readily aware, in every situation, of the need which they have of one-another, and consequently they have an active and permanent feeling of mutual dependence (Durkheim 1972, 184).

---

[9] For a discussion of the political considerations that have led to the adoption of TRCs, see Roper and Barria (2009).

[10] Some human rights activists have claimed that criminal prosecution is a superior response to widespread human rights violations, but that practical limits on the number of lawyers, judges, courtrooms, or time may make TRCs the best available alternative. See Minow (2001: 237). For instance, the formal legal system in Rwanda following the 1994 genocide was so devastated that it was estimated that it would take more than a century for that system to process the hundred thousand prisoners accused of participating in the genocide. See Zorbas (2004). In part, the inability of formal legal institutions to handle the massive number of cases prompted the January 2001 *gacaca* law, which is a form of TRC. See Zorbas (2004).

[11] See Durkheim (1966).

[12] Durkheim (1972).

On this account, the truth-telling function of TRCs is important, not simply because it reveals the truth, but because it reveals certain *kinds* of truths – those regarding connections among people and their effects on each other. Anomie arises when persons become isolated from one another and no longer recognize their obligations to each other or their interdependency. As a forum for bringing oppressors and victims together and airing grievances, a TRC is a way to make different sides of a conflict to acknowledge each other and the effects of their past interactions. Thus the transparency created by TRCs may help create the "active and permanent feeling of mutual dependence" required for individuals' happiness by forcing oppressors, victims, and the rest of the population to acknowledge how their actions affect each other.

9.2 Why TRCs?: Considerations of Justice

The account given in Sect. 9.1 helps to explain the intuitive value of the TRC process. But it also brings out the apparent tension between TRCs and considerations of justice that many observers have noted. Seen as a tool for restoring the internal "balance" of a post-conflict state, the TRC process is concerned with individuals, but principally as a means to a broader end, much as a utilitarian is concerned with individuals' happiness only as a means of maximizing total happiness. And, just as utilitarians have difficulties accounting for moral intuitions about justice, so too advocates of TRCs have been said to give short shrift to considerations of justice for the individual victims of conflict.[13]

It is not hard to see the potential tension between TRCs and justice. Our judgments of the justice of political arrangements rest ultimately on their impact on individual rights, liberty, and dignity. From that perspective, institutions are just only insofar as they support the just treatment of individuals. But if there is no necessary connection between restoring the internal balance among the members of a population and treating each of those members justly, then the internal logic of the TRC process – which is ultimately concerned with publicly recognizing injustices and the role of wrongdoers in perpetrating those injustices – imposes no requirement that individuals be treated justly.[14]

This potential tension between the aims of the TRC process and individual justice has often been recognized. As reported by the authors of South Africa's TRC *Final Report*, for instance, a "common refrain" from observers of the process was

---

[13] See, for instance, Kiss (2001).

[14] I assume that to the extent that the potential clash between the TRC process and justice for the individual is realized, that is generally an unintended consequence of the process. However, as other commentators have noted, there may be particular instances in which TRCs are intentionally used to disadvantage particular groups or to favor certain interests unjustly. See, for example, Rettig (2008).

that "We've heard the truth. There is even talk about reconciliation. But where's the justice?"[15] Another commentator on the South African TRC process noted that while the process helped to create the bases for reconciliation, individual South Africans were unlikely to be compensated for the injustices they suffered:

> Although only a few South Africans are likely to receive prompt and ample state compensation for their injuries, given the parlous state of the economy, they can fully participate in the politics of memory, which easily transmutes into the restoration of their dignity and perhaps in due course, for others, reconciliation with their erstwhile enemies and tormentors.[16]

Indeed, a common criticism of the TRC process is that it forces "messy compromises" that may be "inconceivable or offensive to some" – compromises with deeply held moral intuitions about the importance of giving individuals (both victims and their persecutors) their just deserts for the sake of reconciliation and peace.[17]

Individuals thus occupy an uncomfortable position vis-à-vis the nation in the TRC process. As a method of transitional justice, TRCs are teleological: they are primarily intended to help survivors of conflict realize a new, more just society. But if TRCs (and methods of transitional justice generally) aim at creating or restoring *peaceful coexistence*, there are more and less legitimate ways to achieve that aim. For instance, oppressors could be unfairly coerced into peaceful coexistence by locking them up, gagging some, stripping others of their freedom, ostracizing some, and killing the rest. Alternatively, victims could be required to simply swallow their sense of injustice and move on with their lives for the sake of eliminating conflict. Neither of those "solutions" to the problem of conflict is completely morally acceptable – yet it is unclear precisely how we should compromise victims' legitimate claims for remedies against oppressors' equally valid claims for fair and just treatment and the overarching desire to make peace from conflict.

When considering the legitimacy of TRCs, we must attend not just to the desired outcome of the processes on the population as a whole, but also the compromises on individual justice and individual rights required to achieve that outcome. If politics is to be a genuine alternative to violence, both the destination and the path to that destination must be legitimate. From this perspective, approaches to transitional justice – including TRC – must consider the consequences for the individuals involved.

But for all the understandable concerns about the limits of TRCs to deliver justice to individuals in the aftermath of widespread conflict, I believe we should take those limits as telling us more about when and where TRCs are appropriate than as a general objection to TRCs. Indeed, I argue here that TRCs are really no different from other institutions we use to address wrongs, in that each makes particular compromises vis-à-vis justice in order to promote certain aims or values at the expense of other aims or values.

---

[15] Quoted in Kiss (2001: 70).

[16] Dale (2002).

[17] Zorbas (2004).

First, if we think of justice as a fair allocation of certain types of goods, TRCs actually seem an ideal method of dispensing justice with respect to at least some goods. According to political philosopher John Rawls, for instance, "self-respect" or "self-esteem" is the fundamental social good for a system of justice, and TRCs appear quite capable of dealing with the fair allocation of that good. That is, on Rawls' account, self-respect relates to a person's sense of his own worth, the belief that "the conception of his good, his plan of life is worth carrying out;" and to one's "confidence in one's ability, so far as it is within one's power, to fulfill one's intentions."[18] By helping to publicize the injustices suffered by victims and the culpability of oppressors, TRCs help to acknowledge the importance of the victims and the moral significance of their suffering, and so naturally be seen as a way of supporting their self-respect.[19]

Viewing the TRC process as an institution that aims at supporting the self-respect of victims, we can see that process as a fairly conventional institution of justice, one that shares many of the general problems that arise in more conventional institutions of justice. For instance, to the extent that TRCs are supposed to help fix the facts underlying past injustices, that presumes that there is a single true history to tell. But which history is that? A state in conflict is, almost by definition, a collection of individuals with different experiences, conflicting perspectives, and potentially incompatible goals, all of which may lead to divergent histories of the events. Whose version should be privileged? Do the accounts of the victims automatically trump those of the oppressors? Are the oppressed to be considered a single, undifferentiated mass, whose grievances can be perfectly reflected in a handful of their most articulate representatives? When the oppressed speak, do they speak frankly, i.e., from the bottom of their hearts without duress or fear?

The fact that TRCs do not redistribute other goods such as income and wealth that might also affect victims' self-respect is a limitation, of course. But it is hardly unique to TRCs, for other institutions used to deal with injustices suffer similar limitations. Formal adjudication, for instance, may promise those who have been wronged more tangible remedies than the TRC process does, but may do so by subjecting the victim to embarrassment or humiliation that the TRC process would not.

TRCs share other limits that criminal courts and formal legal proceedings exhibit with respect to delivering justice to victims. In the criminal justice system in the United States, for instance, known wrongdoers are routinely granted immunity or reduced penalties in exchange for providing information used to apprehend and

---

[18] Rawls (1999: 386).

[19] As Shelby Weitzel (2004) has argued, this acknowledgment of wrongdoing by the wrongdoers themselves is essential for the victim of that wrongdoing to exhibit forgiveness, rather than condonation. As presented by Weitzel, forgiveness is an act that is compatible with (and potentially a source of) self-respect, and it implies that someone other than the victim regards the wrongdoing as morally significant. Condonation, in contrast, is an acceptance of the wrongdoing in a way that denies the moral significance of that wrongdoing – and in so doing, undermines the self-respect of the victim.

prosecute other, presumably more dangerous, offenders. So, just as the TRC process trades off the ability to punish wrongdoers in exchange for eliciting facts about wrongdoing (and about other wrongdoers), so too do formal criminal justice systems sometimes deny victims of crime retributive justice for the sake of some other, presumably more valuable, objective.

Similarly, the civil legal system in the United States sometimes trades off considerations of retributive justice for some other purpose. Judges are typically seen as being charged with applying the law fairly and objectively to the parties before it. But to apply the law, judges often must first decide what the law is, and to do that, they look past the parties before them to the effects of a given interpretation on the next parties in a similar situation.[20] That, however, is just another form of balancing the consideration for particular individuals so closely linked to conceptions of retributive justice against legitimate, but quite different, concerns as to what is best for the broader population.[21]

My point here is not to downplay the importance of understanding how justice for the individual can be achieved from within the TRC process. Rather, I want to underscore the fact that a TRC is just one institution among many. Like other more conventional institutions that deal with crime, conflict, and abuse, it necessarily balances a variety of different and legitimate objectives against each other. Are TRCs ill suited to dispense retributive justice in the sense of punishing wrongdoers? Perhaps – but that merely shows that it is incomplete in particular respects, just as alternatives to TRCs are.[22]

Recognizing the limits of TRCs with respect to justice (or rather, justice with respect to certain goods) does, however, prompt us to ask whether the compromises TRCs

---

[20] This is particularly the case for those judges highly influenced by the law and economics approach to the analysis of legal rules and institutions. According to one of the most influential advocates of this approach, Judge Richard Posner, legal rules should be efficient (from an economic point of view). See, generally, Posner (1973). To the extent that adjudication requires formulating a specific rule the court follows, this attention to economic efficiency requires the judge to consider not just what seems right for the parties before it, but also how the rule applied will affect future behavior of other parties.

[21] Similar tradeoffs are made when judges consider exercising their equitable powers. Judges are sometimes thought to be responsible for applying the law so as to do justice, rather than blindly applying rules. The institution of a court of equity, as opposed to a court of law, grew out of a recognition that the letter of the law sometimes imposes a rigidity that is inconsistent with the spirit of the law. In the United States, for instance, while the distinction between courts of equity and courts of law has largely disappeared in the United States, federal bankruptcy courts have very broad equitable powers, and "should invoke [those] equitable principles and doctrines, refusing to do so only where their application would be inconsistent with the Bankruptcy Code." In re Beaty, 306 F.3d 915,922 (9th Cir. 2002). Yet courts are legitimately wary about invoking their equitable powers too often, since that may create moral hazard, i.e., may allow considerations of individual justice to remove the incentives that individuals have to protect themselves against certain types of risks.

[22] Thus objections to TRCs based on their apparent inability to deliver justice are not like similar objections to utilitarianism. The latter purports to be a complete moral theory, in which case its failure to account for strong moral intuitions regarding justice is a serious objection. The former is merely one institution among (potentially) many, and so does not purport to deliver everything we might desire in a system of justice.

make are appropriate in the context in which they are used. For instance, when the injustices to be remedied are principally material – in Rawlsian terms, income and wealth – the justice dispensed by TRCs is bound to be disappointing, even insulting, to the victims of the injustices. In other cases, however, the injustices to remedy relate to matters of recognition or standing in a community, in which case the TRC might actually be the optimal means of dispensing justice. By taking a closer look at precisely what values or ends the TRC process tends to promote or degrade, we stand to learn something about how that process might be more effectively deployed in the future.

9.3   TRCs and Personal Freedom

In this section, I consider the effect that TRCs have on the personal liberty or freedom of the individuals in the affected population. Just as TRCs appear to be better suited to deliver certain kinds of justice than other, I argue here that TRCs also are not neutral with respect to the kind of personal freedom that members of different populations might value.

To do this, I first contrast two different concepts of personal freedom. The first is what Isaiah Berlin famously referred to as "negative liberty," or the right to be left alone to act as one chooses.[23] Negative liberty depends on the absence of constraints on, or interference with, agents' possible action by other human beings. Thus, greater negative liberty means greater isolation or independence from the effects of others' actions.

I contrast negative liberty with what I call "relational freedom". This conception is exemplified in certain traditional African communities such as those of the Nso. In contrast to negative liberty and its equating of independence and freedom, this concept of relational freedom presumes – indeed, requires – a background network of familial relations. On this conception of personal freedom, the thicker the network of affective dispositions available to an individual, the more opportunities there are for the exercise of freedom. As I have explained in greater detail elsewhere, an individual's behavioral and attitudinal patterns towards familial networks constitute that individual's virtues, or his dispositions to act in certain ways toward others.[24] The need for background conditions of a familial network privileges a distinctive set of affects to both promote and deter certain ranges of behavior to give individual persons the opportunity for purposeful action and autonomy.[25]

Relational freedom, then, is a matter of an individual's capacities to act in certain ways by virtue of being highly connected to others, as opposed to an individual's degree of freedom from outside constraints. In the sense I intend, then, relational freedom can be likened to Berlin's own contrast to negative liberty, i.e., positive

---

[23] Berlin (1969).

[24] See generally Wingo (2010).

[25] See Wingo (2010).

liberty. It has been suggested, for instance, that Berlin's notion of positive liberty (as articulated in *Four Essays on Liberty*) indicates that the "self" that enjoys positive liberty "is collective (i.e., national, or rather nationalist), and that its 'realization' might involve very severe restrictions, both on individuals' negative freedom, and (partly in consequence) on the possibility of their *individual* self-realization."[26] The interdependence among individuals implied by positive liberty (at least on this reading) closely tracks the idea that relational freedom arises through an individual's personal ties to others.[27]

There is a quite natural affinity between the TRC process and relational freedom, in that TRCs aim to strengthen or restore relations among people on different sides of conflicts. Widespread conflict severs these relationships, not just by literally causing the deaths of the members of one's network, but by displacing them or erecting barriers of hatred, fear, or resentment. Repairing these connections and forging new ones is a way of undoing at least part of the harm created by conflict. But this process of repairing severed social ties is a leading characteristic of the TRC process, for as one commentator has noted, TRCs and African methods of conflict-resolution are each intimately tied to the repairing of social ties – the same kinds of social ties that form the basis of relational freedom:

> Africans believe that when two people fight, the entire village is affected. Therefore, conflict resolution requires not just a settlement between the two disputants, but also an effort to repair frayed social relationships. ...South Africa's Truth and Reconciliation Commission (TRC), established after the dismantling of apartheid in 1994, based itself on this African tradition.[28]

The distinctive nature of relational freedom in communalistic societies can be brought out by contrasting it to negative liberty, for these two conceptions of freedom are, if not incompatible, at least in tension. One way to see the tension is to note the significant differences in the communities that embrace one or the other conception. Eccentricities, so celebrated by John Stuart Mill, are a hallmark of negative liberty – yet are frowned upon in the communalistic cultures that prize relational

---

[26] Grant (1999: 1221).

[27] There is, to be sure, a sense in which relational freedom will strike one who thinks of personal freedom principally in terms of negative liberty as a kind of interconnectedness or community that, while perhaps valuable in its own right, should be distinguished from personal freedom per se. I take that intuition as resting on the presumption that there can be no distinctive sense of personal freedom within communities that do not share Western liberal presumptions about the primacy of individuals. Recognizing relational freedom as a viable alternative to negative liberty requires in part acknowledging that "Western political systems are based on a concept of the citizen which appears of little relevance to Africa," and that "[t]he notion of the individual in Africa, with due allowance for the differences found in various parts of the continent, is again one which is inclusive rather than exclusive," one on which "individuals are not perceived as being meaningfully and instrumentally separate from the (various) communities to which they belong." Chabal and Daloz (1999: 52). While that conception of individuals appears to be incompatible with negative liberty, it does not imply that Africans have no meaningful sense of personal freedom, but rather that their conception must accommodate their view of the relationship between individuals and the community.

[28] Ayittey (2009).

freedom. Similarly, the association between freedom and home ownership is strongest in the Anglo-American tradition that produced Mill and Berlin.[29] Such a notion of the "home" – a place identified with one's inner self, a essentially private sphere to be shielded from outside interference – is alien to the communalistic world.

More generally, the live-and-let-live attitude cherished by advocates of negative liberty is anathema to those for whom isolation was a sure road to social, spiritual, economic, and even physical death. For those, ancient slavery was not the worst thing that could have happened to an individual person – ostracism was. Banishment was not merely geographical separation, but dispossession of an individual from her relational network, the wellspring of relational freedom.

Recognizing these critical differences between relational freedom and negative liberty sheds light on the role of TRC and the way that it promotes certain values. Significantly, TRCs have been particularly important in resolving conflict in Africa, with TRCs having been used in Liberia, Morocco, Algeria, the Democratic Republic of Congo, Ghana, Sierra Leone, Côte d'Ivoire, Nigeria, South Africa, Burundi, Ethiopia, Chad, Uganda, and Zimbabwe, in addition to those still at work in Kenya and Rwanda. There are, undoubtedly, many different factors that contribute to the use of TRCs in Africa. But one of those factors, I think, is that TRCs are particularly amenable to the sense of relational freedom that has traditionally had a hold on Africans. For those who prize relational freedom, then, TRCs offer not just a means of revealing truths about past injustices and recognizing the moral significance of victims' suffering, but also helps to repair the social basis of personal freedom.

9.4 Models of Responding to Conflict

The TRC process also has a close connection to a particular view of how we should deal with conflict. All human societies face deep conflicts – be they religious, ethnic, cultural, tribal, racial, social, economic or historical – but not all human societies respond to conflict in the same way. Ethnic, cultural, and religious differences simply do not threaten the stability of the United States in the way they do to countries like Nigeria, Liberia, Somalia, Rwanda, Iran, and Sierra Leone. One reason is that the former has generally (at least since the American Civil War) channeled these differences into political action, action that in turn is shaped and constrained by a constitutional system. In contrast, conflict in the latter regularly overwhelm political channels, sending floods of violence across the state despite efforts of well-meaning reformers to quell the cultural, religious, and ethnic storms that feed the deluge.

What accounts for this difference? Why should liberal democracies like the contemporary United States be more dexterous in dealing with the pressures and tensions of differences among individuals and groups than other kinds of systems in the

---

[29] See the distinction and the discussion on private and public sphere in Arendt (2005: 114–15, 122–3, 127–9, 135–40, 142, 149–51).

developing world have? One explanation appeals to the political institutions found in these states. The political institutions of the former can *accommodate* deep differences among individuals and groups and still find it possible to cooperate within a political system; the latter seem much less capable of doing that.

To see why, step back a bit and look at some different ways one might respond to conflict in general. Consider a group of people sharply divided over an issue, with each side both passionately committed to its view and unwilling to continue to live in a divided community. In such a situation, there are at least three general possible outcomes:

$$\text{Fighting} \leftrightarrow \text{Cooperation} \leftrightarrow \text{Flight}$$

"Cooperation" here is intended to be a fairly weak concept, one that implies merely that the conflicting sides agree to carry out their conflict within the political system, and to accept the policy decisions resulting from that system. "Fighting" and "Flight" are what happen when the parties fail to achieve cooperation in that weak sense. Fighting implies that neither side of the conflict relents and the conflict escalates to the point at which violence breaks out; this is the case in a civil war, with the sides slugging it out until either one group is destroyed, conquered, or forced to withdraw or both collapse from exhaustion. Flight entails that one or the other side withdraws from the conflict; this would be the case with secession.[30]

Intuitively, cooperating is preferable to either alternative in most circumstances. For those of a liberal bent in particular, the idea of cooperating suggests a tolerant community, one in which rival parties peacefully reach a position to which each member of that group or community can plausibly be said to have consented.[31]

For purposes of this essay, then, I presume that for most divided populations, it is better to cooperate within a political system and continue to live together rather than resort either to fighting or flight. But even if we assume that cooperation is better than either alternative, it isn't obvious what basis is required for cooperation. Does it require some deep consensus on every policy decision, and if so, must this consensus be morally justified or can it merely be an orthodoxy or set of (potentially unjustified) social norms? Or does cooperation require only the most superficial deal or modus vivendi sufficient for the parties each to endorse the same actions? Does it imply that there is no significant dissent, or can we have cooperation even though the population remains sharply divided on many important issues?

The answers to those questions depend on the particular population involved and how they are prepared, as a matter of their history and political institutions, to respond to conflict. In the United States, for instance, significant proportions of the

---

[30] For a general discussion of the factors affecting individuals' decisions to remain "loyal" to a community, rather than to engage in some form of "exit" from that community (either by engaging in flight or by fighting), see Hirschman (1970).

[31] There are, of course, circumstances in which resolving differences by fleeing or fighting is intuitively preferable to any kind of cooperation. If cooperation requires compromising with the devil (or some sufficiently oppressive party), that will be too high a price to pay.

population usually disagree over certain central policy decisions, such as enacting national healthcare reform legislation or continuing the wars in Iraq and Afghanistan. Despite those differences, however, Americans generally cooperate in the sense that they accept as legitimate those decisions that have been duly enacted, even if they vehemently disagree with those decisions. Consensus is rare – yet there is coopera-tion in the sense that those that disagree do so while continuing to work within the same political community. Indeed, Justice Robert Jackson celebrated the absence of any means of enforcing consensus when he wrote that "If there is any fixed star in our constitutional constellation, it is that no official, high or petty, can prescribe what shall be orthodox in politics, nationalism, religion, or other matters of opinion, or force citizens to confess by word or act their faith therein."[32]

One reason this is possible is because the United States protects the "losers" in that political community. As a liberal state, of course, the United States recognizes minorities' rights and (for the most part) protects those rights against the will of the majority. But the United States also has constitutional features that protect access to the electoral system. That is, the Constitution gives hope to today's electoral losers that they will be winners tomorrow. The effect is to enhance the political system's ability to tolerate internal dissent and disagreement, and give today's losers incen-tive to remain within the system, rather than opting out for fear that a single loss will mean they are forever shut out of power.[33]

This is one approach to achieving cooperation. On it, the electoral process – or more generally, the mechanism used to select policies – is structured not to remove disagreement, but to accommodate it by giving different groups a fair shot in the future at being able to decide which policies are adopted. In simplistic terms, it is like letting everyone have a turn: in that case, everyone still has reason to continue to work within the system – notwithstanding the fact that there may never be con-sensus on any of the policies adopted.

This approach to conflict admittedly leaves much to be desired. In an ideal world, people should be able to reach agreement one issue at a time, deliberating coolly over each issue and coming to an agreement on that matter that each side finds acceptable. The approach I am describing, however, suggests a very different process, one which produces a series of zero-sum outcomes on which one party prevails and the other loses. Parties in such a system are neither aiming to reach a middle ground that respects the desires and objectives of all the disputing groups, nor are they nobly struggling for a principle on which they will not compromise. Such a system does not rest on consensus regarding decisions, but rather a grudg-ing willingness to endure losses today in the hopes that there will be victories tomorrow.

Finding a way to cooperate is important to the extent that we disagree – and we disagree about many, many things. But the aim of cooperation in the very limited,

---

[32] West Virginia Board of Education v. Barnette, 319 U.S. 624, 642 (1943).

[33] The classic source of the view of the U.S. Constitution as policing the political process is Ely (1980), and its themes are echoed in Breyer (2005). I have discussed the role of constitutional protections and other safeguards for the political system in Wingo (2004).

minimalist sense in which I am using the term is not to end these disagreements. Rather, it offers us a tool to act in the presence of disagreement and conflict, and to find ways to "go on" in ways that at best protect the parties from one another, but will usually never totally satisfy each. Cooperation in this minimalist sense, then, is an enterprise devoted to managing conflict: much as the realistic goal of medicine is to control disease rather than eradicate it, the practice of politics is a means of addressing the conflicts that are a natural part of social life rather than eliminating them.

This is, however, not the only way to achieve cooperation within a community. An alternative approach is simply to insist on consensus, and require that everyone "get on board" with a policy before enacting it. This is the approach we find in many traditional African communities. Among the Nso people of Cameroon, for instance, the way to deal with internal dissent over what course of action to take is to sit down and talk: Members of these communities will literally sit down and talk and talk and talk for as long as it takes to iron out their differences and achieve a consensus – not just a promise to go along with a decision they disagree with, but a genuine consensus[34]:

> In crisis-resolution, the African tradition entails consultation and decision-making by consensus. When a crisis erupted in a typical African village, the chief and the elders would summon a village meeting and put the issue to the people. There it was debated by the people until a consensus was reached.[35]

Consider the following example from my own people, the Nso. Like many indigenous African societies, the first option for the Nso in dealing with internal conflict is to expel the difference that led to the conflict. This does mean in the first instance casting out those individuals who have caused the conflict (although eventually it might come to that), but instead calls for certain ritual processes intended to reintegrate the community.[36]

Faced with internal sources of conflict, the Nso first come together in search of the *phamakoi* that divided individuals, with the shared understanding that such divisions – even if they directly affected only a few, would eventually threaten the survival of all. That is referred to as the time of reckoning and atonement (or *suliy* in Lamnso, the language spoken by the people of Nso).

The *suliy* process involves individual family members and family heads – the *a Fai* ("a" stands for plural) – coming together in public before the watching eyes of all and speaking the truth to the listening ears of all. This transparent ritual of truth utterances is followed by a swearing ceremony in which each member swore to the ancestors (believed to be living in the spiritual realm) that their words represent the truth and nothing but the truth. They then stand on a broom, a symbol of purifying

---

[34] I have discussed such approaches to conflict resolution in Wingo (2004).

[35] Ayittey (2009).

[36] In a continent historically plagued by under-population, African communities didn't have the luxury of using exile or imprisonment as a first option for dealing with those who violated social mores.

the differences that led to conflict. The process is then sealed by a blood-letting sacrifice to the ancestors, another symbol of purification of the society. The "polluted" persons involved in the conflict are given small slivers of sticks to clean their mouths, and the ceremony ends with their throwing those slivers – now infused with all that ailed the community – behind them, a gesture symbolizing their determination never again to utter a word on the matter. All this was to ensure survival in a world where the welfare of the whole as a unified body was paramount.[37]

Such a ritual is intended to reintegrate all but the most deviant into the community, and reinforces the values of unity and consensus. Those values are not totally arbitrary, but instead reflect the rational response to the particular demands of their environment and history. Consensus was a key to survival in a harsh environment, and the development of political communities bound together by common lineage, blood, and ritual served as a useful means of achieving such a consensus.[38]

The character of social and political institutions that one finds in different societies around the world reflects not just conscious human design, but also the various pressures, and forces that have acted on those societies over time and the resources available to those societies. In the case of communalistic societies, like those found in Africa and the Middle East, political institutions were developed in response to harsh environments that required individuals and groups to band together for survival.[39] As such, the history of places like Africa and the Middle East is not that of rugged individualists. It is one in which, in evolutionary terms, the environment selected for societies that prized the whole over the part. The interdependence of individuals in communalistic societies is captured by a statement from the Kenyan-born Anglican priest and theologian, John Mbiti: "I am, because we are; and since we are, therefore, I am."[40]

Such communities exhibit a remarkable – even beautiful – internal coherence and structure, and in their particular practices exhibit many virtues. The Nso purification ritual described above, for instance, shares several features of what members of a modern liberal state would regard as a legitimate institution. First, the process recognized and respected the victim as an individual. Second, each individual with an interest in the proceeding was allowed to participate and to voice her interests and

---

[37] See Wingo (2010).

[38] Ryszard Kapuściński, a long-time observer of African politics and culture, remarked on the profound importance of unity and social connections in Africa: "Individualism is highly prized in Europe, and perhaps nowhere more so than in America; in Africa, it is synonymous with unhappiness, with being accursed. African tradition is collectivist, for only in a harmonious group could one face the obstacles continually thrown up by nature." He illustrated this with a revealing anecdote: "One day a group of children surrounded me. I had a single piece of candy, which I placed in my open palm. The children stood motionless, starting. Finally, the oldest girl took the candy, bit it into pieces, and equitably distributed the bits." Kapuściński (2002: 36).

[39] For an excellent overview of how Africa's geographic and environmental features and the selective pressures that those features imply have shaped traditional social and political structures in Africa, see Reader (1998). See, in particular chapter 28, in which Reader discusses how the demands of labor-intensive agriculture shaped a range of African social institutions, from slavery to the tradition of clientalism to the highly communal nature of indigenous communities.

[40] Mbiti (1996: 141).

concerns. Third, the individuals involved are approximately equal economically and socially, a fact that mitigated the risk of exploitation of one group by another. Fourth, free and frank speech was encouraged, by way of creating a special environment for speaking out without fear of reprisal. And fifth, reconciliation grew out of the living experience of the members of the society, a condition I have referred to elsewhere as conferring "living legitimacy" on the result.[41]

But the internal coherence and structure of these communities come at a price, for they cannot easily withstand internal dissent. They take on a wonderful organic unity that seems constitutionally incapable of surviving the internal differences that are a matter of course in any truly diverse modern state. As they have arisen in many parts of Africa, this fragility has not been a handicap, since it traditionally has been easy for dissenters to exit such societies.[42] The effect of this is that those traditional structures have not had to develop the means of dealing with internal dissent. As long as flight was a viable option, it may well have been the rational alternative to cooperation. But when flight has become more difficult – as it has with the modernization of African states, the only alternative to cooperation is fighting. There is no middle ground left.

The limitations of this kind of communalistic consensus approach are evidence in many of the conflicts that have plagued (and continue to plague) Africa in the post-colonial period. That is, while consensus-based politics may have been effective among relatively small, homogeneous, and familial-based communities, the focus on consensus becomes a liability outside the special circumstances of those traditional communities. As applied to modern African states whose borders cut across ethnic and tribal lines and whose populations are diverse multi-ethnic, multi-lingual, multi-cultural, and multi-religious mixes. Consensus among strangers bound together not by common blood or origins can be very difficult if not impossible to find.

Yet to a remarkable extent, modern-day African politics still reflects this consensus-based approach.[43] As Archbishop Tutu has said of South Africa, "social harmony is for us the summun bonum – the greatest good. Anything that subverts or undermines

---

[41] See generally Wingo (2001). Under the conditions of living legitimacy, the process of reconciliation is not foisted onto members, it is their own.

[42] See, for example, the analysis by Jeffrey Herbst (2000), in which he traces the traditional weakness of African states to the traditional difficulties with controlling territory. In a section entitled "The Primacy of Exit," Herbst notes that the large amounts of open land and rain-fed agriculture meant that relatively little investment was needed for persons to move from one place to another. As a result, "it was often easier to escape from rulers than to fight them. Africans, on the basis of sensible cost-benefit equations, would, more often than not, rather switch than fight" (Herbst 2000: 39). See also the analyses of Harms, Asiwaju, and Barfield referenced by Herbst.

[43] One particularly interesting sign of this continuing commitment to consensus is the design of the Apartheid Museum in South Africa. As described by Teeger and Vinitzky-Seroussi, the form and content of the museum is dedicated at creating consensus: "through its controlled form, the Apartheid Museum seeks to offer a consensual reading of the past. . . . The Apartheid Museum is careful to ensure that the consensual form be translated into consensual content. Thus it sets up a content that, much like its architecture, is carefully controlled to elicit consensus and not conflict." Teeger and Vinitzky-Seroussi (2007: 64).

this sought after good is to be avoided like the plague. Anger, resentment, lust for revenge . . . are corrosive of this good."[44] Such a sentiment is attractive on its face, but too firm an adherence to the aim of harmony understood as the absence of disagreement or dissent has an ugly side. For instance, the African institution of "one-party democracy" (or even "no-party democracy") is in part supported by the African practice of consensus and avoidance of conflicts.[45] Kwasi Wiredu has argued for this uniquely African version of consensual democracy on the grounds that multi-party democracy is too divisive, and only helps to further divide ethnic groups in African countries.[46] And in an interesting contrast to the constitutional protections in place in the United States to maintain the integrity of the electoral process described above, corruption of the electoral process by those seeking to quash opposition is a disturbingly regular event across Africa.[47]

African responses to the problems of ethnic conflict also reflect the presumption that the way to control conflict is to eliminate the differences between the conflicting parties (rather than finding some other mechanism for accommodating those differences). In post-genocide Rwanda, for instance, the constitution forbids Hutus and Tutsis to identify with their ethnicities.[48] Similarly, reform-minded Africans in Ghana and Nigeria have written into their constitutions provisions that forbid political parties from identifying themselves along ethnic lines,[49] and the Nigerian constitution

---

[44] Tutu (1999: 35).

[45] In their intriguing analysis of the synthesis of traditional African institutions and modernization, Chabal and Daloz highlight the difficulty in finding a place for opposition in African political systems. They argue that "[w]hereas in the West, the practice of democratic elections is, with the exception of coalition governments, a zero-sum game – there are recognizable winners and losers, each with a proper constitutional role – the same cannot apply in Africa. If the notion of the individual and the meaning of representation are bound up with the identity, defence and furtherance of the interests of the community, then there can be no place in the political system for an opposition with no means of delivering resources to its constituents. To be in opposition is of no intrinsic or even political value." Chabal and Daloz (1999: 55).

[46] Wiredu (Wiredu 1995).

[47] In reporting on the patterns of abuse in African, George Ayittey has remarked that "the destruction of an African country, regardless of the professed ideology of its leader, always begins with some dispute over the electoral process." Ayittey (2009). He also reports that manipulation or blockage of the electoral process set off civil strife or war in several African states, including Rwanda, Sierra Leone, Zaire, Liberia, Congo, Algeria, and Nigeria.

[48] Constitution of the Republic of Rwanda, ch. II, art.9 ("The State of Rwanda commits itself to conform to the following fundamental principles and to promote and enforce the respect thereof: . . . eradication of ethnic, regional and other divisions and promotion of national unity, . . . [and] the constant question for solutions through dialogue and consensus."); id. title III, art.54 ("Political organizations are prohibited from basing themselves on race, ethnic group, tribe, clan, region, sex, religion or any other division which may give rise to discrimination.").

[49] See Constitution of the Republic of Ghana, ch. 7, para.55(4) ("Every political party shall have a national character, and membership shall not be based on ethnic, religious, regional or other sectional divisions."); Constitution of the Federal Republic of Nigeria, Part III.D, para.222(e) ("No association by whatever name called shall function as a party, unless – . . .the name of the association, its symbol or logo does not contain any ethnic or religious connotation or give the appearance that the activities of the association are confined to a part only of the geographical area of Nigeria.").

actually makes it a duty of the national government not only to allow, but to "encourage inter-marriage among persons from different places of origin, or of different religious, ethnic or linguistic association or ties."[50]

The unfortunate effects of this coupling of the traditional African value of consensus and highly diverse populations that lack that consensus are written in blood on recent African history. For instance, even given the intimate connections within small, homogeneous traditional African communities, dissent would arise, but the vast unsettled expanses of Africa in the past provided plenty of room for flight to those who rejected the orthodoxy. The fragile nature of traditional African communities and their inability to accommodate dissent help to account for this time-honored tradition of Africans "voting with their feet." Not surprisingly, then, Africa today accounts for a disproportionate share of the world's refugees, and refugee crises in places like Darfur, Chad, Kenya, Liberia, Sierra Leone, Somalia, and Zimbabwe remind us of the cost of "cleansing" a community of dissent in order to maintain a desired degree of consensus.[51] And this tradition has been complicated by the fact that those who seek to exercise their exit option no longer simply move into unclaimed territory, but into that of a neighboring sovereign state that is often intent on keeping those strangers from settling permanently.[52]

These examples provide a sobering lesson on the need to develop ways to respond to conflict rather than simply avoid it. As I've already noted, for most of African history, the tradition of consensus and conflict avoidance are highly rational, intelligent strategies, given the advantages this attitude provided in an environment where survival was for so long a precarious thing. But however rational or intelligent this commitment might have been then, it has had some disastrous effects in Africa today. The commitment to consensus, after all, does not imply that all differences must be resolved – it only means that differences be eliminated, and often the easiest way to do that is for one party or the other to pick up and leave – a response that has had a negative impact across the continent.[53]

The fragility of the highly consensus-driven institutions and traditions of Africa can be seen in a variety of other systems as well. For instance, while there are legitimate criticisms of the monarchical regimes that cover the Arabian Plate, their survival is not wholly accidental. The regime they support is intertwined with a

---

[50] Constitution of the Federal Republic of Nigeria, ch. II, para.15(3)(c).

[51] According to the UN High Commissioner for Refugees, in 2002 Africa hosted 25.7% of the world's refugees, despite having only about 15 % of the world's population. According to Herbst (2000), "Certainly, one of the reasons that Africa [hade] the largest number of refugees in the world [as of 1994] is that the speed at which boundaries have become consolidated has overwhelmed people seeking, as their ancestors did, to vote with their feet" (230).

[52] See Herbst (2000: 229–30).

[53] For instance, one Cameroonian analyst has attributed sub-Saharan Africa's poor record on development to certain common features of "African culture," in which he includes "a tendency to 'convivial' excesses [and] the primacy of conflict avoidance." Etounga-Manguele (1993), quoted in Chabal and Daloz (1999: 128).

variety of time-honored traditions and "coping strategies" that at least in the past
had value. From the rigid theocracies that admit no accommodation to shifting
realities to the consensus-based indigenous structures, we find a range of practices
and institutions that exemplify fragility. Fragile political institutions have many
virtues: they often embody clear principles, untainted doctrine, impeccable structures,
and perhaps even special aesthetic qualities. What they do not have is the flexibility
to accommodate the kind of conflict that will inevitably arise in any political
system that allows members of a diverse population to voice their honest interests
and beliefs. A fragile system is incapable of tolerating political practice that is nonviolent but competitive, that is built of negotiation, give-and-take, grudging concessions and compromise.

It is surely the case that there is no single, easily identifiable reason why certain
parts of Africa and the Middle East seem so plagued by conflict. Indeed, it may be
that the strife and instability in those regions is inevitable, given the legacy of colonialism and Western dominance, the manipulations of the United States and Soviet
Union during the Cold War, religious differences, and ethic strife – each of which
is an important factor contributing to the problems in those regions. But in addition
to all these factors, the political violence we find in Africa and the Middle East
appears to reflect a certain incapacity to respond to the events and forces that contribute to conflict. That is, the violence we find in these regions does not necessarily imply that differences between parties there are deeper or more passionate than
those found between groups in Western Europe or North America. Rather, the different outcomes may reflect differences in how different states try to foster cooperation within increasingly diverse populations in order to respond to problems as
they arise. Institutions in Western Europe and North America can accommodate
fairly substantial differences among citizens by rejecting the need to ground that
cooperation on consensus. Those in many parts of the Africa and the Middle East,
in contrast, still rely on consensus and orthodoxy as bases for cooperation, and as
a consequence, lack the willingness or ability to engage in the kind of politics – the
give-and-take, the compromising, and the 'unprincipled' deal-making – that seems
necessary to respond to challenges as they arise.

Such unwillingness to engage in this kind of politics does not necessarily mean
one is unreasonable or an ideologue unwilling to bend on the most insignificant
point of principle. Indeed, one of the reasons that violent conflict in so much of the
developing world is so tragic is that while such violence extracts a terrible cost,
there are often rational supports for the institutions and practices that sustain that
violence. As I have already noted in the context of indigenous African communities,
for instance, institutions and the attitudes of members may be so firmly entrenched
that undermining them may just not be an option.

It seems reasonable to believe, given the long history of religious and ethnic
strife, that these forces of religious and ethnic identity are barriers to the kind of
peace and stability required for other kinds of political reform. Unfortunately,
things are not this simple. Differences such as these are often differences between
the most basic touchstones for the identity of people. One does not put on or take

off a religious conviction or ethnic identity like a coat or a pair of shoes. And for that reason, traditions such as these are typically too much a part of people ever to eliminate or significantly reduce.

9.5   Conclusion: The Future of TRCs

As my discussion above should indicate, TRC have a natural affinity for communalistic societies and for those societies in which networks of personal connections are particularly important, insofar as the TRC process is generally directed toward illuminating the ways that individuals (including oppressors and their victims) are related and repairing the connections that have been severed by conflict. What that suggests is that, notwithstanding the apparent broad appeal of TRCs through-out the world, there are general circumstances in which TRCs will be more useful or appropriate than in other circumstances. That is, in those places that are par-ticularly dependent on strong social ties among individuals or that put a premium on consensus as a means of grounding cooperation, TRCs will be a valuable tool for repairing the basis for a functioning state. By examining the particular effects of TRCs with respect to conceptions of personal freedom and approaches to conflict and cooperation, we gain some insight into where they are most likely to be useful in restoring the internal balance of the community disrupted by conflict. This contributes to our understanding of how TRCs operate and the types of effects we should expect from them – two things needed in order to apply this device in an intelligent approach to dealing with the aftermath of conflict. For instance, recognizing the role that TRCs play in shore up the foundations of relational freedom may lead us to consider ways that the TRC process might be tailored in particular applications to focus first on those who have been made most vulnerable by conflict, i.e., those that were made 'socially dead' by being cut off from familial networks.

At the same time, however, there is clearly work to be done in the way of identifying the particular effects of TRCs on different populations. For instance, by providing a forum for individuals to testify to their own experiences and name their oppressors, TRCs provide individuals the chance – perhaps for the first time in their lives – to exercise free speech. This freedom to speak imposes its own special burden, and calls on individuals to exercise certain 'civic muscles' such as self-expression and self-determination that is part of being a citizen in a lib-eral democratic state. The TRC process, then, may have a role to play that goes beyond merely revealing the truth about the conflict and healing divisions, and can play a part in the civic education of citizens of a post-conflict state. TRCs are not a panacea for states torn apart by conflict; as I have argued here, it is impor-tant that we take a realistic view of what TRCs can and cannot deliver, and try to identify with some detail the kinds of values and outcomes that the TRC process is likely to produce. Still, there is reason to think that despite its limits, the TRC process has an important, and perhaps unique, role to play in supporting certain conceptions of freedom and model of cooperation, as well as helping to transform the way citizens of a post-conflict state respond to conflict so as to avoid such widespread conflicts in the future.

References

Abrams RI (2009) Truth and reconciliation in baseball. In: The Huffington Post, February 14. http://www.huffingtonpost.com/roger-i-abrams/truth-and-reconciliation_b_165343.html. Accessed 22 Nov 2011
Arendt H (2005) The promise of politics. Schocken Books, New York
Ayittey GBN (2009) An African solution: solving the crisis of failed states. Harv Int Rev 31(3):24–27
Berlin I (1969) Four essays on liberty. Oxford University Press, New York
Breyer S (2005) Active liberty: interpreting our democratic Constitution. Knopf, New York
Cavallaro JL (2009) We need a truth commission to uncover Bush-era wrongdoing. In: Christian Science Monitor February 20. http://www.csmonitor.com/Commentary/Opinion/2009/0220/p09s02-coop.html
Chabal P, Daloz J-P (1999) Africa works: disorder as political instrument. International African Institute in association with James Currey, Oxford
Cunningham D, Nugent C, Slodden C (2010) The durability of collective memory: reconciling the 'Greensboro Massacre'. Soc Forces 88(4):1517–1542
Dale R (2002) The politics of the rainbow nation: truth, legitimacy, and memory in South Africa. Afr Stud Rev 45(3):39–44
Durkheim É (1966) Suicide, a study in sociology. Free Press, New York
Durkheim É (1972) Selected writings. University Press, Cambridge
Ely J (1980) Democracy and distrust: a theory of judicial review. Harvard University Press, Cambridge
Etounga-Manguele D (1993) L'Afrique a-t-elle besoin d'un programme d'ajustement culturel? Editions nouvelles du Sud, Paris
Grant R (1999) Morality, social policy and Berlin's two concepts. Soc Res 66(4):1217–1244
Hayner P (2001) Unspeakable truths: confronting state terror and atrocity. Routledge, New York
Herbst J (2000) States and power in Africa: comparative lessons in authority and control. Princeton University Press, New Jersey
Hirschman AO (1970) Exit, voice, and loyalty: decline in firms, organizations, and states. Harvard University Press, Cambridge
Ignatieff M (1996) Articles of faith. Index Censorship 25(5):110–122
Kapuściński R (2002) The shadow of the Sun. Vintage, New York
Kiss E (2001) Moral ambition within and beyond political constraints: reflections on restorative justice. In: Rotberg R, Thompson D (eds) Truth v justice: the morality of truth commissions. Princeton University Press, Princeton, pp 68–98
Magarrell L, Wesley J (2008) Learning from Greensboro: truth and reconciliation in the United States. University of Pennsylvania Press, Philadelphia
Mbiti J (1996) African religions and philosophy. Heinemann, London
Minow M (2001) The hope for healing: what can truth commissions do? In: Rotberg R, Thompson D (eds) Truth v. justice: the morality of truth commissions. Princeton University Press, Princeton, pp 235–260
Posner R (1973) Economic analysis of law. Little Brown, Boston
Rawls J (1999) A theory of justice, Revised edn. Cambridge Mass: Belknap Press of Harvard University Press

Reader J (1998) Africa: a biography of the continent. A.A. Knopf, New York

Rettig M (2008) Gacaca: truth, justice, and reconciliation in postconflict Rwanda? Afr Stud Rev 51(3):25–50

Roper SD, Barria LA (2009) Why do states commission the truth? political considerations in the establishment of African truth and reconciliation commissions. Human Rights Rev 10:373–391

Stein S (2009) Leahy talks to white house about investigating bush. In: The Huffington Post. February 10. http://www.huffingtonpost.com/2009/02/10/exclusive-leahy-talks-to_n_165774.html. Accessed 22 Nov 2011

Teeger C, Vinitzky-Seroussi V (2007) Controlling for consensus: commemorating apartheid in South Africa. Symb Interact 30(1):57–78

Tutu D (1999) No future without forgiveness. Rider Books, London

Weitzel S (2004) Forgiving the unrepentant: self-respect and the role of third parties. In: Breen MS (ed) Truth, reconciliation, and evil. Rodopi, New York, pp 223–232

Wing AW (2008) A truth and reconciliation for Palestine/Israel: healing spirit injuries. Trans Law Contemp Probl 17(1):139

Wingo AH (2001) Living legitimacy: a new approach to good government in Africa. New Engl J Public Policy 16(2):49–71

Wingo AH (2004) Learning how to lose: coping with political defeats in honor/shame cultures. UNESCO conference on philosophy and democracy, Beirut, Lebanon

Wingo A (2010) The odyssey of human rights: reply to diagne. Transition 202(1):120–138

Wiredu K (1995) Democracy and consensus in African traditional politics. A plea for a non-party polity. In: The Centennial Review 39. http://them.polylog.org/2/fwk-en.htm. Accessed 22 Nov 2011

Zorbas E (2004) Reconciliation in post-genocide Rwanda. Afr J Legal Stud 29:40–52

Chapter 10
Apologizing for Atrocity: Rwanda and Recognition

Lynne Tirrell

Abstract Apology is a necessary component of moral repair of damage done by wrongs against the person. Analyzing the role of apology in the aftermath of atrocity, with a focus on the genocide of the Tutsi in Rwanda, 1994, this chapter emphasizes the role of recognition failures in grave moral wrongs, the importance of speech acts that offer recognition, and building mutuality through recognition as a route to reconciliation. Understanding the US role in the international failure to stop the '94 genocide raises the question of how any response could mitigate a world-shattering wrong like genocide. With a focus on survivors, this chapter explains the concepts of recognition harm and spirit murder to illuminate what survivors experience and need. The third section develops a theory of apology as offering recognition to the victim of wrongdoing – through both the act of speaking-to and through its content. The chapter examines US President Bill Clinton's 1998 apology to Rwandans, to understand it as an apology, and to see how it began reconciliation between Americans and Rwandans. The chapter concludes with a brief discussion of the inter-related significance of apology and material reparations.

In the hills of Rwanda, people in serious danger make a specific whooping cry, which is re-produced by those who hear it even as they run to the aid of their neighbor. Hearing the call imposes an obligation on hearers to add their voices to the cry and to provide help. Inaction is not an option. A Rwandan explains,

L. Tirrell (✉)
Department of Philosophy, University of Massachusetts Boston
100 Morrissey Blvd, Boston, MA 02125-3393, USA
e-mail: lynne.tirrell@umb.edu

A. MacLachlan and A. Speight (eds.), *Justice, Responsibility and Reconciliation in the Wake of Conflict*, Boston Studies in Philosophy, Religion and Public Life 1, DOI 10.1007/978-94-007-5201-6_10, © Springer Science+Business Media Dordrecht 2013

The people are living separately together. So there is responsibility. I cry, you cry. You cry, I cry. We all come running, and the one that stays quiet, the one that stays home must explain. Is he in league with the criminals? Is he a coward? And what would he expect when he cries? This is simple. This is normal. This is community.[1]

In 1994, the international community did not reproduce Rwanda's distress call and did not come running. As Hutu extremists murdered Tutsis, governments of many nations sent troops to Rwanda to evacuate their own citizens, leaving those Rwandans marked for genocide to suffer and die. This was both literal and normative abandonment. Offering neither diplomatic[2] nor military intervention,[3] the international community did not give appropriate uptake to the Rwandan distress cry. General Roméo Dallaire, commander of the UN peacekeepers in Rwanda, sums up the issue: "at its heart, the Rwandan story is the story of the failure of humanity to heed a call for help from an endangered people" (Dallaire 2003, 516).

The Rwandan distress cry is a speech act that engenders immediate action from those within its range who are also part of the linguistic community that understands its conditions of use. Those who do not respond appropriately are held morally accountable and must explain their failure. This scenario raises questions concerning what post-hoc explanation might accomplish, which sorts of explanations are sufficient to the task, and which individual and social needs are met by such linguistic responses. Demanding an explanation from those who fail to intervene keeps secure the victim's moral status as a person; the non-responder risks loss of status. Explanation is a first step in the multi-directional process of restoring moral statuses of (and perhaps relations between) victims of crimes, perpetrators, and—our focus here—those who stood by or walked away. Explanation alone might get a non-responder off the moral hook, so to speak, but if it does not, then apology becomes a crucial part of moral restoration. Explanation is a

---

[1] Gourevitch (1998, 34, emphasis). It is important to hear this "cry" as a call, like the low-tech "911," automatic, without involving emotional investment in the particular event.

[2] Louise Mushikiwabo, testifying at a U.S. Congressional hearing in 2004, said, "all that was needed was a clear and unequivocal signal to the government of Rwanda back then, that violence will not be tolerated...Rwanda depended very heavily on foreign aid, therefore the international community had an easy and sure tool to use with a government that no longer did its primary job, protecting its people. The planners of the Rwandan genocide were intelligent and world savvy, and there is no doubt that they could have taken the clue from the international community's words if not actions." USHR (2004, 71).

[3] Dallaire (2003, 141–151), Neuffer (2002, 116–117), Power (2003, 343), Shattuck (2003, 76). Consider Shattuck: "The catastrophic consequences of failing to act at an early stage—when minimal intervention might have saved lives—are magnified because the world paid little attention to the warnings coming from Rwanda. By denying General Dallaire and his troops the tools they needed to do their job, and then withdrawing them at the very moment when they might have been able to stop the violence, the international community sealed the fate of 800,000 Rwandans." For an argument that military success would have been unlikely, see Kuperman 2001.

key part of an effective apology, but apology, through both its action and its content, offers the victim moral and social recognition that explanation alone does not provide. Apology is necessary for full repair of harms that threaten or undermine the victim's moral status, and it opens the door to renewing the moral standing of the one who apologizes.

Apology is most necessary—and least likely to seem sufficient—when an offense undermines a person's status as part of a human community, i.e., when the offense attacks their very personhood. Genocide is such an offense, and more, a wrong so grave that apology seems trivial. And yet, apology can be reparative through showing recognition for our mutual basic humanity. It can shape the meaning of actions that follow. Although Rwanda is not a person, it is nevertheless a collective of persons, each of whom experienced the genocide from a particular embodied stance; individuals were targeted *qua* Tutsi, but each suffered individual degradations and losses. In 1994, Rwanda's Tutsi were abandoned by their own government, which planned the genocide, as well as by their neighbors, who implemented it, and by the world at large, which mostly looked away (Melvern 2000; Munro 2001; Power 2001). International silence and active non-intervention in the Rwandan genocide illustrates failure to be moved by common humanity. In 1994, terrified Tutsi expected more support from the US and Belgium than either country delivered, so they particularly valued official apologies from US President Bill Clinton (1998) and Belgian Prime Minister Guy Verhofstadt (BBC 2000). Survivors of genocide need acknowledgement of their experience as part of the process of returning to community with those who neither shared that experience nor tried to stop it. Without apology, reparations and humanitarian aid offer insufficient recognition of this particular damage to another's life. Understanding what apology offers to victims of grave wrongs shows why speech, particularly apology, is a necessary component of both healing and reconciliation. Clarifying the powers of apology and promises, of "mere" words and material support, this paper examines the power of apology for reconciliation in a global context.

The analysis here draws upon several features of apologizing, which will be further explained in what follows. First, apology offers recognition from the wrongdoer to the victim. In this way, apology restores some of the moral and normative status that the wrongdoing challenged or undermined. The apologizer's attention—to the victim *qua* victim, to the action as a wrong, to the damages done—each of these acts of attention creates the possibility for, and may in some cases constitute, recognition of the dignity and humanity of the victim. This highlights the second feature, which is that the primary function of apology is other-regarding, seeking the restoration of the victim's damaged moral status. Apology may be made with or without any attempt to gain forgiveness or to forge reconciliation. Seeking forgiveness is a self-regarding motive for apology; a self-regarding apology may still help heal recognition harms, but this would depend on how serious the wrongdoing was and how self-serving the apology is. Third, as an other-regarding act of recognition, apology does not actively *seek* reconciliation or forgiveness (insofar as these are self-regarding ends), but apology is usually oriented towards or offered in the spirit of repair, and thus often plays a role in fostering reconciliation. Forging reconciliation always involves an element of mutuality, of creating a restored "we." In understanding the role of apology in the aftermath of atrocity, we must emphasize the role of recognition failures in moral wrongdoing, the importance of speech acts that offer recognition, and the role played by building mutuality through recognition along the route to reconciliation.

In the first section, we will look at the behavior of the US in 1994 with respect to the genocide of the Tutsi in Rwanda. The US was neither the only, nor the primary, international actor that mattered; France and Belgium were far more significant. From 1990 to 1993, Rwanda, one of the smallest countries in the world, became one of the largest African importers of machetes and other weapons, mostly from China, using international aid money from France, Germany, Belgium, and the US (Melvern 2004, 56–58). There were many dirty hands. Understanding the US role in the international failure to stop the genocide sets the stage for asking how any response could mitigate a world-shattering wrong like genocide. Intensifying our focus on survivors, the second section examines the concepts of recognition harm and spirit murder to illuminate what survivors experience and need. The third section develops an analysis of apology as offering recognition to the victim of wrongdoing, achieved through both the act of speaking-to and through its content. We then examine US President Bill Clinton's 1998 apology to Rwandans, to understand it as an apology, and to see how it began reconciliation between Americans and Rwandans. The paper concludes with a brief discussion of the inter-related significance of apology and material reparations.

10.1 The Adequacy Problem

Any particular apology follows a precipitating situation, which involves a moral or normative offense—a wrong against a person or a shared norm. The apology is undertaken as part of a process that seeks to repair the damage done. Clearly, just as wrongs can range from minor to overwhelming, the requirements of apology can vary. Sometimes, particularly with grave wrongs, an apology is needed from a secondary participant, not the main agent. The Rwandan distress call sets up just such a demand upon secondary persons.

The Rwandan says: *…the one that stays quiet, the one that stays home must explain. Is he in league with the criminals? Is he a coward?* Both kinds of explanation have been given for the US role in the international non-response to the genocide of the Tutsi. In October 1993, only 6 months before the onset of Rwanda's genocide, the desecrated bodies of 18 American Army Rangers, an elite military force, were dragged through the streets of Mogadishu, Somalia. Analyses commonly cite the psychological and political damage done by these horrific deaths as undermining America's political will to intervene in Africa, particularly where we have no "strategic

interest." This charges the US with cowardice.[4] Charging the US with criminality is
more complex. First, the longstanding US alliance with France puts us *"in league
with the criminals"* due to France's support for Rwanda's Hutu Power government
(Wallis 2007). More directly, the US decision to classify the genocide as "tribal or
civil war" generated a cognitive fog, giving cover to international neglect and
legitimating the Hutu Power government. Further, evidence suggests that US
non-assistance was active and intentional. During the first weeks of the genocide,
Madeline Albright (2003), US ambassador to the UN, not only stopped the UN from
adding peacekeepers in Rwanda, but also worked to diminish UN peacekeepers
by 90%, thus actively preventing other nations from sending help. So there is a case
to be made that the US was directly or indirectly *"in league with the criminals"*
(Morris 1999, 1).

Not wanting to accept the moral charges of being cowardly or criminal, the US
government, as "the one who stayed home," claimed *cognitive* failure. In his 1998
speech at Kigali Airport, US President Clinton told Rwandans that his government
"did not fully appreciate the depth and the speed with which you were being engulfed
by this unimaginable terror." Perhaps. This is parallel to a Rwandan in the hills
saying, "I heard the call but thought it was something else." Claiming cognitive
failure is meant to evade the charge of moral failure. Nevertheless, forewarned by
independent observers, by the UN, and by it own military, the US government had
the information it needed for an accurate assessment of the situation in Rwanda, as
became clear when documents were de-classified in 2000. So, the cognitive failure
excuse fails. If you don't hear the cry because you stop your ears, your lack of
response is culpable (Tirrell 2009). Further, the US's conceptual contortions to
avoid calling it "genocide" reveal an *effort* to disregard the distress cry, a cry that
brings with it a moral obligation to help, as made explicit in the UN Genocide
Convention of 1948. Ignoring the Rwandan distress cry was both a moral and political
failure (see Neuffer 2002, 124; also Morrow 1999).

The failure of the international community to stop the genocide of the Tutsi in
Rwanda constituted a *recognition harm*, a fundamental moral failure. Deciding that
Rwanda was irrelevant to their strategic interests, they failed to treat the Tutsi as persons,
as beings with moral claims that must be honored. Rwandan Tutsi experienced

---

[4] An Associated Press wire story, 25 March 1998 says: "At the time, the United States was still
stunned by the deaths of U.S. Rangers in Somalia in October 1993 and feared further military intervention in Africa." http://www.news-star.com/stories/032598/new_clinton.html   The Radio
Netherlands Internet Desk, 23 August 2001: "Fearing to get embroiled in yet another vicious civil
conflict, the UN, the United States, Rwanda's former colonial ruler Belgium and other nations did
little to prevent the killings. The Rwandan-based UN Force known as UNAMIR, which could have
helped protect civilians, was withdrawn on the advice of US and other diplomats," (http://www2.
rnw.nl/rnw/en/currentaffairs/region/northamerica/us010823.html). See "Rwanda: The Preventable
Genocide," for an OAU panel discussion of the influence of Somalia on US policy in West Africa.
(OAU Doc. IPEP/Panel (May 29, 2000) at 12.33), Prunier (1995–2005). Gibney and Roxstrum, note
38, Taylor (1999, 3–4), Gourevitch (1998, 149–150), Kuperman (2001, 4), and Power (2003, 335).

normative abandonment by the rest of the world (see Walker 2006). Survivors are keenly aware of this normative abandonment, which is why Rwandan President Paul Kagame still sometimes speaks with contempt of the so-called "international community." Normative engagement—participation in shared norms and practices—defines a community, a world (Lugones 2003); normative abandonment shatters it.

The overwhelming damage done by the mass atrocities of the twentieth century lingers in the lives of millions of survivors, compelling responses from bystanders, who in turn seek to compel responses from perpetrators. Addressing the issue of finding an adequate response to atrocity, Martha Minow says, "…no response to mass atrocity is adequate. The sheer implication of adequacy is itself potentially insulting to the memory of those who were killed and to the remaining days of those who were tortured, and to those who witnessed the worst that human beings can do to other human beings" (Minow 2000, 235). Minow is right; there is no adequate response to atrocity. And yet, lack of response is also deeply inadequate. Non-response shades into erasure, which opens the door to denial. The adequacy problem is a double-bind, leaving us damned if we do and damned if we don't. Clearly, some ways of being inadequate are worse than others, and aiming for adequacy is at best an ideal. Apology helps us aim.

The adequacy problem asks: "*How can anything we say or do after an atrocity make any difference at all to survivors?*" Contrasted with saying, doing suggests material action—we use our bodies and our resources to rescue, feed, and clothe survivors, reunite families, rebuild infrastructure, and restore communities as best we can. These important actions send an expressive message of care and concern that is necessary, but insufficient, for restoring personal and social equilibrium. Also necessary are speech acts that set such actions into social and historical context, giving meaning to material actions, settling, for example, whether the action is a generous gift or the repayment of a debt. The difference is crucial. Aid from those who had a direct or indirect hand in the suffering should be offered as reparations; the transformation from aid to reparations is achieved through being offered with an apology.

10.2 Lifting Lazarus: Spirit Murder as Recognition Harm

To see what an apology must accomplish, we must understand the damage it attempts to repair. The focus of our account is the survivor, as it should be for the perpetrator who must apologize. As we have seen, responding to grave wrongs is challenging. This is partly because, as Hannah Arendt understood, the impact on survivors is almost unintelligible. Its scope and scale are overwhelming, making the testimony of survivors suspect, even to themselves. She writes that if the survivor "has resolutely returned to the world of the living, he himself is often assailed by doubts with regard to his own truthfulness, as though he had mistaken a nightmare for reality." This nightmare—which was their reality—reminds us that

> the psyche can be destroyed even without the destruction of the physical man; that indeed,
> psyche, character, and individuality seem under certain circumstances to express themselves

only through the rapidity or slowness with which they disintegrate. The end result in any case is inanimate men, i.e., men who can no longer be psychologically understood, whose return to the psychologically or otherwise intelligibly human world closely resembles the resurrection of Lazarus (Arendt 1973, 439–441).[5]

Raising such a Lazarus would require understanding the harm that Patricia J. Williams calls "spirit murder," which is a species of what I call *recognition harms*.[6] The world-shattering wrongs of genocide cast the person out of the realm of norms and values that define his/her community. To bring her back requires recognition of her personhood, through the exercise of typically human functions, with language primary among these. Apology offers recognition of and regret about the harm, plus hope for a better future.

Spirit murder starts with practical behaviors in which physical and normative abandonments are intertwined. Genocide survivors live each day with the damage done to their families, communities, and the infrastructure of their society. UNICEF estimates that after Rwanda's genocide, over 600,000 children were orphaned, and about a million children were made "vulnerable." Nearly half of the children under five were malnourished, over 400,000 school-aged children were not in school, and over 100,000 children were heads of their households.[7] In light of the enormous psycho-social damage resulting from experiencing and witnessing heinous crimes, Gourevitch argues that

Hutu Power's crime was much greater than the murder of nearly a million people. Nobody in Rwanda escaped direct physical or psychic damage. The terror was designed to be total and enduring, a legacy to leave Rwandans spinning and disoriented in the slipstream of their memories for a very long time to come (Gourevitch 1998, 224; cf. Hatzfeld 2005, 133).

The terror endures by shaping the survivors' daily interpretations of themselves and those around them. A 2004 Amnesty International report on the violent legacy of the genocide for women and girls notes that "Many were raped at barriers erected by the *interahamwe* youth militia and/or held as sexual captives in exchange for temporary protection from *interahamwe* militia and the military. *Their bodies and spirits were mutilated, humiliated and scarred.*"[8]

---

[5] Arendt here references the story of Lazarus's miraculous resurrection from the dead, found in *The Bible* at John 11: 1–46. Briefly, Lazarus was the brother of Mary and Martha, and all three were friends of Jesus. Jesus was in Bethlehem when Lazarus died in Bethany, about 2 miles away (15 furlongs). Martha went to find Jesus, and met him on the road, returning to Bethany; she criticized Jesus for failing to save Lazarus. Jesus told her to go get Mary, and meet at Lazarus's tomb. Lazarus had been dead for 4 days. At the tomb, Jesus wept over the death of his friend, and then told those assembled to move the stone blocking the entrance to the tomb (a cave). Jesus said a prayer of thanks to God, and cried out "Lazarus, come forth" (11:43). Lazarus is said to have arisen from the tomb, still bound in linen wraps. Lazarus, like Jesus, is a symbol of resurrection.

[6] The concept is drawn from Hegel, and has had many incarnations in existentialist, phenomenological, and idealist philosophies that developed since Hegel. The most recent and thorough is found in the writings of Axel Honneth. My concept of recognition harm is independent of but compatible with Honneth's account of recognition as foundational to ethics. See Honneth (2007).

[7] http://www.unicef.org/infobycountry/23867_20292.html

[8] Amnesty International. 6 April 2004. Emphasis added. See Hatzfeld (2005, 86, 97, 134).

   The damage of spirit murder is a form of alienation from oneself and from others. It is widespread, enduring, and generated by the actions of others, particularly those exhibiting casual or cruel disregard for one's status as a person. Its ripple effect spreads beyond its immediate victims, infecting the culture. Witnessing brutality at close range, at the hands of people one formerly trusted, shatters the foundations of one's social and psychological world. One Rwandan says, "We have all lost something. We even have a name for it: *bapfuye buhagazi*. It means the walking dead. This is the land of the walking dead" (Neuffer 2002, 251).

   Serious recognition harms are partly a moral phenomenon and partly metaphysical. The world-shattering damage of these crimes undermines an agent's sense of having a legitimate claim to moral status. Hannah Arendt's "living corpses" are *bapfuye buhagazi,* a concept underscored by Raphael Lemkin's view that genocide is a "double murder," an actual murder of many and a murder of the spirits of those who survive. Susan Brison describes the feeling of "outliving oneself" as common to Holocaust survivors and others who experience life-threatening and life-shattering assault. Orlando Patterson charges that slavery led to social death, and Claudia Card draws on Patterson to analyze genocide as inflicting social death. Card emphasizes genocidal destruction of forms of life, especially social norms and practices that must be abandoned to maintain physical survival.[9] Each variation on the articulation of recognition harm shares the core concept that the behavior to which the person is subject somehow shatters her sense of self and place in the world. These are world-shattering wrongs.[10]

   Arendt's analysis of the implementation of totalitarianism, a political process of reshaping individuals and their worlds, identifies two steps toward preparing "living corpses": first "to kill the judicial person in the man" and second, "to murder the moral person in the man." The dissolution of the individual almost always follows. In genocide, even more overwhelming than the vast numbers killed, are the facts about how and why they were killed, and by whom. The murders of the Tutsi were enacted up close, hand to hand, often by neighbors and even family members, who left the dead and dying unburied, unnamed, unclaimable. Or they buried them in unspeakable ways, in latrines, covered ditches, and mass graves. Arendt argues that in making death anonymous, the Nazis "robbed death of its meaning as the end of a fulfilled life. In a sense they took away the individual's own death, proving that henceforth nothing belonged to him and he belonged to no one. His death merely set a seal on the fact that he had never really existed" (Arendt 1973, 452).

   Such denial of existence is part of the core of spirit murder. Marie Louise Kagoyire, a survivor of the genocide of the Tutsi, explains,

> We shook hands cordially over deals we struck, we lent them money, and then, they decided to hack us to pieces. They wanted to wipe us out so much that they became obsessed with burning our photo albums during the looting, so that the dead would no longer even have

---

[9] Arendt (1973, 425, 431, 435, 437), Brison (2002, 38–39, 45–46, 49–59), Patterson (1982), Card (2003), and Power (2003, 28).

[10] See Stolorow et al. (2002, especially chapters 7 and 8). Also De Zuleuetta (2007).

the chance to have existed. To be safer, they tried to kill people and their memories, and in any case, kill the memories when they couldn't catch the people. They worked for our extermination and to erase all signs of that work, so to speak. Today many survivors possess not even one tiny photo of their mama, their children, their baptisms and marriages, a picture that could have helped them smooth a little sweetness over the pain of their loss (Hatzfeld 2006, 130–131).

Genocide is about erasure on every level: physical and material, cultural, historical, everything. No traces left behind. In thus describing what the *génocidaires* did, Kagoyire also reveals what internationals turned away from, as if we thought that in turning away we could convince ourselves that these crimes were not wrongs against persons. See no evil, indeed.

In a community, mutual recognition makes our forms of life possible. *When I cry, you cry. When you cry, I cry.* Within a healthy and vital community, your very being is reinforced by the vision, understanding, and cooperation of others. When community shatters, we fail to provide this kind of being-affirming recognition to each other, and so each undermines the other's efforts to construct her or his life. In a society of equals, such recognition is mutual, and not shaped by social, political, or economic power. Such a society is a myth, of course. Consider the inequalities of power between the US and Rwanda in light of Patricia Williams' observation: "There is great power in being able to see the world as one will and then to have that vision enacted. But if being is seeing for the subject, then being seen is the precise measure of existence for the object" (Williams 1992, 28; Cf. Frye 1983). Many supporters of truth tribunals take the tribunal's value to be "seeing" survivors back into being *as* members of human community through the recognition that acknowledgement affords. Survivors often focus on the harms done to their loved ones and their community, overlooking the lingering recognition harms they still experience. They struggle for recognition, remaining mystified by its loss. In targeting the Tutsi for genocide, Hutu extremists not only sought to rob them of dignity and respect, casting them out of human community, but sought to erase the Tutsi from the earth.[11]

Long after buildings have been rebuilt, water supplies cleaned, and services restored, the complex work of rebuilding persons remains. Material support is crucial, but insufficient, for regaining psycho-social and moral equilibrium. If humanitarian aid is to be truly humane, something must be done to restore to its recipients their basic human dignity and a sense of community belonging. This is where it matters what is said; as speakers, we help to articulate and construct each other and ourselves as social beings, highlighting some aspects of reality and obscuring others with our words. What we say about what happened, about our own role in it,

---

[11] Minow (1998) writes that the trial process is not the best means to meet the "twin goals" of gaining public acknowledgment of wrongs done, and allowing survivors an official forum for which to develop and within which to present their own narrative accounts of those wrongs is a better way of achieving those goals. For that, she argues, truth and reconciliation commissions, of the sort developed in South Africa, are better suited (Minow 1998, 58–59, and elsewhere. See also Kritz 1996, Rotman 2000).

our moral accounting of events, can make the difference between lingering hostilities and slowly earning trust between individuals. National narratives play similar roles in constructing national identities and building relations amongst nations. Reports, stories, analyses, accusations, denials, and acknowledgments: all these speech acts obviously make a difference to the progress of social and human restoration. Speech acts shape the social reality within which we live and as such are acts of normative engagement (Tirrell 2012).

International refusal to hear the Rwandan distress cry, thereby abandoning the endangered Tutsi, damaged survivors' spirits and undermined their status as persons. Williams says spirit murder is rooted in a "disregard for others whose lives qualitatively depend on our regard" (Williams 1992, 73). Spirit murder is possible because "part of ourselves is beyond the control of pure physical will and resides in the sanctuary of those around us; a fundamental part of ourselves and of our dignity depends on the uncontrollable, powerful, external observers who make up a society" (Williams 1992, 73). When others with whom your conception of self is intertwined brutally murder your friends and family, the inhumane message of disregard comes through loud and clear. When those you counted on for help do not come, the message is also clear. Interestingly, many Rwandans today distrust the regard of "the whites" (*muzungu*), a catch-all term for Europeans and Americans who walked away in 1994. Today, Rwandans seek internal control, allowing outsiders less power over these strong recognitive functions.

In the context of heinous murder and torture, it seems strange to focus on refusing to give a person's speech uptake, but it is important to see such refusals as an effective way to erase a person—a survivor—from the social landscape, through signaling a lack of reciprocity. A great deal of what we do as persons depends upon the cooperation of others to make it what it is, and by extension, key aspects of one's identity depend upon this social cooperation. Particularly in dire circumstances, the fact that your endangerment is deemed irrelevant renders ineffective any claim you might make upon the help and concern of others, and thus calls your very personhood into question. Amongst nations, mutual recognition or refusal of recognition is clearly important to both internal and international development. Trade embargos and travel bans illustrate the dramatic consequences of isolation. Evacuating American and European citizens from Rwanda was a way of abandoning Rwanda to itself, marking its distress as no longer relevant. Disregarding genocide in progress certainly excludes that nation and its people from international community, denying them the mutual recognition and interdependence that marks a human community.

10.3   Apology, Recognition, and Repair

To understand the reparative power of apology, one needs to understand it as both a speech act and as a moral action, other-regarding to its core. The speech act side of the analysis shows how an apology uses social conventions to offer recognition to its recipient. The moral side of the analysis reveals why this matters. Even a very official, somewhat *pro forma,* apology offers recognition through its utterance. The quality of the recognition it offers will depend on both the way in which it uses mutually understood conventions and the quality of its content. This section will make these claims clearer.

Consider first the speech act dimensions of the Rwandan distress cry. This simple, loud, signaling sound is non-compositional, requiring no parsing. It is a basic speech act using conventionalized sounds with a particular force; it conveys a meaning that imposes an obligation on all who comprehend it. Like promising, apologizing, or saying "I do" in a wedding, the Rwandan distress call is an illocutionary act: it is conventional, not achieved by other means, and requires hearer uptake for its completion (Austin 1962, 116–117). Its force is achieved through conventions, and it requires certain kinds of subsequent actions. Using Austin's example, being married is an illocutionary effect of saying "I do" (as spouse-to-be) within a properly officiated wedding ceremony. Making your mother happy is a perlocutionary effect of that same act. The difference between illocutions and perlocutions depends on how closely the effect is tied to operative conventions. The effect of being married is achieved through specific conventions; the effect of making Mom happy can be achieved in a variety of ways, not all conventional. Further, once the speech act is done, the illocution achieved is independent of the perlocutionary effects. You are married whether Mom is happy or sad. When the Rwandan makes the distress call, that illocutionary act has been issued; others hear it, grasp the responsive action required, and comply or not. The moral scorecard has changed.

The sounds of the Rwandan distress cry might alarm anyone, but only a Rwandan would understand it as a conventionalized and morally obligatory call to action. It alerts the hearer to trouble and need (this is the illocution), carrying with it a demand that the hearer reproduce the cry (extending its range) while coming to the aid of the victim. In this way, the speech act engenders action. A speech act, because of its thorough conventionality, is possible only because both speaker and hearer are involved in a normative framework, a system of values, a community. These community-based practices are what make it possible for the hearer to give the call appropriate uptake, to know what to do with it. The core concept behind the distress call in the Rwandan hills is community.

When people respond appropriately to your distress, they remind you that you and they form one community. *"I cry, you cry. You cry, I cry. We all come running."* When they fail to respond appropriately, explanations are required to either restore community or to break it down explicitly. On a large scale, the United Nations is supposed to be such a community for member states, and although it often fails, this normative imperative is one of its reasons for being. Rwanda's sense of international participation was strengthened in 1994, for it held one of the rotating seats on the UN's Security Council that year. And yet, when Hutu extremists unleashed genocide, the UN turned away. Beneath the Rwandan demand for an explanation of why the international community did not heed their distress call is a need to restore trust in the values and norms that bind the members of the community. Beneath the demand for an explanation is a need for *reconciliation*. Apology, in offering recognition to the victim, is a start.[12]

The recognition inherent in offering an apology is also shaped by how well the basic elements of apology are achieved. Most theories analyze apology into several key components, emphasizing confession or acknowledgement, remorse or contrition, and offers of reparations. Aaron Lazare, concerned to explain the healing power of apology, analyzes an effective apology into four parts: (1) acknowledgement, (2) attitudes and behaviors (including remorse, shame, humility, and sincerity), (3) explanation, and (4) reparations (Lazare 2004, 79). Acknowledgement, which is both cognitively and morally substantive, is at the heart of his account. Acknowledgement involves specifically naming the offense and saying how it violated a moral norm or how it undermined an understanding of a relationship.[13] Identifying the impact of offense on the other person is part of its other-directedness, whereas explanation is focused on the perpetrator's actions.

On the account developed here, the primary task of apology is to offer recognition to the victim, aimed at restoring damaged moral standing. Through this, it may foster other forms of repair. Centering on recognition, my account emphasizes two overarching components of an apology. First, there is the Account, which offers recognition of the victim and her experience through acknowledgement of the wrong done and its damage, plus an explanation of the precipitating situation and the perpetrator's motives, which may or may not have countenanced the victim's agency. The Account is thus a backward-looking view of the moral wrong. Equally important is the Response, which discloses the wrongdoer's present attitudes about the past wrong, with its ongoing effects. This attitude is a stance toward himself, his victim, his community, and is conveyed not only in descriptions but also in how the perpetrator treats the victim and similar persons now. A *génocidaire* who states his regret but continues to mistreat Tutsi is sending a mixed Response. Speech and other actions are evaluated together in judging the reliability of the Response. A *génocidaire* who follows through on his expressed remorse with reparative gestures, such as helping widows to plough their fields, sends a solid reparative message. The Response includes affect and action, expressing affective attitudes and behaviors

---

[12] Who seeks reconciliation, and under what circumstances, matters. My concern with the Rwandan demand for an explanation is about a process set in motion by atrocity survivors. One Rwandan, whose family had been stuffed live down a latrine and left to die, said: "People come to Rwanda and talk of reconciliation. It's offensive. Imagine talking to Jews of reconciliation in 1946. Maybe in a long time, but it's a private matter" (Edmund Mrugamba, in 1995, quoted in Gourevitch 1998, 240). Personal decisions about how to cope with the aftermath of genocide are ongoing, excruciating, and beyond prescription by any analysis an outsider could offer. In contrast, it is not a private (personal, individually decided) matter whether reconciliation is possible between Rwanda and the US or Belgium, and at issue is what those who looked away can do now.

[13] Lazare maintains that acknowledgement is the *essential condition* of apology–without it, there is no real apology. Govier (2002) also emphasizes the role of acknowledgement, but holds that moral apology includes a request for forgiveness. Neither Lazare's view nor mine requires this; forgiveness is a response that the recipient of the apology might choose, but the apology itself is not about what the perpetrator may try to get from the victim.

and offering promises for reparations and reform. Through this amalgam, the perpetrator shows that gaining a clearer understanding of the victim's experience
has changed his/her stance toward the victim. In the Response, the wrongdoer presents changed attitudes and promises reparations.

Both the Account and the Response play important roles in repairing the normative
damage done by the wrongdoing. The apologizer must acknowledge the wrong
done, qua wrong, and own up to the damage his actions did to the victim. Here,
empathy and moral imagination are necessary; the wrongdoer must imagine the
action from the victim's perspective in order to fully grasp the wrong. Explanation
discloses the wrongdoer's motivations and causes, making the apologizer vulnerable
to deeper criticism. Explanations fail when they turn into excuses, for excuses are
designed to prevent the very vulnerability that real disclosure opens up. Exposing
regret, remorse, and sincerity also makes the perpetrator vulnerable to the victim
and enables the victim to regain a sense of trust in the apologizer. These affective
states are important to consider alongside reparations, because without them,
victims worry that promises for changed behavior and reparations will go unfulfilled.
Sincerity generates trust, but so does a good track record, and the track record can
be guaranteed in a variety of ways. The affective question of what is in the mind and
heart of the apologizer is often less important than whether he/she follows through
on the promised behavioral changes that are part of reparations.

Some apology theorists, like Tavuchis, take the central purpose of apology to be
"to convey sorrow through speech," thus treating apology as an expression of regret,
a report of the perpetrator's feelings, through which exposure the wrongdoer makes
himself vulnerable to his own victim (Tavuchis 1991, 32). On such a view, apology
is construed as an outward visible sign of an inward mental or emotional state, but
this cannot be the whole story. Except in trivial harms, such as jostling someone on
the street, apology is not just saying you are sorry, and it is not only or primarily
about the speaker's emotional states. Apology is what J.L. Austin called a
performative utterance: it is a speech act that, in being said, *does* something beyond
describing or reporting.[14] A mere expression of remorse describes the speaker's
state of mind, so is made true or false by how the speaker feels. When I say, "I am
so sad about that," I describe my own feelings, and my sentence is true or false
depending on the feelings I have. As Austin argues, when I say "I am running," it is
the fact that I am running that makes the statement true or false. In the case of a
performative utterance, in contrast, we think more about its success than about its
truth. Austin explains, "it is the happiness of the performative 'I apologize' *that
makes it the fact* that I am apologizing; and my success in apologizing depends upon
the happiness of the performative utterance 'I apologize'."[15] An effective (successful,

---

[14] Austin (1970, 136). Tavuchis misses this performative aspect of speech acts when he says both
that "apology is essentially a speech act" and that "an apology cannot and does not attempt to
accomplish anything outside of speech" (1991, 31).

[15] Austin (1962, 47, emphasis added). "Happiness" here is a technical term, akin to Austin's use of
"felicity." Others might call it success, but Austin is not emphasizing outcomes at the expense of
processes. Both the process and the outcome factor into the happiness of the speech act.

"happy") apology undertakes a set of commitments, including a particular interpretation of past events, as well as committing to future actions relevant to that interpretation. An apology is thus a performative utterance that undertakes ongoing commitments. As a performative utterance, apology changes the moral relations between the parties; this is its illocutionary force. A mere expression of remorse or regret lacks this crucial performative dimension.

Specifically, apology is a speech act that undertakes a set of ongoing linguistic, social, and moral commitments. Austin treats apology as a *behabitive,* such as thanking, greeting, blessing, cursing, deploring, etc.; these are inherently social acts that tend to be responsive to the acts of others. Responsiveness to the other is certainly a component of apology. Austin treats promises, on the other hand, as *commissives*; these commit the speaker to an undertaking or course of action (Austin 1962, 151–152; cf. Celermajer 2009). On my view, apology is best understood as a commissive with a behabitive component: just like a promise, I undertake a complex commitment when I apologize, and that commitment is to a person whom I have harmed. This commitment is about the past, the present, and the future: ideally, it acknowledges the past, assesses the impact of the past on the present, and makes sincere promises about the future which seek to repair the damage done.

Many theorists assume that an apology is inherently a request for forgiveness, thereby treating apology as more self-regarding than other-regarding. An apology based on self-interest treats the other as an instrument to release one's own guilt, as a tool for the improvement of one's situation; it *uses* the victim once again.[16]

In contrast, I urge that the paradigm of apology is *other-regarding*; apology must be understood as an *offering* to the wronged party. Apology is primarily other-regarding, acknowledging the wrong done to the other person, restoring recognition of the other through that acknowledgement. Forgiveness, when given, is a per-locutionary effect of the apology—an outcome beyond the apology, which is foreseeable but distinct from the apology itself (Austin 1970, 131–132). Official apologies can fall into either category. Critics of Rwanda's *gacaca* system, for example, cite testimony from *génocidaires* who confess and apologize insincerely in order to manipulate the system. As unsatisfying as an insincere or remorseless apology is, it remains an apology; the performative aspect of the speech act ("I apologize") is distinct from and trumps the descriptive report ("I'm sorry" or "I'm not sorry"). Austin would count an insincere apology an *abuse* of the speech act, because it technically meets the criteria for being an apology and yet is designed to achieve the end without substantively fulfilling the means.[17] Similarly, an apology

---

[16] About forgiveness in political contexts, see Digeser (1998). About self-interested apology, see Hatzfeld (2005, especially 157–164 and 195–207).

[17] Could one coherently say: "I apologize and I am not sorry"? Would it count as an apology? Tavuchis claims that "sorrow is the energizing force of apology" (Tavuchis 1991, 122) so on his view such a claim would be a contradiction. It is not so clear. The first clause marks the illocutionary force, while the second simply states the speaker's attitude, so the second clause does not neces-sarily undermine the first. Such a conjunction would still have the illocutionary force of apology but it would fail to achieve the perlocutionary effects at which apologies typically aim. It is unlikely to be an *effective* apology.

that is a *de facto* demand for forgiveness does not respect and does little to rebuild the victim's status as a person. A truly other-regarding apology matters, even in cases in which forgiveness may be impossible.

10.4 President Clinton's 1998 Apology to Rwanda

Once we recognize that apologies function as a way of restoring social and moral standing, we can see apology as an instrument of *justice*. As an instrument of justice, apology shapes or frames the status of any package of more concrete reparations. Apology is often overlooked as an instrument of justice in the aftermath of atrocity because it is so readily seen as cheap and easy, as "only words," which simply offer regret or remorse (e.g., Gibney and Roxtrum 2001). Edward Royce, Chairman of the US House of Representatives Subcommittee on Africa, on traveling to Rwanda with President Clinton in 1998, said, "Expressions of regret are fine, but words without action are worse than useless" (USHR 2004, 7). Royce is right about mere regrets and words without action, but fails to consider words which themselves are actions, namely performative utterances (Austin 1970). Apology serves restorative justice because it offers acknowledgment of harms done; its connection to restorative justice is through its illocutionary force. Apology serves retributive justice insofar as the perpetrator's Account leads to punishment and sacrifice; this service would be through its perlocutionary effects. From the perpetrator's perspective, apology is often seen as putting one's guilt on record and so making too strong a commitment, whereas to the victim it may seem too weak. Negotiating these issues and others is part of how apology creates the potential to restore moral equilibrium (Govier and Verwoerd 2002, 71).

More fundamentally, the speaker's *very* speaking, in addressing the survivor, recognizes the survivor as part of a normative community (see Kukla and Lance 2009). Apologies of state are most often offered for transgressions long past, over which the current administration had no control. In President Clinton's watershed 1998 apology at Kigali airport, for the first time in recent memory, a sitting head of state apologized for actions that *occurred on his watch* and for which he was responsible. Although this apology falls short in many respects, it was well received in Rwanda for several reasons. First, President Clinton's travel to Rwanda, speaking with survivors and listening to their stories, was an act of attention that stood in opposition to his own administration's egregious neglect. One Rwandan official, who attended the speech, said "To genocide survivors, Clinton's decision to visit was an apology in and of itself, or at the very least, an acknowledgement that he should have done things differently" (Sebarenzi 2009, 124). Second, in offering an apology to the *people* of Rwanda, not to their government, President Clinton came across as *both* official and personal. Third, the content of Clinton's speech, offering an explicit apology and forthrightly labeling the massacre of the Tutsi as "genocide," also constituted renewed recognition. For these reasons, Clinton's apology won the hearts of survivors.

The Account elements of Clinton's apology present a mixed bag, a solid acknow-ledgement, but a disingenuous explanation—really a set of excuses and lies. At the time, Clinton got away with the false explanation (mostly). Although the explicit apology is brief, Clinton's acknowledgment of American complicity is complex and attenuated. Seeing the weaving of different elements in the apology throughout Clinton's speech makes it possible to understand why Rwandans found his words a source of comfort and inspiration and yet many Americans did not. Rwandans wanted and received strong acknowledgement of their experience; American critics sought a more honest and detailed explanation, and were disappointed (Morrow 1998; Cassel 2000).

Clinton's main avowal of culpability is explicit and succinct, accepting significant backward-looking responsibility. He said:

> We did not act quickly enough after the killing began. We should not have allowed the refugee camps to become safe haven for the killers. [Applause.] We did not immediately call these crimes by their rightful name: genocide. [Applause.]

News reports indicate that Rwandans appreciated Clinton's directness. Elsewhere in the apology, Clinton shows a grasp of the extent of the damage, admits that it was not inter-tribal warfare, and affirms that it was really a structured and planned genocide, supported by the Rwandan government. This new official description takes six paragraphs early in the speech, explaining that the US was wrong in its earlier descriptions of the events, and in its actions based on those descriptions. This re-interpretation is a crucial contribution of the apology; its overturning of earlier denials was a real service to the Rwandan people. Clinton's acknowledgements are the strength of his speech, for they help to restore a sense of shared values and shared vision. On the other hand, they are limited and too often vague. About the international community, for example, he says only that it "must bear its share of responsibility for this tragedy." Such vagueness is a key way apologies fail, and is often reason for their rejection (Lazare 2004, 86–88).

The one that stays home must explain… Acknowledgement without explanation damages the Account, limiting the apology's effectiveness. Lazare notes that victims often

> make comments such as "You owe me an explanation" or "Please tell me why you did this," or, "You could at least have had the decency to explain yourself." These statements suggest that the failure to offer an explanation is often perceived as an inadequate apology or even an insult. (Lazare 2004, 119)

Owning up to the full facts would have required Clinton to call the US obstruc-tionist and to explain the motives for the obstruction; failing to do so, he leaves the US demand for withdrawal of UN forces unexplained, and so shirks responsibility for America's more egregious actions. The most serious flaw in Clinton's apology is its lack of adequate explanation.

Surely no explanation for turning away from genocide could be adequate, but still, the question lingers: what kind of explanation should be offered to a genocide survivor, and what kind of explanation could be accepted? We see again the double bind that no explanation is sufficient and failing to explain adds to the offense.

In the weakest part of the speech, Clinton offered the cognitive failure excuse: "All over the world, there were people like me sitting in offices, day after day, who did not fully appreciate the depth and speed with which you were being engulfed by this unimaginable terror." In 1998, most Rwandans did not know that this was patently false. Still, one survivor in attendance, Joseph Sebarenzi, whose family perished in the genocide, writes of his frustration with this very part of the speech, saying that, even then, he thought:

> He could not claim that he didn't know what was going on. No one could. The murders were carried out in broad daylight. Footage of people being hacked to death was broadcast on television. It was reported in newspapers. It was told in gruesome detail by those fleeing the violence. Whatever excuse anyone could give about the decision not to act, lack of awareness was not one. Again, I thought of my family. *If someone had acted, they would be alive today.* (Sebarenzi 2009, 130)

A front-page commentary in the *Wall Street Journal* said: "Clinton's dishonesty here conceals complicity in a truly horrible crime" (Morris 1999). Surely this cognitive failure excuse is what Austin would call an abuse, seeming to offer an explanation but instead preying upon survivors' needs for recognition.

An accurate Account would require addressing America's limited perceived interest in Africa, from strategic, material/economic, and even humanist standpoints. Clearly such explanation was not and will not be forthcoming. This is the closest Clinton comes:

> So let us challenge ourselves to build a world in which no branch of humanity, because of national, racial, ethnic or religious origin, is again threatened with destruction because of those characteristics, of which people should rightly be proud. Let us work together as a community of civilized nations to strengthen our ability to prevent and, if necessary, to stop genocide.

This exhortation highlights the role of race and ethnicity in genocide without directly acknowledging its role in international neglect of Rwanda's genocide. Clinton leaves that implied. Clinton's suggestion for developing an international anti-genocide coalition lacks specifics, and seems oddly oblivious to the founding mandate of the United Nations (Pendergast and Smock 1999). Had the UN lived up to its mandate, and had its "peacekeepers" been allowed to keep the peace, hundreds of thousands of lives would have been saved (Dallaire 2003; Shattuck 2003, 76). Surely this promise to prevent genocide has not been fulfilled, given the ongoing genocide in Darfur.

Part of Clinton's task in Kigali was to be the face of American concern. This required him to be vulnerable to the experiences of the genocide survivors who spoke, but strong in his acknowledgement and offers of reparations. The Account and the Response elements of Clinton's apology work together. The Account shows respect in offering an improved interpretation of events, and the Response reinforces this interpretation as Clinton listened attentively with an emotionally expressive face to the testimony of survivors. Throughout the speech, Clinton's expressive response flouted long-standing conventions of presidential behavior in order to show human connection instead of positional distance, thus reinforcing his message. He concluded his remarks with an invocation of shared values in basic human unity, highlighting both cognitive and moral aspects of the situation.

You see countless stories of courage around you every day as you go about your business
here—men and women who survived and go on, children who recover the light in their eyes
remind us that at the dawn of a new millennium there is only one crucial division among the
peoples of the Earth. And believe me, after over five years of dealing with these problems I
know it is not the division between Hutu and Tutsi, or Serb and Croatian and Muslim in Bosnia,
or Arab and Jew, or Catholic and Protestant in Ireland, or black and white. *It is really the line
between those who embrace the common humanity we all share and those who reject it.*

This emphasis on the value of basic humanity countermands the message of the
genocide. It fits the aspirations of American ideology, but not our actual foreign policy,
which too often stands on the wrong side of the line Clinton draws. Embracing common
humanity as a shared value offers crucial recognition to the dispirited survivors, a recognition that needs reinforcement through future actions and improved foreign policy.

The Account and the Response need to work together to restore recognition and
rebuild a sense of shared values. Ongoing commitments in the form of promises and
reparations are important to this normative project, providing the ultimate test of sincerity.[18] Clinton concluded his speech by pledging to follow through on the promises
he had just made, particularly the promise of international cooperation and support
for Rwanda and Africa. Ultimately the value of his speech is judged by whether the
US lives up to these promises. Our track record is inauspicious, although USAID
estimates its 2010 spending in Rwanda at over $208 million, on health, education, and
economic development. They report that in 2008 over 700,000 Rwandans benefitted
from U.S. food assistance (USAID 2011, also Great Lakes Policy Forum 2003). Since
leaving office, Clinton's own philanthropy in Rwanda has made him well liked and
respected there. He used his own money to help finish the genocide memorial in
Kigali, and the Clinton Foundation has worked effectively, according to Partners in
Health, to reduce dramatically the prices of anti-retroviral medicines that fight HIV
and AIDS (Farmer 2005). These important actions, among others, give material
weight to Clinton's apology.

Promises offered as reparations, like most promises, must offer what the injured
party needs. Promising something the receiver does not want or that undermines her
well-being is not a promise but a threat, and a promise to do what would already
happen in the ordinary course of affairs is also in an important sense not a promise
(Searle 1969, 58–59). A promise needs to take the promiser out of herself and her
own needs and into the needs of the recipient. Like apology, it is other-oriented. Of
Clinton's five explicit official promises, only two offer to directly rebuild Rwanda.[19]

---

[18] Lazare, for example, says, "in the end, it is reparations—or the lack of them—that determine the
success of the official apology" (Lazare 2004, 65).

[19] Specific Promises: 1. Early warning systems: "I am directing my administration to improve, with
the international community, our system for identifying and spotlighting nations in danger of genocidal violence." 2. Readiness: "we must as an international community have the ability to act when
genocide threatens" 3. Economic support: US will donate $2 million to Survivors Fund, "continue
our support in the years to come, and urge other nations to do the same, so that survivors and their
communities can find the care they need and the help they must have." 4. Legal Infrastructure:
Citing the importance of re-establishing the rule of law, Clinton promises $30 million from his
Great Lakes Initiative to reestablish criminal justice system. 5. International Court: Clinton pledges
to support establishment of a permanent international criminal court, guided by United Nations.

Donating to the Genocide Survivors Fund and rebuilding the legal infrastructure both provide immediate assistance to survivors and so are both valuable promises. In contrast, Clinton's promises to develop early warning systems and readiness to intervene correlate to his disingenuous avowal of ignorance, and since this was false, these two promises seem at best unnecessary, and at worst, a smokescreen (Dallaire 2003, 514–522).

Despite this, Clinton's promise to make it impossible to claim ignorance in the future can be seen as more substantive in light of the Rwandan survivor's challenge: *the one that stays home must explain*... Such early warning and readiness programs should eliminate future invocations of the ignorance excuse. Seen in this light, we can remain skeptical of Clinton's cognitive failure excuse while seeing how these promises comforted Rwandans. While drawing Rwanda back into international community, Clinton also indicates that this is a community worth rejoining, one that promises not to make this mistake again. The weakness of Clinton's apology is its unacceptable cognitive ignorance excuse parading as an explanation. The strengths of Clinton's apology are in the recognition he offers through what he acknowledges, in the human connection he forges through breaking out of his positional role, and in the promises that he makes for future policy.

10.5 Neither Apology nor Reparations Alone

In our skepticism about the words of world leaders, it would be natural to ask whether their speech is superfluous, whether reparations alone can bring repair and lead to reconciliation. If the test of official apologies is in the reparations, then perhaps apology is not really necessary. Reparations can feed people, strengthen public health and safety, and rebuild roads and infrastructure, but without apology, reparations fail to restore the dignity of the recipient. Reparations may help recipients to rebuild their own dignity, but this is not the same as our recognizing their inherent dignity. Apology without reparations seems weak, insincere, and immaterial; offering reparations without apology seems cowardly or coercive.

Where all responses are inadequate, the need for *both* speech and action is unmistakable. Apology without reparations misses the point of continuity between the illocutionary shift of moral ground and the subsequent behavior required by that shift. Reparations without apology seem cowardly because the perpetrator avoids the hard work of recognizing the experience of the other and evaluating oneself as an agent.

Making the Account and Response explicit to the victim is crucial for situating future action. Without the Account elements of apology, acknowledgement and explanation, the Response, i.e., international aid flowing into Rwanda, could be a way to buy influence, or to gain the indebtedness of the Rwandan people or their government. Without apology, aid could be seen as largesse, and perversely make those to whom a debt is owed feel indebted.[20] Aid without explanation is always

---

[20] Thanks to Claudia Card for this observation. See also Gill (2000, 23).

open to multiple interpretations. More importantly, aid alone does not address the recognition problems that constitute recognition harm and maintain spirit murder. To let you know that I see you as a person, I must behave in certain ways, and among them is using language and linguistic conventions to reinforce our mutual recognition of each other's situation. Apology and promises are crucial among these.

The credibility and power of our speech acts depend upon the overall context within which they are issued and their coherence (or incoherence) with our attendant and consequent actions. It is a package deal. The speech act undertakes commitments, which subsequent material actions either support or undermine. Each is judged in terms of the other because they are part of the same whole. The timing and delivery of the several components of an apology matter; in apology, the distinction between word and deed may mislead. Clearly, moral and social repair after a crime against the person, from rape to genocide, requires recognition of the victim's personhood. Such recognition need not come from the perpetrator, but when it does, the effect is powerful. Apology has the power to achieve recognition through the balance and amalgamation of its elements.

In looking for human connection in the speech act of apology, an atrocity victim not only wants justice, but also seeks understanding—an understanding that carries an emotional burden. "*I cry, you cry. You cry, I cry. We all come running....*" This kind of understanding is not compartmentalized into an Account and a Response; rather, it traverses them. Cognitive, emotive, interpretive, and behavioral elements all intertwine. The understanding sought by the recipient is often thickly moral and emotional, not simply a thin restating of events, and so apology demands that those who did not experience the survivor's ordeal must use their imagination to ascertain the full moral gravity of the wrong.[21] This is a masterful aspect of Clinton's apology: stepping out of positional distance as the US president and allowing himself to express an emotional connection to the survivors with whom he met. He showed them empathy, and that is a deeper form of understanding than anyone expected, particularly from one who did not come running. This exercise of the moral imagination is the connective tissue that allows apologies and attendant promises to rebuild relationships.

The task of the moral imagination is daunting in the face of the horror of genocide, where the mind confronts its own limits. Like Hannah Arendt, Samantha Power holds us responsible for our own incredulity (Power 2002, 15). Philip Gourevitch recounts his lonely visit to Nyarubuye church, 13 months after over 20,000 were massacred there. Seeing decomposing bodies strewn throughout the church and grounds, still lying where they fell, Gourevitch's imagination resists encompassing what his intellect more readily comprehends. Gourevitch writes: "Yet looking at the buildings and the bodies and hearing the silence of the place, with the grand Italianate basilica standing there deserted, and beds of exquisite, death-fertilized flowers blooming over the corpses, it was strangely unimaginable. I mean one still has to

---

[21] This use of "moral imagination" should be neutral across ethical theories and is not bound to Burke's or Kirk's or others.

imagine it" (Gourevitch 1998, 19). In the very presence of horrific evidence, full comprehension requires imagination and yet the imagination resists. Imagining involves activating the relevant sensory portions of the brain; it requires seeing not just the line on the skull left by the machete blow, but somehow sensing, feeling, the blow. Even writing or reading this is hard enough. Really imagining the experience of the massacred is overwhelming. The well-protected imagination takes energy to unleash, and an attentiveness to do its work.

Atrocity's scale distorts comprehension for all involved. Considering the tendency of concentration camp survivors to doubt their own experiences, Arendt writes:

> This doubt of people concerning the reality of their own experience only reveals what the Nazis have always known: that men determined to commit crimes will find it expedient to organize them on the vastest, most improbable scale. Not only because this renders all punishments provided by the legal system inadequate and absurd; but because the very immensity of the crimes guarantees that the murderers who proclaim their innocence with all manner of lies will be more readily believed than the victims who tell the truth (Arendt 1973, 439).

Such denials are easier to believe because they maintain our sense of the limits of human possibility. They let us ignore the depths of human depravity. Truthful comprehension of atrocity requires imaginative involvement that no one wishes to endure. It is painful and dis-integrating to engage the imagination to fully grasp the enormity of such crimes.

An effective apology makes clear to both the apologizer and the recipient that the nature of the harm is fully understood, a daunting task in cases of grave wrongs. This is why apologies are often negotiated, offered in stages, and revised (Lazare 2004, 204–227; Digeser 1998, 707). In seeking apologetic sincerity from a perpetrator, we seek an engaged moral imagination, which may, in some cases, make forgiveness or reconciliation possible. Appropriate feelings are a sign of the impact of the moral imagination; clinical acknowledgement alone does not restore the human bond. Ultimately, this is where Clinton both succeeded and failed in 1998.

To overcome the recognition harm of spirit murder, to restore humanity where it has been viciously assaulted, the conventions of human life need to be invoked and restored. Normative abandonment can only be repaired through normative engagement. Speech acts like apology are a necessary component of such restorative actions. Overcoming recognition harm requires speech conveying recognition. Those who failed to heed the call of common humanity need to disclose their own humanity while recognizing the personhood of survivors. Those who stayed home should apologize, offering *both* acknowledgement and explanation, which in turn give meaning to their reparative gestures. Without offering an Account—without offering meaning, especially acknowledgement and explanation—we offer no balm to a spirit damaged by the onslaught of ethnic and racial politics. Without appropriate Responses, we fail to engage with aftermath of the inhumanity the Account discloses. Only speech acts, embedded in engaged restorative material acts, can rebuild the humanity so damaged by genocide. Only such speech acts mitigate recognition harms.

Acknowledgments A very early version of this paper was presented as "Apology, Promises, and the Politics of Reconciliation" at "Pathways to Reconciliation and Global Human Rights",

Sarajevo 2005, sponsored by the United Nations Development Program in BiH, and The Globalism Institute of RMIT, AUS. I am grateful to Claudia Card, Danielle Celermajer, Tom Ferguson, Robert Gakwaya, Alice MacLachlan, Mary Kate McGowan, Robert K. Shope, Arthur Ripstein, Ajume Wingo, Ed Herman, David Gibbs, and Janet Farrell Smith, for suggestions and criticisms.

References

Albright M (2003) Madam secretary. Hyperion, New York

Amnesty International (6 April 2004) Report: "Rwanda: 'Marked for Death', rape survivors living with HIV/AIDS in Rwanda" AI Index: AFR 47/007/2004

Arendt H (1973) The origins of totalitarianism. Harcourt, New York

Austin JL (1962) How to do things with words. In: Urmson JO, Sbisà M (eds) The William James lectures at Harvard University. Harvard University Press, Cambridge, MA

Austin JL (1970) Performative utterances. In: Urmson JO, Warnock GJ (eds) Philosophical papers. Clarendon, Oxford, pp 233–252

BBC (2000) Belgian Apology to Rwanda. Friday, 7 April 2000 at 18:27GMT, 19:27UK. http://news.bbc.co.uk/2/hi/africa/705402.stm

Brison S (2002) Aftermath: violence and the remaking of a self. Princeton University Press, Princeton

Card C (2003) Genocide and social death. Hypatia 18(1):63–79

Cassel D (2000) The Rwanda genocide: failing the test case. Northwestern Law Center for International Human Rights: World View Commentary 73, http://www.law.northwestern.edu/depts/clinic/ihr/display_details.cfm?ID=246&document_type=commentary

Celermajer D (2009) The sins of the nation and the ritual of apology. Cambridge University Press, Cambridge

Clinton WJ (1998) Remarks by the President to Genocide Survivors, Assistance Workers, and U.S. and Rwanda Government Officials, Kigali Airport, March 25, 1998. http://www.clintonfoundation.org/legacy/032598-speech-by-president-to-survivors-rwanda.htm

Dallaire R (2003) Shake hands with the devil: the failure of humanity in Rwanda. Carroll & Graf, New York

De Zuleuetta CF (2007) Mass violence and mental health: attachment and trauma. Int Rev Psychiat 19(3):221–233

Digeser P (1998) Political forgiveness: dirty hands and imperfect procedures. Polit Theory 26(5):700–724

Farmer P (2005) Global health equity and the future of public health, Speech, Wellesley College, 4 April, 2005. Available online: http://forum-network.org/lecture/global-health-equity-and-future-public-health

Frye M (1983) The politics of reality. The Crossing Press, Trumansburg

Gibney M, Roxstrom E (2001) The status of state apologies. Human Rights Quart 23(4):911–939

Gill K (2000) The moral functions of an apology. Philos Forum 31(1):11–27

Gourevitch P (1998) We wish to inform you that tomorrow we will be killed with our families. Picador (Farrar, Straus and Giroux), New York

Govier T, Verwoerd W (2002) The promise and pitfalls of apology. J Soc Philos 33(1):67–82

Great Lakes Policy Forum (2003) Meeting Report, March 20. www.sfcg.org/Documents/GLPF/GLPF032003.pdf – Aug 25, 2005

Hatzfeld J (2005) Machete season: the killers in Rwanda speak (trans. Coverdale L (2005)). Farrar, Straus and Giroux, New York. Initially published as Une saison de machetes, Éditions du Seuil, 2003

Hatzfeld J (2006) Life laid bare: the survivors in Rwanda speak (trans. Coverdale L (2006)).
    Farrar, Straus and Giroux, New York. Initially published as Dans Le Nu de La Vie, Éditions
    du Seuil, 2000
Honneth A (2007) Disrespect: the normative foundations of critical theory. Polity Press, Cambridge/
    Malden
Kritz NJ (1996) Coming to terms with atrocities: a review of accountability mechanisms for mass
    violations of human rights. Law Contemp Probl 59(4):127–152
Kukla R, Lance M (2009) 'Yo!' and 'Lo!': the pragmatic topography of the space of reasons.
    Harvard University Press, Cambridge, MA
Kuperman AJ (2001) The limits of humanitarian intervention in Rwanda. The Brookings Institution
    Press, Washington, DC
Lazare A (2004) On apology. Oxford University Press, New York
Lugones M (2003) Pilgrimages/Peregrinajes: theorizing coalition against multiple oppressions.
    Rowman and Littlefield, Lanham
Melvern L (2000) A people betrayed: the role of the west in Rwanda's genocide. Zed Books,
    New York
Melvern L (2004) Conspiracy to murder: the Rwandan genocide. Verso Books, New York
Minow M (1998) Between vengeance and forgiveness: facing history after genocide and mass
    violence. Beacon, Boston
Minow M (2000) The hope for healing: what can truth commissions do? In: Rotberg RI, Thompson
    D (eds) Truth v. Justice: the morality of the truth commissions. Princeton University Press,
    Princeton
Morris SJ (1999) Clinton's genocide confusion. In: Wall Street Journal, 12 Jan 1999:1
Morrow L (1998) Rwandan tragedy, Lewinsky Farce. Time 152(15):126
Morrow JH (1999) America's Choice: if Kosovo, why not Rwanda? Emerge 10(8):62–66
Munro G (2001) US 'Ignored' Rwanda genocide: documents reveal full extent of official knowledge.
    In: The Voice. London: 3 Sep 2001. 976:11
Neuffer E (2002) The key to my neighbor's house: seeking justice in Bosnia and Rwanda. Picador,
    New York
OAU (Organization for African Unity) (2000) Rwanda: the preventable genocide. In: OAU Doc.
    IPEP/Panel, 29 May 2000 at 12.33
Patterson O (1982) Slavery and social death. Harvard University Press, Cambridge
Pendergast J, Smock D (1999) Postgenocidal reconstruction: building peace in Rwanda and
    Burundi. United States Institute of Peace; Special Report 53. http://www.usip.org/pubs/special-
    reports/sr990915.html
Power S (2001) Bystanders to genocide. In: The Atlantic Monthly, September, pp 84–108. http://
    www.theatlantic.com/magazine/archive/2001/09/bystanders-to-genocide/4571/
Power S (2002) Genocide and America. New York Rev Books 49(4):15–18
Power S (2003) A problem from hell: America in the age of genocide. Harper, New York
Prunier G (1995a) The Rwanda crisis: history of a genocide. Columbia University Press, New York
Prunier G (1995–2005) Interviewed by Fergal Keane. http://www.pbs.org/wgbh/pages/frontline/
    shows/rwanda/etc/interview.html
Rotberg RI, Thompson D (eds) (2000) Truth v. Justice: the morality of the truth commissions.
    Princeton University Press, Princeton
Searle J (1969) Speech acts. Cambridge University Press, Cambridge
Sebarenzi J (2009) With Laurie Anne Mullane. God sleeps in Rwanda. Atria Books, New York
Shattuck J (2003) Freedom on fire: human rights wars and America's response. Harvard University
    Press, Cambridge, MA
Stolorow RD, Atwood G, Orange DM (2002) Worlds of experience. Basic Books, New York
Tavuchis N (1991) Mea culpa: a sociology of apology and reconciliation. Stanford University
    Press, Stanford
Taylor CC (1999) Sacrifice as terror: the Rwandan genocide of 1994. Berg Publishers, Oxford

Tirrell L (2009) Epistemic aspects of evil: the three monkeys meet the atrocity paradigm. In: Veltman A, Norlock K (eds) Evil, political violence and forgiveness: essays in honor of Claudia card. Lexington Books/Rowman & Littlefield, Lanham, pp 35–51

Tirrell L (2012) Genocidal language games. In: Maitra I, McGowan MK (eds) Speech and harm: controversies over free speech. Oxford University Press, Oxford, pp 174–221

UNICEF. http://www.unicef.org/infobycountry/23867_20292.html

USAID (2011) http://www.usaid.gov/locations/sub-saharan_africa/countries/rwanda/index.html, and http://www.usaid.gov/locations/sub-saharan_africa/countries/rwanda/rwanda_fs.pdf

USHR (2004) 93-231PDF: Rwanda's genocide: looking back: hearing before the Subcommittee on Africa of the committee on International Relations House of Representatives one hundred eighth congress second session April 22, 2004 Serial No. 108–96. http://commdocs.house.gov/committees/intlrel/hfa93231.000/hfa93231_0.htm

Walker MU (2006) Moral repair: reconstructing moral relations after wrongdoing. Cambridge University Press, Cambridge

Wallis A (2007) Silent accomplice: the untold story of France's role in the Rwandan genocide. I.B. Taurus & Co., London/New York

Williams PJ (1992) The alchemy of race and rights. Harvard University Press, Cambridge, MA

Chapter 11
Government Apologies to Indigenous Peoples

Alice MacLachlan

Abstract In this paper, I explore how theorists might navigate a course between the twin dangers of piety and excess cynicism when thinking critically about state apologies, by focusing on two government apologies to indigenous peoples: namely, those made by the Australian and Canadian Prime Ministers in 2008. Both apologies are notable for several reasons: they were both issued by heads of government, and spoken on record within the space of government: the national parliaments of both countries. Furthermore, in each case, the object of the apology – that which was apologized for – comes closer to disrupting the idea both countries have of themselves, and their image in the global political community, than any previous apologies made by either government. Perhaps as a result, both apologies were surrounded by celebration and controversy alike, and tracing their consequences – even in the short term – is a difficult business. We avoid excessive piety or cynicism, I argue, when we take several things into account. First, apologies have multiple functions: they narrate particular histories of wrongdoing, they express disavowal of that wrongdoing, and they commit to appropriate forms of repair or renewal. Second, the significance and the success of each function must be assessed contextually. Third, when turning to official political apologies, in particular, appropriate assessment of their capacity to disavow or to commit requires that consider apologies both as performance and as political action. While there remain significant questions regarding the practice of political apology – in particular, its relationship to practices of reparation, forgiveness and reconciliation – this approach can provide a framework with which to best consider them.

A. MacLachlan (✉)
York University, 4700 Keele Street, Toronto, ON M3J 1P3, Canada
e-mail: amacla@yorku.ca

A. MacLachlan and A. Speight (eds.), *Justice, Responsibility and Reconciliation in the Wake of Conflict*, Boston Studies in Philosophy, Religion and Public Life 1, DOI 10.1007/978-94-007-5201-6_11, © Springer Science+Business Media Dordrecht 2013

"Finally, we heard Canada say it is sorry."
– *Chief Phil Fontaine, Chief of the Assembly of First Nations, June 13, 2008*

11.1 Introduction

The year 2008 saw two historic government apologies offered to indigenous peoples, in surprisingly short succession.[1] On February 13, newly elected Australian Prime Minister Kevin Rudd gave an official apology on behalf of his government (Rudd 2008) and 4 months later, on June 8, so did Canadian Prime Minister Stephen Harper (Harper 2008). These apologies are notable for several reasons; they were both issued by heads of government, and both spoken on record within *the space of government*: namely, the national parliaments of both countries. Both apologies can be traced to years of indigenous campaigning and, lobbying – and, in the Canadian case, to a series of lawsuits – as well as government-initiated independent investigations launched a decade earlier, which strongly recommended apology as a measure of reparation to each country's indigenous peoples, and whose recommendations had been strongly resisted by the government of the time, in each case.[2]

The substance of these apologies is also notable. While both refer generally to a long history of displacement, appropriation, assimilation, and inequality, they also focus on two specific government policies; the Canadian apology is addressed to former students of Indian Residential Schools, and the Australian apology reflects "in particular on the mistreatment of those who were Stolen Generations" (Rudd 2008). The impact of both policies on indigenous individuals, communities, and tribal cultures cannot be overestimated. In the Canadian case, the policy was explicitly articulated as a way to "get rid of the Indian problem" by "killing the Indian in the child" (Harper 2008). Young children were separated from their families and placed in church-run schools, which denied them their language and cultural practices, as well as access to the warmth of family and community. Conditions in these schools were notoriously poor, and many suffered from physical and sexual abuse at the hands of their so-called "civilizers". Australia's Stolen Generations have a not dissimilar story; government policy was to forcibly remove primarily

---

[1] The Canadian apology was directed towards members of the tribes represented by the political body of the Assembly of First Nations, the Canadian Métis peoples and the Canadian Inuit people. The Australian apology identified the Aboriginal and Torres Strait Islander peoples by name. The naming of indigenous peoples is itself a contested issue, with a history of colonization, misunderstanding and racism behind it. In this paper, I will use "aboriginal" "indigenous" and "native" interchangeably to describe the first peoples of the territories of present-day Canada and Australia, while recognizing that none of these is unproblematic. In doing so, I acknowledge the damage of not naming tribes and communities individually.

[2] Royal Commission on Aboriginal Peoples; "Bringing them Home". Both are available online: http://www.ainc-inac.gc.ca/ap/pubs/rpt/rpt-eng.asp#chp6; http://www.humanrights.gov.au/Social_Justice/bth_report/report/index.html

"half-caste" Aboriginal children from Aboriginal families, and place them in orphanages, group homes, or with white families. The rationale offered was that the plight of Aboriginal peoples was hopeless – they were a dying race – but that half-caste Aboriginals could be saved and, indeed, "whitened". As in the Canadian case, there is significant evidence that a culture of physical and sexual abuse permeated the institutions in which they were placed.

The policies and attitudes that led to the Residential Schools and the Stolen Generations were undoubtedly racist and colonial. They were also genocidal, as defined in the UN Convention on the Prevention and Punishment of Genocide in 1948, which lists "forcibly transferring children of the group to another group" as an act of genocide in Article 2. This convention was signed and ratified by both countries before either saw fit to cease their domestic policies of indigenous displacement, undermining any potential claim of ignorance regarding the wrongness of these policies. Indeed, the government of Canada did not begin to close a significant number of schools until the 1980s, and the last residential school in Canada closed as recently as 1996.[3] Moreover, the collective and multigenerational traumatic impact of the seizure of children from close-knit communities cannot be overestimated. Both cases reflect Claudia Card's insight into genocide, when she notes how it includes "the harm inflicted on its victims' social vitality… its survivors lose their cultural heritage, and may even lose their intergenerational connections" (Card 2007, 11, 20). The harm inflicted in these cases is not a discrete past harm; it is an ongoing one, played out in indigenous communities and families today, as the survivors of schools become parents and grandparents to children of their own. Native scholar Andrea Smith also argues forcibly for recognizing the role that widespread tolerance of sexual violence toward indigenous peoples (including children) played in genocidal policies in North America (Smith 2005, 35–54). Although, in most cases, residential schools were run by Canadian churches and not by the Canadian state, the decision to enact these policies cannot be neatly separated from the conditions they created.

In addressing these policies and acknowledging the attitudes that produced them as endemic to and representative of the history of both "settler societies", the Canadian and Australian apologies challenge the founding myths of both states. That which is apologized for, in both cases, comes closer to disrupting the *idea* both countries have of themselves – and their image in the global political community – than any previous apologies made by either government. Perhaps as a result, both apologies were surrounded by celebration and controversy alike, and tracing even their short-term consequences is a difficult business.

Both are excellent examples of the burgeoning global phenomenon of the official political apology: that is, an apology offered by political representatives or heads of state, *on behalf of a political body or state*, for wrongs committed in the recent or

---

[3] Information about the history of the residential schools is available on the Assembly of First Nations website http://www.afn.ca/residentialschools/history.html (last accessed March 24, 2010).

the distant past. What then can we learn about the phenomenon of political apologies, and how to think about and theorize them, from these two examples?

I see two dangers lurking for theorists who try to take up this question. The first is the danger of *piety* – that is, of being caught up in the solemnity of such ceremonial occasions, and the weight of history that they seem to carry. In the face of powerful phrases like "reconciliation" and "a new chapter", daring to critically analyze apologies can feel a little like talking in church.[4] On the other side sits the danger of too-easy cynicism. Such cynicism dismisses all political apologies as cheap, gestural politics awash in self-interest and crocodile tears, which enable politicians to win public acclaim and diffuse angry minority groups, without committing any actual resources to problems of injustice and exclusion (Cunningham 2004). These dangers are magnified by a certain degree of confusion regarding the nature and purpose of official political apologies: that is, what exactly qualifies as such, what role they are meant to play or what purpose they accomplish, and what criteria or standards exist for distinguishing between better or worse instances. Given the kinds of serious and longstanding wrongs for which states and governments are called upon to apologize, these questions can seem almost unanswerable. It is hard to imagine what could possibly qualify as a *good* or a satisfying apology.

In this paper, I explore how theorists might navigate a course between piety and cynicism in thinking critically about apologies, by focusing on these two government apologies to indigenous peoples. Such a course can be found, I argue, when we take several things into account. First, apologies have multiple functions: they narrate particular histories of wrongdoing, they express disavowal of that wrongdoing, and they commit to appropriate forms of repair or renewal. Second, the significance and the success of each function must be assessed contextually. Third, when turning to official political apologies, in particular, appropriate assessment of their capacity to disavow or to commit requires that consider apologies both as performance and as political action. While there remain significant questions regarding the practice of political apology – in particular, its relationship to practices of reparation, forgiveness, and reconciliation – this approach can provide a framework with which to best consider them.

11.2   What Is an Apology? What Does It Do?

As apologies have become increasingly accepted in the public realm, taxonomies of apology have become increasingly complex. Theorists distinguish between collective and individual apologies (Tavuchis 1990, 48) and between contemporaneous

---

[4] Consider for example, the usually acerbic and critical Canadian columnist Rex Murphy, famous for his vigorous and spirited attacks on Canadian politicians. Murphy wrote of the Canadian apology: "the day of apology called from our sometimes all too predictable politicians a better version of themselves, gave them words and substance that may bring a hopeful new energy into play. For once, then, yes, they have the benefit of every doubt." (Murphy 2008).

and retrospective apologies (Weyeneth 2001, 20). They also take note of the *kind* of authority the apologizer is taken to have, whether representative, ceremonial, corporate or celebrity, (Nobles 2008, 4) and of the identity of the individual or group demanding an apology in the first place, whether these are primary victims, their political representatives, or indeed their descendants (Thompson 1992). The focus of these taxonomies is revealing: the status, import and even the function of a particular apology may vary along with the role or authority of the apologizer, the content of what is being apologized for, and the identity of the intended addressee. As these vary, so too does the meaning of the apology.

But this does not yet tell us what an apology is, in general – if indeed a singular meaning can be taken from the wealth of examples available. So, for example, an apology is something we *say* or *utter*, in speech or writing, but it is also something we *offer* and that we offer to *someone* in particular; this is part of what distinguishes apology from confession. Furthermore apologies – and certainly political apologies – are usually *performed* on a certain occasion, in a certain context. All of these factors contribute to whether or not we succeed in apologizing: the words we use, the timing and circumstances in which we say them, the person we offer them to, and what we are taken to be giving or offering that person in speaking at all. How ought we to go about theorizing apologies, so that we remain attentive to all these elements?

For the most part, theorists have followed J.L. Austin in thinking of apologies as speech acts, that is, social actions "that can only be done with words and, by corollary, if [they] not done in the words, [they have] not been done" (Bavelas 2004, 1). Nicolas Tavuchis refers to their "secular verbal magic" (Tavuchis 1990). But it is not clear that apologies *are* always done in words – and certainly, not the same words each time. In some close intimate relationships, much can be communicated with a single glance or gesture. Even in formal relationships, it seems, "apologies can be communicated in a wide range of ways, through verbal statements issued publicly, joint declarations, legislative resolutions, documents and reports, legal judgments, pardon ceremonies, apology rituals, days of observance, reconciliation walks, monuments and memorials, even names bestowed on the landscape" (Weyeneth 2001, 20). But perhaps these other avenues are substitutes for words, or come to perform the function of words. If so, then apologies ultimately reduce to the communication of key propositions: "I'm sorry," "I apologize," "I was wrong" or "I hurt you," "I won't do it again".

To reduce apologies to their propositional content, even with the understanding that such content must be communicated, is to miss the extent to which apologies may be ritualistic and ceremonial, and to ignore how these non-verbal performative elements contribute to the meaning and success of the apology itself. Some theorists of apology have begun to recognize this fact. Sanderijn Cels argues that we should focus less on apologies as speech and more on apologies as performances, drawing on the resources of dramaturgical theory to interpret their ceremonial significance.[5] Nick Smith also includes performance among the elements of what he calls a

---

[5] This point is taken from personal correspondence with Cels. For more information on her work in progress on this topic, see http://cbuilding.org/about/bio/sanderijn-cels (last accessed March 23, 2010).

"categorical apology," to his mind, the regulative ideal guiding our various practices of apologizing (Smith 2008, 74). Finally, Mark Gibney and Erik Roxtrom argue for two non-vocal performative elements, publicity and ceremony, as crucial criteria for an authentic public apology (Gibney and Roxstrom 2001). There is more to the import of apologies than what gets literally communicated; this is particularly true for the examples I consider, because of their status as *official* apologies.

11.3   The Functions of an Apology

In understanding apologies as speech, Austin assigns apologies to the class of behabitives: performatives concerned with attitudes and feelings (Austin 1975, 83).

But it is far from clear that feelings and attitudes *are* the primary things with which apologies concern themselves. Indeed, even when we consider apologies purely as speech acts – and not more broadly, as symbolic performances or dimensions of repair – I would argue that emotions play only a secondary role in apologizing. They are not the main purpose of apologies, though they do, in many instances, play a role in conveying or guaranteeing the success of that purpose. In fact, both political and personal apologies potentially aim to accomplish five things, not all of which are necessarily a matter of emotion. Put differently, apologies have *narrative* functions (identifying the wrong, the wrongdoer and the victim) as well as expressing and performing the apologizer's *disavowal* of her past acts and her *commitment* to some form of repair; they are thus simultaneously backwards and forwards looking. Indeed, we can look to our examples to see how in apologizing, apologizer aims to accomplish most or all of the following five tasks:

1. She identifies an act, or series of acts that took place, and characterizes them as wrong, bad, harmful, injurious. That is, she locates the wrongdoing as such (this is not insignificant, especially in highly contested histories of events).

This can be seen in both the Australian and the Canadian apologies: in the Australian case, Rudd names the wrongfulness of past policies in the official motion, naming the "mistreatment of those who were Stolen Generations," "the removal… of children," and "the breaking up of families and communities." In the longer speech that follows the motion, he goes into detail: first describing one individual history of a woman in the audience, Nanna Nungala Fejo, then offering specific statistics, percentages, and dates, naming the *Bringing Them Home* report as an authoritative source for the stories and statistics, and also quoting some of the more reprehensible articulations of the policy at various points, as evidence for its racism (Rudd 2008). The Canadian apology is shorter, but it also provides numbers, dates and other details in the very first two paragraphs, as well as the most infamous articulation of that policy, namely "to kill the Indian in the child." It also details the conditions of the schools themselves, as well as the abuse suffered, and mentions ongoing detrimental effects: "The legacy of Indian

Residential Schools has contributed to social problems that continue to exist in many communities today" (Harper 2008).[6]

2. She takes on responsibility for these events and, in doing so, accepts (or takes on, in a representative capacity) the role of the wronging party, that is, the wrongdoer.

In the case of official apologies, this is often the most controversial element, as political responsibility is closely linked both to material liability and, on occasion, to domestic or international criminal responsibility. In the Australian apology, this function emerges in two ways in the text of the official motion: first and directly, "We apologise for the laws and policies of successive Parliaments and governments that have inflicted profound grief, suffering and loss on these our fellow Australians." – and then, in the repetitive litany of "for...we say sorry," listing each harm inflicted. Rudd also forestalls any deflection of blame for past wrongs, by noting "this was happening as late as the early 1970s. The 1970s is not exactly a point in remote antiquity."[7] The most blunt statement of responsibility is the following: "The uncomfortable truth for us all is that the parliaments of the nation, individually and collectively, enacted statutes and delegated authority under those statutes that made the forced removal of children on racial grounds fully lawful" (Rudd 2008).

In this aspect, the Canadian apology is both less detailed and more equivocal. At first, Harper states: "In the 1870s, the federal government, partly in order to meet its obligation to educate Aboriginal children, began to play a role in the development and administration of these schools." Two phrases lessen the extent to which responsibility is taken: the reference to meeting an obligation (which sounds like an excusing or a justifying condition) and the idea of "playing a role." While it is true that the schools were administered by the churches and overseen by the government, this has the effect of seeming to "split hairs" regarding responsibility for the policies. Luckily, the statement continues with a more accurate assertion of responsibility: "The Government of Canada built an education system in which very young children were often forcibly removed from their homes." Furthermore, it is not only

---

[6] Note also how, as a potential *aim* of apology, this narrative function is also a point of criticism: in apologizing for specific policies, both governments succeed in avoiding the broader question of apologizing for a much longer history of genocidal appropriation and displacement.

[7] There is political and philosophical significance to this remark. One standard objection to official apologies concerns the difficulty of shouldering responsibility for distant injustices – and indeed, of applying contemporary moral standards to past eras. In his response to Rudd's motion, Australian Liberal Leader Brendan Nelson emphasized, "our generation does not own these actions, nor should it feel guilt for what was done in many, but not all cases, with the best of intentions" (Nelson 2008). Indeed, former PM John Howard refused to apologize for precisely these reasons: he argued that because the policies leading to the Stolen Generations did not violate domestic or international laws of their time, and did not constitute gross human rights violations, they should not be judged by contemporary standards (Nobles 2008, 96). To do so would be to inflict a kind of chronological colonialism of our own, he claimed, via the unfair imposition of alien moral standards. Rudd's history reminds his audience that the era of the Stolen Generations is *not* alien. Australia's signature on the UN Convention also undermines Howard's position.

the policies that must be acknowledged as wrongful, but the worldview that motivated them: since, "these objectives were based on the assumption Aboriginal cultures and spiritual beliefs were inferior and unequal" (Harper 2008).

3. She acknowledges what she takes to be the effect of her acts on the addressee or recipient of her apology; that is, she locates the addressee as the wronged party or victim.

It might seem that the effects of the forcible removal of children, the separation of families and communities, and the systematic devaluing and destruction of a culture are obvious, and not in need of emphasis. But this is far from true: indeed, official apologies can play a crucial role in ceasing (or curbing) formal and informal practices of victim-blaming. In these examples, the present states of indigenous communities, still reeling from collective trauma, are taken out of their causal and historical contexts – not to mention ongoing systemic injustice. In the case of the Canadian apology, for example, the experience was very nearly marred by the radio comments of a parliamentary secretary in Harper's government, Pierre Poilievre, MP for Nepean-Carleton, who suggested just hours beforehand that the apology and subsequent reparations were wasted money, and that Canadians would do better to "engender the values of hard work and independence and self-reliance" in indigenous communities.[8] The 1996 Royal Commission on Aboriginal Peoples had emphasized, in its recommendations, how "*acknowledging* responsibility assists in the healing process because it creates room for dialogue" (Govier and Prager 2003, 68). Rudd's speech describes these effects quite viscerally, in discussing the stories captured in the *Bringing Them Home* report:

> "The pain is searing; it screams from the pages. The hurt, the humiliation, the degradation and the sheer brutality of the act of physically separating a mother from her children is a deep assault on our senses and on our most elemental humanity" (Rudd 2008).

Harper is more circumspect, and – again – not without equivocation:

> "The government now recognizes that the consequences of the Indian Residential Schools policy were profoundly negative and that this policy has had a lasting and damaging impact on Aboriginal culture, heritage and language. *While some former students have spoken positively about their experiences at residential schools*, these stories are far overshadowed by tragic accounts of the emotional, physical and sexual abuse and neglect of helpless children, and their separation from powerless families and communities" (Harper 2008, italics added).

There is a very real sense in which this nested minority report misses the point: the wrongness of the residential schools policy cannot be measured in terms of individual student satisfaction. Even if a majority of students had spoken positively, it remains true that the policy would still have been wrong. In qualifying his description of the effects of the schools, Harper undermines the act of recognition mentioned above, namely, that the residential schools were wrong in *objective* as well as in

---

[8] Mr Poilievre subsequently apologized for his remarks in the House of Commons. See http://www.cbc.ca/canada/story/2008/06/12/poilievre-aboriginals.html (accessed March 25, 2010).

practice. Furthermore, in alluding to a wide range of experiences at the schools, he also subtly displaces top-down responsibility, hinting that the bad experiences of some – or most – might well be attributed to particularly abusive "bad apples" in the schools themselves, and not a bad system. Finally, while there may be some appropriate time to celebrate the experiences of happier survivors, an official apology is simply not that moment. Of course, the Canadian apology does acknowledge suffering survivors, as the appropriate recipients of acknowledgment, in a slightly different manner:

> "It has taken extraordinary courage for the thousands of survivors that have come forward to speak publicly about the abuse they suffered. It is a testament to their resilience as individuals and to the strength of their cultures."[9]

This acknowledgement is especially significant since it notes how the burden of a culture of silence was also inflicted on survivors; it was left to them to come forward, to initiate justice, to demand what was rightly theirs. Harper goes on to say, "the burden of this experience has been on your shoulders for far too long. The burden is properly ours as a Government and as a country." In other words, the *absence* of an apology and gestures of reparation – up until this point – is itself an ongoing source of grievance and pain.

4. She disavows her acts as wrongful. This may include expressions of remorse, agent-regret, guilt or shame. It may involve the identification of individual wrongs, and explanations of *why* they are wrong (thus demonstrating an appropriate attitude to these wrongs in particular, and wrong acts or policies in general).

Disavowal and repentance are a complicated business. To fully take responsibility for the act, the agent must identify herself with the wrongdoings in some way; that is, she must own them. And yet – to disavow these acts – she must distance herself from them. At least in our interpersonal relationships with others, we achieve disavowal and distance from past actions in part through our attitudes towards them. We experience and express remorse, guilt, and shame, and others test and measure our disavowal by the sincerity of these expressions.

Of course, attitudes can be misleading, as Alice learns in hearing the story of the Walrus and the Carpenter (who lured and ate a number of oysters) from Tweedledum and Tweedledee, in Lewis Carroll's *Through the Looking Glass:*

> "I like the Walrus best," said Alice, "because you see he was a *little* sorry for the poor oysters."
>
> "He ate more than the Carpenter, though," said Tweedledee. "You see he held his handkerchief in front, so that the Carpenter couldn't count how many he took: contrariwise."
>
> "That was mean!" Alice said indignantly. "Then I like the Carpenter best—if he didn't eat so many as the Walrus."
>
> "But he ate as many as he could get," said Tweedledum.

---

[9] This resembles a feature that, in his discussion of apologies, Louis Kort describes as a "gesture of respect" – additional words acknowledging the victim's perspective, or some further indication of respect that counteracts the initial disrespect conveyed by the wrong itself (Kort 1975).

This was a puzzler. After a pause, Alice began, "Well! They were *both* very unpleasant characters—" (Carroll 1960, 237).[10]

Clearly, the wrongdoer's actual behavior also plays a crucial role in disavowal. But in interpersonal contexts, at least, feelings and attitudes cannot be discounted; most victims would regard with suspicion and hostility a perfectly well behaved and reformed wrongdoer who nonetheless experienced no regret.

Feelings and attitudes cannot play the same role in official apologies as they do in interpersonal apologies, though this does not mean public figures have been unwilling to exploit them. Apology politics have emerged, in part, alongside a new "self-reflexive" approach to political leadership, exemplified by charismatic figures like Presidents Bill Clinton and Barack Obama, or Prime Minister Tony Blair. Leaders are more willing to bare their souls, and their emotions: on camera, on talk shows, or on paper. Nevertheless, the irony of this supposedly personal style of politics is apparent in an exhibit by Canadian artist Cathy Busby (2009), titled *Sorry*. The exhibit consists of extremely large photographic prints of politician's mouths, captured whilst "baring their souls" in apology (in these cases, usually for their own, individual, misdeeds). In these photographs, the intimacy of the personal – here, represented visually by the close-up on a face – is hyper-accelerated by a camera that has zoomed in too far. Visual intimacy *in extremis* actually robs the speaker of recognizable identity, and thus of personhood: a mouth is just a mouth after all. Lined next to one another on display, the apologizers are uniform, faceless, and anonymous. Busby's images are far more impersonal than photographs taken at a distance, such as traditional formal photos of government officials engaged in formal treaty negotiation, and the "souls" that are supposedly bared are revealed so intimately that they become utterly soul-less. The text of each apology is printed only in excerpts: the artist's comment on style over substance in the modern practice of political apology.[11]

---

[10] In the edition of *The Looking Glass* annotated by logician Martin Gardner, Gardner somewhat officiously informs the reader in a footnote that in fact, Alice is puzzled because she faces the familiar dilemma of judging someone by their acts or their intentions. This footnote has always bothered me. Both the Walrus and Carpenter had fairly devious intentions and abhorrent actions (at least from an oyster-sympathizer's perspective). Instead, Alice seems unsure about the end of the story: that is, their reactions in the *aftermath* of the crime – especially given Tweedledee and Tweedledums' narrative additions and adjustments. What lies in question is not the intention or action of the wrongdoers, but their stance following the wrongdoing – and, more broadly, what we do or do not want to see in a story of wrongdoing.

[11] Busby references both individual and official apologies, by both political and other public figures, and almost all her examples are for contemporaneous not retrospective apologies. www.cathy-busby.ca/sorry/ (accessed March 17, 2009). Interestingly, Busby has chosen to represent the two apologies I focus on today very differently: in her latest exhibits, *Righting the Wrongs* and *We are Sorry*, Busby has imposed the texts of the apologies by the Canadian and Australian Prime Ministers along the front or side of public buildings. The effect is very different from that of *Sorry*: the words of contrition literally cover the public face of a public building, suggesting that, in these cases, perhaps substance has trumped style [reproductions of *Righting the Wrongs* and *We are Sorry* received from private correspondence with the artist].

The sense that personal emotions have no place is compounded when the public apology is official. The acknowledgment, disavowal, and commitment necessary for a successful political apology cannot depend merely on the sentiments and feelings of the individual(s) who will utter it. Whether or not the Canadian government faces its responsibility for a legacy of residential schools will not depend on PM Stephen Harper's inner life. The appearance of the wrong emotional tone can certainly cause a political apology to misfire, but it is not clear that the right tone can guarantee its success.

In the absence of interpersonal feelings and attitudes, what appropriate moral motivation is there to drive political apologies? The cynical answer is, of course, that they lose meaning *qua* apologies altogether: because they are public, formal and pre-negotiated, they are empty gestures. This cynicism is not limited to academics and media commentators. Consider the following somewhat representative response to the Canadian government's apology, taken from an online news forum:

> "I can't believe it! Some of you are complaining that the apology didn't have enough "emotion." What the heck did you want the [Prime Minister] to do... get all misty eyed and start crying/talking as he gave his speech...Many of these comments are made from people who can't see the reality of the [public relations] value of this apology. The apology garners [sic] PC party support during the next election. Also the [sic] PC party made the apology because it was the politically correct thing to do... THAT'S IT."[12]

Should we endorse this commentator's assessment of the Canadian apology? Certainly, it is true that the motivations of political actors may be more complex than those of private individuals: politicians are elected to serve the interests of their constituents, after all, and not always for some wider moral purpose. Furthermore, their own interests are very much bound up in continuing to serve that purpose, through re-election. Official apologies are the result of complex negotiations and calculations. For this reason, we do better if we do not model political apologies too closely on the personal and emotional qualities of apologies made by individuals (Thompson 2008, 36), but look to other measurements of disavowal, based on their nature as *official* acts.

In some sense, even uttering the word "apology" is a kind of disavowal. Governments, unlike the Catholic Pope, do not claim infallibility – but neither are they known for rushing to admit mistakes. Harper says "apology" twice in his speech, "apologize" four times, and "sorry" once. Rudd, in his longer speech, says "apology" 14 times, "apologize" five times, and "sorry" nine times. Unlike the Canadian government's previous 1998 "Statement of Reconciliation" or the previous Australian government's policy of "practical reconciliation," both aim at the idea of apologizing, explicitly.[13] While this effect may fade as the "age of apology" continues, it is still

---

[12] The comment wrongly identifies the governing party of Stephen Harper as the (now defunct) Progressive Conservative party, rather than the present-day Conservative Party of Canada. Posted by commonsenseman, 2008/06/12 at 1.12 PM ET, http://www.cbc.ca/canada/story/2008/06/11/pm-statement.html#articlecomments (accessed March 12, 2009).

[13] The previous Australian Prime Minister, John Howard, consistently refused to issue an apology for the "Stolen Generations," and instead advocated pursuing a policy of "Practical Reconciliation": a vision of formal equality with no distinctions in citizenship, with involved no land claims, no self-governance and few special rights for Aboriginal Australians, and which took no responsibility for the policies of past governments.

the case that government apologies possess sufficient novelty for this act, in itself, to indicate an important change of stance and policy.

Furthermore, the authoritative articulation of right values can itself function as disavowal of widespread wrong values (Harvey 1995). In describing Australian Aboriginals as "a proud people… and a proud culture," Rudd refuses to endorse stereotypes to the contrary. In identifying "reconciliation" as the expression of a "core value of our nation – … the value of a fair go for all," and noting that a "fair go" was not had by the Aboriginals, Rudd – in his leadership capacity – puts the lie to any story to the contrary. Rudd describes collective encounter with "the cold, confronting, uncomfortable truth" of Australia's history as the "wrestling with our own soul" and insists that as far as reconciliation and justice are concerned, "old approaches are not working." Thomas Brudholm writes, "a kind of reconciliation between peoples can build on a common refusal of reconciliation with the past" (Brudholm 2008, 116). Rudd's speech returns, again and again, to the idea that the past has *not* passed, in many significant senses; rather, it remains something to be "wrestled with" and repaired. In refusing either to reconcile with or to simply accept the past, his words do much to disavow it.

Harper's apology relies partly on the image of a journey to express his disavowal: "You have been working on recovering from this experience for a long time and in a very real sense, we are now joining you on this journey." There is an appropriate humility in this expression. The metaphor is not unproblematic, however; Harper says, four times, "the Government of Canada now recognizes that it was wrong" or "we now recognize that it was wrong," implying that Canadian failures were ones of (possibly culpable) moral ignorance and not knowing wrongdoing. Yet the "Royal Commission on Aboriginal Peoples" (1996) documents *available* testimony and evidence dating back to the early days of both policies, indicating the generally poor conditions at state-run schools and orphanages. In a 1907 report, for example, the Canadian Indian Affairs' chief medical officer admitted, "50% of the children who passed through these schools did not live to benefit from the education which they have received therein" (Rolfsen 2008, 30). In other words, disavowal must be balanced with responsibility to avoid appearing disingenuous.

The final element of an apology is the most forward-looking. Not coincidentally, it is also the element that resists analysis in terms of speech. For commitment in particular, it seems, contra Bavelas, apologies *cannot* be done *only with words* at all (Bavelas 2004). The fifth function of an apology is as follows:

5. She commits herself to a future in which apologies are *not* necessary; that is, she commits herself to further appropriate acts and attitudes on her part ("I won't do it again"). If appropriate, she may also indicate a willingness to change things for the wronged party, either through amends and compensation, further gestures of respect, or perhaps the initiation of a more appropriate moral relationship.

Both Rudd and Harper make commitments to a different future between indigenous and non-indigenous citizens, in their official apologies. Rudd speaks of a new "partnership" aimed at the very practical goals of closing the gap in life expectancy, literacy, numeracy, employment outcomes, and opportunities – and sets some concrete goals for childhood health and education. He also proposes that the commission established to achieve this might consider "the further task of constitutional recognition of the first Australians," suggesting a commitment to both symbolic and material change. Harper's commitments on behalf of his government are perhaps less voluntary, since they originate in the settlement agreement from a lawsuit (Indian Residential Schools Settlement Agreement 2011), but he also refers to the implementation of this agreement as a new "partnership." Indeed, the agreement included individual compensation packages, support for a general "healing fund" and other forms of commemoration, as well as a $60 million Truth and Reconciliation Commission, dedicated to uncovering the history of Indian Residential Schools, and making these stories known to non-Indigenous Canadians.[14] The commitments listed are not only practical; in naming aspects of the new partnership, Harper gestures towards "a relationship based on the knowledge of our shared history, a respect for each other, and a desire to move forward together with a renewed understanding that strong families, strong communities and vibrant cultures and traditions will contribute to a stronger Canada for all of us" (Harper 2008).

11.4 Assessing Apologies

As I mentioned above, my purpose in itemizing these five features has been to demonstrate a given apology may have multiple purposes. First, there are *narrative* purposes: apologies identify the wrongdoing as such, the apologizer as responsible for it, and the victim or addressee as wrongfully harmed by it. Second, apologies communicate and even demonstrate *disavowal*; in apologizing, the wrongdoer distances herself from her acts even as she takes responsibility for them: repudiating the attitudes, motivations, and circumstances that led her to perform them. Finally, apologies represent a form of *commitment*, both to the apologizer's ongoing disavowal and her good-faith efforts to repair the wrongs as she is able and as is appropriate. Feelings and attitudes only appear as the vehicles for these primary functions. Remorse and guilt can communicate a sense of wrongdoing and acknowledgment of its effects; such attitudes also motivate our desire to disavow past wrongs, and our intentions to be and behave otherwise, and to repair past wrongs.

Not every element I have described is fore-grounded and explicit in every apologetic utterance – in our everyday lives, there is much we can take for granted or communicate non-verbally. But an utterance that failed even to imply any of these five things, or implied their opposite, would not be recognizable as an apology; collectively, they shape the boundaries of our recognizable practices of apology, even if instances of apology within those boundaries share only a family resemblance to one another.

---

[14] In terms of individual compensation, the settlement specifies $10,000 for each student who attended a Residential School, with $3000 for each subsequent year of school. Individual settlements with survivors of sexual and physical abuse will be negotiated beyond these lump sums. To my mind, the Truth and Reconciliation Commission is one of the most exciting aspects of the settlement agreement and subsequent apology.

These features help us to distinguish apologies from close cousins like confessions, which need not identify the addressee as a victim, expressions of sympathy ("I'm sorry you feel that way"), which do not necessarily identify the speaker as the wrongdoer or the act as wrong, or even rueful or unrepentant admissions of fault ("I guess that's just the way I am"), which fail to perform the distancing function of disavowal.

Indeed, we can see just how each of these elements functions in locating practices of apology, if we consider a speech widely recognized to be a *failure* of apology: namely, the 1998 Canadian "Statement of Reconciliation."[15] Unlike the two 2008 examples, Stewart never utters the words "apology" or "apologize" and her single use of "sorry" is questionable. She does identify the wrongful harms of the past and their effects on indigenous culture and peoples, but both the second and fourth elements, i.e. taking responsibility as wrongdoer and disavowing past acts, are absent. Stewart (1998) says that Canada must "recognize" and "acknowledge" the effects of its history, and she formally expresses "regret" at the actions of past governments, but that regret is never transformed into the admittedly stronger terms of "responsibility," "remorse," or even "guilt." The statement rather puzzlingly tells survivors of residential schools that "we wish to emphasize that what you experienced was not your fault and should never have happened," a remark which – in this context – is almost patronizing, since it does not go on to take on that same fault (responsibility). While the statement does say, "to those of you who suffered this tragedy at residential schools, we are deeply sorry," the word "sorry" in this context is highly ambivalent and, it appears, intentionally so; it could express remorse, but equally, it could be merely sympathetic. Similarly, the use of "reconciliation" without responsibility has the effect of suggesting a purely forward-looking approach, or hints that past relationships have faltered because of mutual misunderstanding and not because of an asymmetrical relationship of injustice or oppression. It is hardly surprising that in Chief Fontaine's response to the 2008 apology, 10 years later, he emphasized, "finally, we heard Canada say it is sorry" (Fontaine 2008).

Of the elements of an apology, the fifth and final – commitment – is perhaps the most contentious. There are certainly interpersonal apologies that fail to communicate this element, or fail to communicate it sincerely, while still being recognizable as apologies. In the case of chronic re-offenders, who know they cannot in good conscience promise to be different, but nonetheless acknowledge and disavow their behavior – no doubt experiencing a high degree of self-loathing and alienation as a result – we may recognize the helpless "I wish I could say I won't do it again, but I can't" as a *kind* of apology, albeit one marred by self-conflict and moral dissonance. What is interesting in these cases is that the apologizer appears to be apologizing for who she is, and no longer what she has done.[16] Indeed, this may explain why official apologies, unlike interpersonal apologies, are held to

---

[15] For a discussion of "non-apologies" and "quasi-apologies" in the Canadian context, see the contribution by Matt James in Gibney et al. (2007).

[16] For an interesting and related discussion, see Bell (2008).

stricter standards of commitment; we have little sympathy for a chronically re-offending state, and would have trouble understanding what it meant that such a state simply *could* not subject itself to appropriate reforms and reparation.

Thus, I would suggest that when we approach the assessment of apologies (in any context), it is important first to take into account what Austin's categorization overlooks: namely, their narrative and their commissive functions. Apologies have a historical or recording function; they tell a *particular kind of story* about the events apologized for, and the participants' role in them. They also have a future-oriented commissive function; in apologizing, I often implicitly or explicitly attempt to persuade you that I am not likely to do this again – indeed, that I am not the kind of person to do this again. In political and in personal contexts of contested histories and the ongoing need for mutually acceptable coexistence, these may come to play a primary role in the success and assessment of the apology itself.

Furthermore, the fact that apologies have multiple functions is significant for their assessment. It is not clear that each element of the apology, or its purpose, will be equally important in all cases. So, for example, where there is significant dispute over what actually took place or when the apology follows a long period of time in which the wrongs were covered over or denied, the most important aspect of the apology for all concerned may be its narrative functions: getting clear on who did what, to whom, and when. In other instances, when these details are not in dispute, the roles of disavowal or commitment may come to the fore.

The measurement of each potential function will be highly particularistic; what counts as an appropriate narrative, or a satisfying expression of disavowal, or even a sufficient commitment for the future, will depend on the nature and extent of the wrong, the pre-existing relationship between apologizer and recipient, and other features of the context, including broader social norms surrounding social status, the taking of responsibility, rituals of apology, and acceptable moral relationships. The upshot of these two features – the multiple functions of apologies and the contextual way in which these functions apply – is that there is no overarching singular standard, that is, no "ideal," "paradigmatic" or "categorical" apology against which all individual apologies ought to be measured.[17] Our practices of apologizing are simply too varied, and the norms they obey too tied to contextual features, for such an ideal to function fairly and universally.

11.5 Assessing Official Apologies: Some Complications

Are there aspects of official apologies, beyond their multiple and contextual functions – a feature they share with interpersonal apologies, after all – that prevent us from easily assessing them? Why is it harder to pick out appropriate measures of narration, disavowal, and commitment in political contexts? Certainly, government apologies,

---

[17] Here I part ways from two recent influential treatments of the topic: Charles Griswold's (2007) treatment of apologies and Nick Smith's concept of the categorical apology as normative ideal (Smith 2008).

like individual apologies, can recount appropriate narratives of wrong, responsibility, and harm. Both the Australian and the Canadian example employed narrative imagery in their opening phrases: Harper described the Residential Schools as a "sad chapter" and Rudd a "dark chapter." Rudd also resolved, "that this new page in the history of our great continent can now be written." Few Canadians had previously challenged so-called "common wisdom" (i.e. gross stereotypes and misunderstandings) about poverty, laziness, and substance addiction in Native communities – or connected it to the fact that a generation of sexual-abuse survivors, isolated from all their cultural and community resources as children, is now raising a second generation of children themselves (Rolfsen 2008, 31). Chief Fontaine noted that following the apology, 73% of Canadians surveyed were aware of the apology, and of those, 83% supported it (Fontaine 2008b).[18] The apologies, in naming the wrongs done to generations of indigenous children, succeed in re-counting their history.[19] Indeed, testimonial responses to the Australian apology emphasized this acknowledgment.[20]

More contentious are the latter two functions: it is not clear what plays the analogous role in political life that feelings and attitudes do in personal relationships. What appropriately demonstrates the disavowal and commitment of a government, rather than of a single individual? What would give us reason to trust or to doubt the motivations behind expressions of disavowal and commitment made by Rudd and Harper? Plausible candidates include the success of the material compensation and commitments offered, the effect of changes to the historical record, the affective responses of addressees and witnesses, or perhaps whatever renegotiated political relationships emerges from those initial responses.

Material compensation appears to be an obvious source of measurement; as some have argued, "questions of social justice and legal liability cannot and should not be separated" (MacDuff 2008, 1). Indigenous groups criticized the Australian government for not attaching a compensation package to the apology.[21] While the Canadian

---

[18] Several indigenous commentators on a comment thread on the CBC news website echoed this sentiment: the most moving aspect of the apology was that, for the first time, their non-indigenous friends and neighbors were curious about residential schools and their experiences. See comments posted at http://www.cbc.ca/canada/story/2008/06/11/pm-statement.html. When asked by journalist Rolfsen what white Canadians can do "to repair what's broken?" Canadian Aboriginal Lyana Patrick answered, "Listening would be great. Listening would be great." (Rolfsen 2008, 32).

[19] That it was a government and not an indigenous voice who successfully recounted the history raises entirely different questions of appropriation and silencing. But it is important to remember that when governments tell stories, they get heard.

[20] One woman recounted how she remembered being identified by number and not name in a state-run orphanage, how she was given an arbitrary collective birthday and a uniform token present. She notes the apology with its emphasis on survivor stories was "a final kind of recognition that I exist. My name is Veronica Ann McDonald." http://www.qldstories.slq.qld.gov.au/home/digital_stories/apology_responses

[21] "In fact, that there has been a denial of any [sic] monetary or any compensation that has been talked about in our country, I think is a blight on our history. I think it is morally correct to offer some olive branch here in terms of compensation." Jackie Huggins, deputy director of Aboriginal and Torres Strait Islander Studies at the University of Queensland and a former co-chair of Reconciliation Australia, http://www.abc.net.au/news/stories/2008/02/13/2161979.htm (accessed March 19, 2009).

government's apology was issued alongside material reparations payments and a comprehensive settlement agreement, it was also expressed by a government who had recently slashed funding to First Nations communities and rejected the Kelowna accord (promising $1billion for anti-poverty initiatives, mental health programs, and clean water, and signed by the previous, *less* overtly apologetic, government) and who had stalled a number of land claims negotiations. If we look to material measurements of apology, the verdict is still out on whether either apology has successfully disavowed the past or lived up to its promised commitments.

On the other hand, the scope of political responsibility is not exhausted by notions of legal liability or rectificatory compensation.[22] Neither can the significance of an apology cannot be reduced to its attached reparations; after all, there are victims who reject reparations unless accompanied by some form of apology. The symbolic features of apology matter as much as the material features do.

Both Aboriginal and non-Aboriginal Canadians commented consistently that the most moving aspect of the apology was the sight of Chief Phil Fontaine of the Assembly of First Nations (the political body representing over 50 native tribes) standing on the floor of the parliament in full ceremonial headdress, alongside leaders from Canada's Métis and Inuit populations. This was the first time native leaders had been overtly invited onto the floor of the house in their capacity as representatives of *nations*, and had been granted permission to speak in that capacity. As one commentator remarked, "Never discount the energy and communicative power of symbolism and ceremony. Chief Fontaine's speech was a power in itself, the best of the day… Wearing the appurtenances of his office, standing in that chamber, in the company of other aboriginal leaders… he embodied the occasion" (Murphy 2008).

Receiving and responding to a formal apology, when understood as a gesture between political bodies and peoples, not individuals, cemented recognition in Canadian consciousness that the Assembly of First Nations *was* a political body deserving of formal address, in a way that expressions of feelings could not do alone.[23] In a later speech, Chief Fontaine spoke movingly of what it meant "to be on the floor of the House of Commons – to speak in one's own voice, in one's own right (capacity) to the country…" (Fontaine 2008b). In other words, it was not the speech – or the speaking – of apology itself that achieved the third function, that of recognizing

---

[22] In fact, because the responsibility and recognition expressed in apologies is not necessary tied to material compensation, even those who *reject* the idea of historical reparations may still accept apologetic or symbolic gestures. Jeremy Waldron – who famously argued that commitments to present-day distributive justice supercede the claims of historic injustice – acknowledges that his point applies only to proportionate reparation payments understood as rectificatory justice. Smaller payments attached to apology or other symbolic gestures "symbolize a society's undertaking not to forget or deny that a particular justice took place" (Waldron 1992, 6).

[23] Perhaps for this very reason, whether or not the native leaders would be *allowed* to speak from the floor was a hotly contested issue, almost until the last minute. It was largely because of the intervention of an opposition party – the left-leaning New Democratic Party – the government eventually relented.

and acknowledging the apology's addressee. The recognition required, in this instance, was symbolic and political. It could only be achieved by the apology as public ceremony. Since part of the harm done to Canada's indigenous peoples had been the refusal of such recognition, this also represented (at least) symbolic disavowal of past policies of paternalism and disrespect.

Measuring the need for symbolic gestures of reparation against material and financial is difficult. There is understandable fear that, unless apologies are necessarily tied to reparations, the symbolic nature of apology replaces or circumvents other material efforts to repair damage. Of course, this only holds true if apologies are taken to be a *complete* response to historic injustice in themselves, and not a component of a broader project – indeed, a component that can actually *bind* governments to further action. If part of what an apology accomplishes is commitment, then we are right to measure the success of apology in part by what exactly is committed. In both these cases, that commitment was in part material, and unfortunately, that material commitment remains very much in question.

Recognizing the functions of an apology and learning to evaluate them in terms of those functions is not a guarantee that every good or successful apology is without political risk. For one thing, an apology is, by definition, a wrongdoer's narrative, and thus it remains to some extent within the wrongdoer's control. She still determines the story being told, even if that story involves her best effort to sympathetically incorporate and acknowledge the victim's perspective. Even the most well-intentioned of wrongdoers will dwell just a little too long on the state of their own soul, while castigating it; there is something peculiarly narcissistic in a too-repentant apologizer.[24] Furthermore, an apology does not simply perform one's (prior) guiltiness. Through the ability to narrate that wrongfulness *as* wrong, and through the expression of disavowal and one's commitment to that disavowal, it also performs one's (current) rightfulness – or at least, one's right *thinking*-ness. As Elizabeth Spelman says, apology is a vehicle "for vice nested in virtue," and it allows the apologizer to "wrap herself in a glorious mantle of rehabilitation" (Spelman 2002, 96–97). In doing so, apologies may redirect us from – and even foreclose – other investigations into the misdeeds and motivations of the past, shutting down further inquiry.

Finally, while the call for apology demands something of the wrongdoer, the apology itself may return that demand to the victim. The Canadian apology asks "… the forgiveness of the Aboriginal peoples of this land for failing them so profoundly" (Harper 2008). This request jars with the earlier, humbler acknowledgment that non-indigenous Canadians have only just joined indigenous survivors on a journey of recovery – forgiveness, if relevant at all, seems a little premature.

---

[24] Columnist Salutin described how, leading up to the 2008 apology, "there was a smug sense on the part of some apologizers that it's all about us. CTV's Dan Matheson asked Mike Duffy, 'Do you think we are ready as a people to say we are guilty?' 'Oh I think we are, Dan' cogitated Duff" – much like sports commentators assessing our chances for making the playoffs this year (2008).

It is telling that Chief Fontaine's eloquent response bears no mention of the word forgiveness. While he ends by reaching out to all Canadians in a spirit of reconciliation, he does so by noting: "we still have to struggle." Rudd's speech makes no mention of forgiveness, although he asks that, "the apology be received in the spirit in which it is offered" and further, he states, "it is time to reconcile."

Grasping the risks of apologies requires that we reflect on the differences between requesting or even demanding a response, on the one hand, and providing an opportunity to be heard, on the other. After all, the chance to respond is sometimes a *relief* to victims. Precluding a response from the victims is just as much a danger for official apologies, if the apologizer is given the last public word on the subject. The apology then reinforces the original harm of silence, exclusion, and *being spoken for.* One Australian columnist remarked,

> Throughout the coverage of the apology, I couldn't shake the sense that the indigenous Australians included in the televised spectacle – whether invited guests in Parliament House or the dozens of emotion-filled faces from around the country – were little more than props. Their role was to express and register the emotional content of the event. But the apology was not intended for them. The true recipients of the apology were those white Australians who watched and wanted to be made to feel as if they had taken part in something good...[25]

The most contested aspect of the Canadian apology was the last-minute negotiations to allow the Chiefs to speak from the floor of the Parliament. In both cases, it seems, the danger was not the *demand* for a response, but the refusal to allow one. Recounting one's sins may provide an inner glow, but listening to someone else recount them is far more uncomfortable. There was a distinct and collective intake of breath in Canada, when Chief Fontaine said "racist policy."

One final danger of political apologies emerges from their narrative power and their potential character as already-identified stories of closure and change. Both government apologies mention "new partnerships" between Aboriginals and non-Aboriginals, going forward. Yet the language of reconciliation, often appealed to in apology, suggests the revitalization of an old relationship, not the beginning of a new one. In Harper's apology, the first mention of the word "apology" is: "The government recognizes that the absence of an apology has been an impediment to healing and reconciliation," and in the final paragraph "healing, reconciliation and resolution" are named as the express goals of the settlement agreement. But as Gerry Oleman, a residential school survivor and community support worker remarks, "I think *reconciliation* is the wrong word. When have we been in harmony? I don't think we've had a relationship we're going to mend" (Rolfsen 2008, 30). Thus the value of both apologies may depend to a large extent on how *new* the relationship forged really is: as measured out in political and civic recognition, and in equal conditions and opportunities for civic life and cultural flourishing.

---

[25] Scott Stephens, "The Apology and the Moral Significance of Guilt," http://www.abc.net.au/news/stories/2008/02/25/2171795.htm (accessed March 20, 2009).

11.6   Conclusions: Apologies and Their Aftermath

It seems unlikely that we will ever have purely theoretical grounds for judging one apology an unqualified success, morally or politically speaking, and another a failure. In this paper, I have focused on two recent apologies made by heads of government and directed towards representative bodies of each nation's indigenous peoples. Moreover, I have argued, these two examples demonstrate the complications inherent in understanding and assessing official apologies. In both cases, it is not clear that success or failure in apologizing is something that can be drawn from the text itself or even its ceremonial context – some serious concerns cannot be resolved within the space of a speech, and will very much depend on what happens next for Canada and Australia's indigenous peoples. And yet, the significance and meaning of the apology as performed text does not disappear when we acknowledge this. The various strengths and weaknesses of both apologies highlighted here do matter and have mattered to those who received them and to those who witnessed them. Identifying how these strengths and weaknesses play out along axes of narrative, disavowal, and commitment – even while recognizing that these shift and overlap, according to each particular circumstance – goes some way towards untangling and deciphering the meaning, the relative successes, and the shortcomings of both. Reorienting our approach to apologies in this way allows us to see tremendous potential in these two recent apologies, without assuming that potential has come close to fulfillment.

References

Austin JL (1975) How to do things with words. Oxford University Press, Oxford
Bavelas J (2004) An analysis of formal apologies by Canadian Churches to first nations. Occasional Paper presented to the Centre for Studies in Religion and Society, University of Victoria. web. uvic.ca/psyc/bavelas/2004ChurchApol.pdf. Accessed 4 Nov 2011
Bell M (2008) Forgiving someone for who they are (and not just what they've done). Philos Phenomenol Res 77(3):625–658
Brudholm T (2008) Resentment's Virtue: Jean Améry and the Refusal to Forgive Temple University Press, Philadelphia
Busby C (2009) Sorry. www.cathybusby.ca. Accessed 17 Mar 2009
Card C (2007) Genocide and social death. In: Card C, Marsoobian AT (eds) Genocide's aftermath: responsibility and repair. Blackwell, New York
Carroll L (1960) The annotated Alice: Alice's adventures in wonderland and through the looking glass. With an Introduction and Notes by Martin Gardner. New York: Bramhall House
Cunningham M (2004) Apologies in Irish politics: a commentary and critique. Contemp Br Hist 18(4):80–92
Fontaine P (2008) Justice, responsibility, and reconciliation: legacies of the Holocaust and the persecution of aboriginal Canadians. Talk given at Ryerson University as part of Holocaust Awareness Week, 3 Nov 2008
Fontaine P, Chief of the Assembly of First Nations (2008) Response to Canadian Government Apology, 11 June 2008. http://www2.canada.com/vancouversun/news/story.html?id=18133d91-b8aa-4fbe-956e-20298d79c1d5. Accessed 18 Mar 2009

Gibney M, Roxstrom E (2001) The status of state apologies. Human Rights Quart 23(4):911–939

Gibney M, Howard-Hassmann RE, Coicaud J-M, Steiner N (2007) The age of apology: facing up to the past. University of Pennsylvania Press, October 24

Griswold C (2007) Forgiveness: a philosophical exploration. Cambridge University Press, Cambridge

Harper S, Right Honourable, Prime Minister of Canada (2008) Statement of apology to former students of Indian Residential Schools. June 11. www.fns.bc.ca/pdf/TextofApology.pdf. Accessed 4 Nov 2011

Harvey J (1995) The emerging practice of institutional apologies. Int J Appl Philos 9(2):57–65

Indian Residential Schools Settlement Agreement. http://www.residentialschoolsettlement.ca/ settlement.html. Accessed 4 Nov 2011

Kort LF (1975) What is an apology? Philos Res Arch 1:80–87

MacDuff A (2008) Do sorry statements make you liable? The Australian Legal Context. Forgiveness: probing the boundaries (First Global Conference), Salzburg, Austria

Murphy R (2008) The day the house stood still. Globe and Mail, Saturday June 14

Nelson B, Leader of the Australian Liberal Party (2008) Response to government apology. February 13. Reprinted online in The Australian http://www.theaustralian.news.com.au/story/0,25197,23206522-5013172,00.html. Accessed 17 Mar 2009

Nobles M (2008) The politics of official apologies. Cambridge University Press, Cambridge

Prager CAL, Govier T (2003) Dilemmas of reconciliation: cases and concepts. Wilfrid Laurier Univ. Press, Waterloo

Rolfsen C (2008) After the apology. This Magazine. September/October

Rudd K, Right Honourable, Prime Minister of Australia (2008) Apology to Australia's indigenous peoples. February 13. www.aph.gov.au/house/rudd_speech.pdf. Accessed 18 Mar 2009

Salutin R (2008) Issues of apology and power. Globe and Mail. Friday June 13

Smith A (2005) Conquest: sexual violence and the American Indian genocide. South End Press, Cambridge

Smith N (2008) I was wrong: the meaning of apologies. Cambridge University Press, Cambridge

Spelman E (2002) Repair: the impulse to restore in a fragile world. Beacon, Boston

Stewart J, Honourable, Minister of Indian and Northern Affairs (1998) Statement of reconciliation on behalf of Canada's Government to Canada's Aboriginal Peoples. January 7. http://www.deal. org/content/index.php?option=com_content&task=view&id=889&Itemid=1082. Accessed 18 Mar 2009

Tavuchis N (1990) Mea culpa: a sociology of apology and reconciliation. Stanford University Press, Stanford

Thompson J (1992) Taking responsibility for the past: reparations and historical injustice. Polity Press, Cambridge

Thompson J (2008) Apology, justice and respect: a critical defense of the political apology. In: Gibney M et al (eds) The age of apology: facing up to the past. University of Pennsylvania Press, Philadelphia

Waldron J (1992) The supercession of historical injustice. Ethics 103(1):4–28

Weyeneth RR (2001) The power of apology and the process of historical reconciliation. Publ Historian 23(3):9–30

Chapter 12
The Expressive Burden of Reparations: Putting Meaning into Money, Words, and Things

Margaret Urban Walker

Abstract I propose a novel account of the essentially expressive nature of reparations. My account is descriptive of new practices of reparations that have emerged in the past half-century, and it provides normative guidance on conditions of success for reparative attempts. My account attributes to reparative attempts a dual expressive function: a communicative function that requires the gesture to carry a vindicatory message to victims; and an exemplifying function that requires the gesture to model the right relationship that was absent or violated in the wrongdoing to which reparations respond. This account is able to explain the breadth and variety of measures now recognized as reparations; how reparative attempts can fail in two distinct ways; and why material compensation is never sufficient and not always necessary to reparations.

Making reparations is one practice of doing justice in response to wrongs. Reparations, in the sense I will examine, consist in acts, on the part of those responsible for a wrong or its repair, of intentionally giving appropriate goods to victims of that wrong in order to acknowledge the wrong, their responsibility for the wrong or its repair, and their intent to do justice to the victim precisely for the wrong.[1] What is

---

[1] I speak of those "responsible for wrongs or for their repair," for theoretical and practical reasons. The current practice of reparations for human rights and humanitarian abuses places upon states responsibility to discharge obligations of repair for such abuses, even if the government that must discharge the obligation is a successor to one who was causally responsible by omission, commission, or complicity. I avoid here defending the claim, now embedded in international standards for redress and reparation, that successor governments are responsible for repair of wrongs even if they were not causally responsible for the wrongs. In addition, I believe that there are communal responsibilities of moral repair, some of which are ever-present and have to do with the unique

M.U. Walker (✉)
Department of Philosophy, Marquette University, Coghlin Hall 132,
Milwaukee, WI 53201-1881, USA
e-mail: margaret.walker@marquette.edu

A. MacLachlan and A. Speight (eds.), *Justice, Responsibility and Reconciliation in the Wake of Conflict*, Boston Studies in Philosophy, Religion and Public Life 1, DOI 10.1007/978-94-007-5201-6_12, © Springer Science+Business Media Dordrecht 2013

given to or done for the victim of wrong, however appropriate in light of the harm caused by the wrong, is not in itself what constitutes reparations, for it must be given or done by those responsible for wrong or its repair, and given in a certain spirit and with a certain intent. Others may give aid, comfort, support, or compensation, and in some instances may do so in the spirit that "it is only right" that someone respond in this way to those who have suffered wrongful harms or losses; but if those who do so are not responsible parties who intend to redress wrongs that it is their obligation to redress, this is indemnification or good works but it is not reparations.[2] Nor does it suffice in itself that the persons or entities who give something to or do something for victims of wrongful harms are responsible in the relevant ways, if they do not intend to redress wrongs and to express that intention by what they give or do.[3] A government who by its policies has contributed to a group of citizens becoming impoverished and marginalized might decide at some point to ameliorate the poverty and exclusion of this historically unfortunate group. If the newly offered goods or opportunities are not tendered with the intention to accept responsibility for wrong and offer just redress, however, then the action might be a just redistributive exercise and might be intended to fulfill requirements of distributive justice, but it is not an exercise of reparative justice and the benefits newly offered are not reparations.[4]

My discussion is keyed to the practice of reparations that has taken shape in the past half-century. Reparations were once a transaction between nations that required

---

abilities of communities to address victims, perpetrators, and wrongs in particular ways, and others which need to be taken up by default when the perpetrators of wrongs are unknown, unavailable, unable, or unwilling to engage in repair, including specific measures of reparations. See Walker (2006a, 29–34) on the significance of communal responsibilities of repair.

[2] For an interesting discussion of the non-standard sense in which the U.S. government's compensation plan for victims and survivors of 9/11 may be seen as "reparations", see Issacharoff and Mansfield (2006). See also Brooks (2003, 107) on distinguishing between reparations that "seek atonement for the commission of an injustice" and settlements "in which the government does not express atonement." Admittedly, common usage, as in newspaper articles, often calls settlements that terminate a course of litigation pursuing compensation for injustice "reparations." And there can be a political stake in calling payments reparations even when they are not intended as such, or are denied to be reparations, if this implies that the party making amends is in fact conceding wrongdoing. On one such case, see Jennifer Lind's discussion of Japanese compensation payments to Korea in the 1960s, in Lind (2008, 47). I do not mean here to deny that the term "reparations" is used in both looser and rhetorically opportunistic ways. I mean, instead, to focus on cases, however various in detail, that are clearly intended as acts of acknowledgment and redress. It is by reference to these central or canonical cases that we can better understand the analogies that underlie non-standard uses.

[3] See Boxill (1972, 119).

[4] Some who see "backward-looking" attempts at reparative justice as practically troubled or lacking in sufficient justification sometimes argue that essentially "forward-looking" distributive approaches should either supersede reparative demands based on past injury or should replace reparative attempts with robust distributive ones that address inequalities or injustices in the present. A much discussed argument for supersession of historical injustice by forward-looking considerations is Waldron (1992). Recent arguments for the distributive route include Pierik (2006) and Wenar (2006).

losers to pay tribute to winners for their losses – as in the familiar case of reparations exacted from Germany after the World War I. The landscape of reparations shifted rapidly after World War II with the upsurge in human rights standards, changes in international humanitarian law, and in the unprecedented program of massive reparations by the Federal Republic of Germany to individual victims of the Holocaust. It was further transformed by the decisions of international judicial bodies.[5] In the current state of things, reparations are often programs implemented by states in fulfillment of their internationally recognized obligations to address individual victims of serious violations of human rights or international humanitarian law, often in large numbers, in the aftermath of specific patterns of abuse, repressive and violent authoritarian governance, or armed conflict. The obligation of repair can fall upon successor governments that were neither the source of the abuse nor a culpable bystander to it, but who inherit undischarged duties to repair the grave wrongs of a former regime. More than a legal device, this understanding addresses the need, in the aftermath of mass violence, to provide assurance that the dignity, civic standing, and political equality of those victimized or disregarded is recognized in the post-conflict political order.[6]

The basic principle of reparations, affirmed by the UN General Assembly in 2006 after a decade of study, is that victims of gross violations of international human rights law or serious violations of international humanitarian law should be provided with "full and effective reparation," which takes forms that include restitution; material compensation; rehabilitation through legal, medical, and social services; guarantees of non-repetition through institutional reform; and "satisfaction" (a category of diverse measures that include truth-telling, exhuming human remains from atrocities, public apology, commemoration, and educational activities, among others).[7] The increasingly clear definition of forms and grounds of reparations in international understandings can also put pressure on societies, state or local governments, and institutions, such as corporations, churches, universities, or other collectivities to reckon with legacies of profound injustice in their pasts. It is this moving front of interdependent principle and practice in reparations that my account addresses.

Until recently, the normative literature on reparative justice and reparations has been slight, and has been dominated by a juridical or tort paradigm of restitution or compensation for unjust loss or injury that seeks to restore the status quo ante in order to "set things right." On this view, reparative (or corrective, or compensatory) justice is done when victims are rescued from losing what they should not have

---

[5] On this dramatic historical shift, see Falk (2006), Teitel (2000, 119–128), Torpey, "Introduction: Politics and the Past," in Torpey (2006), Barkan (2003, 95–98). Specifically on the post-World War II German case, see Colonomos and Armstrong (2006). I do not here defend state responsibility for reparations, although I believe it is defensible and it is, in any case, the existing standard.

[6] de Greiff (2006a, b) and Verdeja (2007) offer distinctly political rationales for reparation in cases of mass violence and repression.

[7] United Nations, Basic Principles and Guidelines on the Right to a Remedy and Reparation for Victims of Gross Violations of International Human Rights Law and Serious Violations of International Humanitarian Law, United Nations Document A/RES/60/147, 21 March 2006.

lost, by either its return or equivalent replacement.[8] As newer political practices of reparations have developed in recent decades, this legalistic understanding of reparation as proportionate compensation has come under criticism as inapt or impracticable for large-scale programs of reparations in the political context of reckoning with heinous wrongs of conflict and repression or with historical injustices of dispossession, slavery, enforced inequality, and cultural destruction. Newer moral and political conceptions of reparations that focus on affirming human dignity and equal citizenship, and creating the basis for respectful, trustworthy, and mutually accountable relationships, have been argued as necessary, if not superior, alternatives to the juridical view.[9] It is not my intention to enter that debate. Instead, I begin on the side of those who argue that reparative justice is about redress for injustice and wrongful harms that aims at the reordering of individuals' standing, their relationships, and their communities, and I will give a particular account of what this reordering consists in. This in no way eliminates or diminishes the role of restitution or monetary compensation when these measures are particularly meaningful and effective in providing redress to victims and in expressing the intention of responsible parties to do reparative justice. Rather, I seek to put these transactions into a broader context, where restitution and compensation are never, in themselves, sufficient to repair grave harms, and where it is the meaning of the interaction, and not only or by itself what is tendered in it, that puts the repair in reparations.

By exploring the expressive functions of reparations, and so identifying the expressive burdens that gestures and programs of reparations must meet, whether they entail material transfers or other kinds of acts, we can better understand the human interactions that justice requires when grave wrongs have been done. On my account, gestures of reparation involve a double symbolism: they communicate and exemplify. Their *communicative* function is to deliver to victims, wrongdoers, and communities a vindicatory message that acknowledges the reality, the wrong, the responsible parties, and their intent to do justice. The communicative function may be carried explicitly by apology, but also or alternately by the expressive suitability of the vehicle of reparations – what is given. The *exemplifying* function of an act of reparations is to exhibit the right relationship between the wronged party and those responsible parties who make reparation. The reparative act must exemplify a kind of relationship between victim and responsible parties that was rejected or lacking in the circumstances in which the wrong was done.

---

[8] Brooks (2004) calls this approach the "tort model." Examples include Nozick (1974, 57–58), MacCormick (1977–1978), Nickel (1976), Sher (1980), Coleman (1994), and Winter (2006). On some complexities of compensation, see Goodin (1989).

[9] Political conceptions include de Greiff (2006b) and Verdeja (2007). Brooks (2004) rejects a "tort model" of reparations to African Americans. Roht-Arriaza (2004) argues for collective and symbolic reparations for communities. Thompson (2002) argues for "reparation as reconciliation" within or between communities, rather than "reparation as restoration" of the status quo ante. Satz (2007) explores limitations of compensation as repair for political violence. See also Walker (2006c) for a restorative justice framework as a superior alternative to a corrective justice one for some cases of historical injustice.

My account of these dual expressive functions is normative: it aims to explain a particular kind of practice, and in doing so to identify conditions for the success of that practice. I am saying that reparations gestures – for instance compensatory payments of money for an unjust loss or suffering – may rightly fail to be seen or accepted as reparations if they fail to include or to achieve the necessary expressive dimensions, or may be correctly judged as more or less successful reparative efforts to the extent that they do achieve them. At the same time, my account is meant to stay close descriptively to what has actually been found to happen in attempts, successful and unsuccessful, at making amends for grave wrongs. Finally, it is meant as to underscore how limited and fragile are the effects that even sincerely intended and well-considered reparations measures and programs can have.

12.1 What Are Reparations Intended to Repair?

I begin my account, necessarily, at the end: what is it that reparations are intended to repair? What is the goal of "reparation" at which specific reparations measures aim?[10] In psycho-social perspectives, reparations seek relief of the suffering, distress, anger and sense of violation experienced by victims.[11] Legal perspectives focus on restoring the status quo ante or making the victim whole, drawing on well-established principles of corrective or compensatory justice, which may be of limited guidance in massive reparations programs. Political and moral conceptions of reparations stress the kinds of standing and recognition that reparations must affirm for victims within their communities, and the forms of social and political relationship that they promise (and repudiate) in offering reparations.[12]

Drawing on my work on moral repair, I offer a particular way of understanding the regulative ideal of reparations that foregrounds *moral* aims, while recognizing the importance of psychological and political conditions to expressing and achieving these moral aims. On my view, there are three central conditions of functioning moral relations that are threatened or damaged by serious wrongs. One is the *confidence* that there are mutually recognized and defensible shared standards that define reciprocal normative expectations of mutual respect between parties to these understandings. A second is *trust* that parties may rely on each other to be responsive to these standards, either by conforming to them, or by acknowledging that failure to conform creates liabilities to accountability, sanction, or repair.

---

[10] Hamber (2006) distinguishes "reparations," the particular measures, from "reparation", the end or effect desired. For Hamber, a psychologist, this aim is a kind of psychological state. I adopt his distinction, but use "reparation" to cover desired effects not only of psychological but of moral and political kinds. For a fuller discussion of the psychological needs of victims, see Hamber (2009).

[11] Herman (1997) is a classic text on the trauma of victims of individual abuse and political violence. See Hamber (2009) and Walker (2006a, b).

[12] See note 9 on political conceptions. A defense of the necessity and complementarity in practice of civil litigation and mass political programs is found in Malamud-Goti and Grosman (2006). See also Bernstein (2009).

The trust in question may be general or it might involve specific expectations of relationships with distinct histories. Third, and less commonly recognized, parties must sustain *hopefulness* about the authority and mutual acceptance of moral standards and about the trustworthiness of individuals to be responsive to them. I suggest that reparation aims at the creation or restoration of these conditions of morally adequate relationship – confidence, trust, and hope – on the social and civic level, thus repairing moral relations for common and public life.[13]

Discussions of reparations in political cases (and responses to serious violence and injustice generally) often emphasize the affirmation of the victims' dignity and equality and the creation or reestablishment of common standards of respect among victims and perpetrators and within their communities. The creation or restoration of trust between victims and their communities that shared standards apply to and protect them are also central themes of political accounts.[14] What is most distinctive in my own account is the claim that hopefulness is a fundamental condition of moral relations, more fundamental than trust. The trust we repose in each other to act on defensible shared standards is often disappointed and, in cases of gross injustice and violence, trust will be severely shaken or destroyed at least for victims of grave wrongs, and perhaps for others. The readiness to rely on each other's responsiveness to shared standards is one of the casualties of serious wrongs for individuals or for whole communities. Hopefulness is more fundamental than trust because it can be essential to restoring trust.

Hope is an attitude constituted by a belief in the possibility of some desired situation, by the positive value placed on that situation, and, most characteristically, by an effective motivation, displayed in feeling, imagination, and behavior, to seek, invite, or attempt to bring about the desired yet uncertain reality. The hopefulness at the root of moral relations involves a motivating belief that there is a real possibility, even if slight, that defensible standards are shared and that individuals are disposed to respond to what the standards require. Trust involves actual reliance on others; trust can be maintained, or at extremity to be entertained again, only if there is room for hopefulness, if not about those who have committed grave wrongs, then at least about the general reliability of others of our fellow moral actors. If trust is the stream in which we swim in shared lives organized largely by reliance on the acceptance of common norms, hope is the spring that feeds that stream.

The centrality of hope has important consequences for understanding the repair of moral relations and, more specifically, reparations measures, for one-off displays of acknowledgment, responsibility, and intent to do justice by those responsible for wrongs or their repair would not seem, in the wake of terrible wrongs, to give reasonable grounds for resuming confidence and trust. What a gesture or an orchestrated process of negotiating and making reparations might do instead is to make available, and to make more or less vivid and convincing, the possibility that

[13] Walker (2006a, 23–28).

[14] The recognition of victims and recreation of civic trust are core themes of Pablo de Greiff's political approach to reparations (and other transitional justice measures) for mass violence and repression in political contexts. See de Greiff (2006b, 2008, 2012).

those making reparations really do intend to make themselves worthy of trust. This is the possibility that: (1) they understand the nature of the wrong, loss, suffering, resentment, and alienation they seek to repair; (2) they realize the flawed or malignant kind of relationship, and the violated or perverse standards, that they have visited on the victims or that the victims have suffered; and (3) they are capable of undertaking and willing to undertake the establishment or guarantee to the victims of the sort of standing and relationship that would have prevented such wrongdoing.

To expect an act or process of reparations in and of itself to reinstate or create confidence in shared standards that affirm the dignity of each and respect for all, and trust in others' responsiveness to them, seems wishful. It seems more realistic to view the success of reparations as hinging on the ability of the gesture to animate hope, to kindle a concrete sense of possibility that can motivate actions, feelings, and engagements with others that in turn could permit the regeneration of morally adequate relationships. It is the regeneration of relationships of the right kind, under tests and over time, that in turn might make possible the substantial confidence and trust that adequate moral relations require and upon which stable civic and political relations of respect and equality depend.

12.2   One Expressive Function of Reparations: The Vindicatory Message

Many discussions of reparations distinguish material reparations (money compensation, restitution of property, or goods or services with monetary value) from symbolic reparations. "Symbolic" reparations are those that do not involve a transfer of property or something of monetary value; they can be as diverse as the publication of the truth about abuses, public apologies, memorials, or educational projects. This well-established and useful distinction among kinds of reparations should not obscure, however, that *all* reparations have an essentially symbolic – that is, expressive or communicative – function. Even when monetary compensation or other material goods are offered as reparations, it is their role in carrying the relevant communication that distinguishes reparations from indemnification, payment of a settlement, or compensation on other than reparative grounds.[15] Nor should the fact

---

[15] See Hamber (2009). Based on extensive work with victims of political violence in several contexts, Hamber says: "All objects or acts of reparations have a symbolic meaning to individuals – they are never merely acts or objects," (98). Another common usage in the reparations literature distinguishes between "material" and "moral" reparations. I find this terminology more illuminating, since it allows for the communicative (and in that sense, symbolic) dimension of all reparations while marking the difference between reparations that involve an exchange of monetarily valued goods from those that involve other interpersonal exchanges that convey respect, recognition, compassion, contrition, and so forth. On moral reparations, see United Nations Commission on Human Rights, (1997) "Question of the Impunity of Perpetrators of Human Rights Violations (Civil and Political), Revised Final Report Prepared by Mr. Joinet Pursuant to Sub-Commission Decision 1996/119," United Nations Document E/CN.4/Sub.2/1997/20/Rev.1, 2 October 1997, paragraph 42. On the conceptual terrain and the established terminology of material and symbolic reparations, see de Greiff (2006b, 452–453).

that nonmonetary or nonmaterial reparations are called "symbolic" suggest that what is offered is somehow only a surrogate or stand-in for what would be "real" reparations, money or other materially valuable objects. Studies of victims of political violence in many contexts reveal that measures called symbolic reparations are often more highly valued than monetary ones, and that monetary payments are unacceptable or take on problematic meanings in the absence of other gestures that convey acknowledgment and respect.[16] Whether material or symbolic, all reparations are seen by victims as communicative gestures, and these communications produce real effects of psychological, moral, social, and political kinds. If the reparative communication misfires or is poorly executed, very real effects often follow: the victims may be insulted, outraged, or bitterly disappointed, and may react with protest, withdrawal, or litigation. I don't seek to trouble these entrenched distinctions; rather, I refer to the "expressive" function of reparations to avoid confusion, arguing that the expressive function is essential to all reparations gestures, whether material or symbolic.

That reparations gestures or programs have a crucial expressive dimension is widely recognized, and is recognized as marking the difference between reparations proper, on the one hand, and simple indemnification or compensation, on the other. Yet little has been said about what it is that reparations express and how they do so. A common idea is that reparations gestures acknowledge a wrong (and thus the reality of an event or course of events as well as a norm of conduct that identifies the wrongfulness) and accept responsibility for the wrong that entails an obligation to redress it.[17] Hence my formula for the vindicatory message that reparations must carry: it communicates the reality and wrongfulness of the event in question, as well as a responsibility for the wrong or its repair and an obligation to make amends as a matter of justice. Whatever is given as or in a gesture of reparations needs to come with or to carry this message. If it does not, there can be unclarity about the wrongdoers' or responsible parties' understanding of, and attitude toward, past wrongs and their duties of justice in respect of them, or the act may fail to show proper respect or real

---

[16] An interview study of 102 victims of human rights abuses in a follow-up study of truth commissions in five countries (Argentina, Chile, El Salvador, Guatemala, and South Africa), finds that symbolic measures are most demanded and valued by victims. See Czitrom (2002) and Hamber (2009).

[17] Boxill (1972), for example, argues that reparation cannot be equated with compensation, because reparation requires an acknowledgment that what the bearer of reparations is doing is required of him because of a former injustice he has done, and so involves an assumption of the moral equality of the wronged party and a rejection of the imputation of inferiority in the unjust treatment. Corlett (2001) specifically attributes to reparations an "expressive" function, including disavowal of the wrong and of the wrongdoer, sending "messages to citizens...which seek to build and strengthen social solidarity toward justice and fairness" (237). Hamber (2006) holds that all objects or acts of reparation have two levels of symbolism. They represent or express something to the victims, such as an acknowledgment of their suffering or a focus for their grief or sense of loss, and they represent something about those giving or granting the reparations, such as society's willingness to deal with the past and the victim's suffering or an admission of responsibility. Radzik's (2009) view makes communication and the symbolism involved in a tender of material compensation central elements of atonement.

care for those to whom reparations are owed. Whatever is given as or in a gesture of reparations needs to come with or to carry this message. How is this message sent?

Obviously, the message can be sent explicitly by means of a careful and complete apology: one that identifies the offending event; characterizes its wrongfulness clearly (and ideally identifies the specific values or norms violated and the actual harmful impact on victims); takes responsibility for the wrong or its repair; and repudiates the behavior involved in the wrong.[18] In personal relations, apologies may often be the whole of a reparative gesture and in many cases may suffice as adequate amends. In some historical and political cases involving groups of victims, public apology may also be specially meaningful for its establishment of an historical record (often in the face of persistent denial), and for its public acknowledgment of the injustice, suffering, and loss born by victims. For these reasons apology may be so crucial that the offer of other goods in the absence of the right kind of apology is unacceptable as reparations; but it is equally true that apology, in both personal and political cases, can appear as cheap talk or idle ritual without the tender of something else as amends. Finally, it is possible that tendering the right goods in the right way might by itself send the vindicatory message that an apology makes explicit in words.

There is a need, then, for a fuller and more general understanding of the features that an expressively successful *vehicle* of reparations – the good actually given – will have. Despite widespread recognition of the expressive nature of reparations gestures, there is not much guidance on the general dimensions that determine expressive adequacy. The principle of proportionality in compensation that figures in the juridical conception of corrective justice, is but one guideline, and a meager one in face of the varieties of reparations now recognized. I offer the following general scheme as a start on explaining the features that make a particular vehicle of reparations adequate to the expressive task, whether it be money, services, special opportunities, access to relevant information, apology, concerted truth-telling, educational projects, or commemorative activities.

I suggest four dimensions along which reparations vehicles can be assessed for adequacy to the expressive burden. Reparations vehicles must be *interactive, useful, fitting*, and *effective*.

First, a reparations vehicle must be suitable to be the focus or embodiment of an *interaction* between responsible parties and victims. Responsible parties include the actual perpetrators of wrong, but also parties otherwise responsible, for example, by complicity, culpable inaction, or a legacy of undischarged reparative obligations. Communities also have their roles to play in affirming the authority of norms and the victims' deservingness of repair, either as participants in or as guarantors of repair. Victims are construed for the purposes of this interaction as those who have suffered intentional harms directed at them. In keeping with current legal and

---

[18] Some philosophical accounts of apology that overlap in their main features but are distinguished by more or fewer requirements are found in: Kort (1973), Gill (2000), and Govier and Verwoerd (2002). The most detailed account is Smith (2008). Two thorough and useful nonphilosophical discussions are those of Lazare (2004) and Tavuchis (1991).

political understandings, however, reparations may be offered to others unavoidably and severely affected by wrongs, such as families, close relations, and dependents of direct victims. This interactive aspect is crucial, because it represents *acknowledgment of relationship and the intent to repair it.* Whatever the nature of the relationship, if any, prior to the wrong, in all cases of wrongs that seriously harm there is a charged and negative relationship created by the wrong that is one of the costs suffered by victims. A reparations vehicle must be suitable to acknowledging the existence of a relationship as the context of reparation and the achievement of a morally adequate relationship of reciprocity and respect as its aim.

Second, a reparations vehicle must be *useful* for victims, that is, it must be suitable to their own use in coming to terms with the loss and harm suffered due to the wrong. Reparations are called for when wrongs cause serious harms. Nothing given by responsible parties can be adequate without offering victims something they can do to address the harms and losses, especially in ways that they themselves need and choose to do so. This is not only a matter of respect for their loss, but of their right to exercise agency and control in the aftermath of being unjustly, even violently, subjected to the will of others. A reparations vehicle is useful when victims can use it to replace what was lost; as a means to pursue interests otherwise thwarted by the wrong and its harms; as a means to pursue interests that replace and in some degree compensate for those interests that can no longer be pursued due to the wrong and its harms; or to achieve some degree of satisfaction or relief for the specific pain, suffering, and grief caused by the wrong and its harms.

The limiting case is restitution, where the very thing lost or destroyed is returned or restored in a way that affirms rightful ownership and the wrong of interference. More commonly, reparations offer something the victim of wrong can use to deal with the loss and damage the wrong has caused, and since these losses and harms are various, so may reparative measures vary. In many modern societies money is the all-purpose currency of this interaction, but a memorial that contains individualized references to victims can also be intensely valued as a concrete site or receptacle to focus grief and to point to as durable public acknowledgment of the responsibility of others.[19] Usefulness reminds us that collective measures of reparation must be assessed for their individual impact on relief of individual isolation and suffering and on their contribution to individuals' agency and well-being. Usefulness in a reparative vehicle is crucial to represent the *acknowledgment of the individual victim's experience of suffering and loss and respect for their agency.*

Third, a reparations vehicle must also be *fitting.* The vehicle needs to be related to the wrong and harm that was endured in such ways as to seem fitting and deserved, especially to the victim but also to others in their community, as a response to that *particular* sort of wrong and loss, to the specific damage to opportunities and well-being it causes, and to the kind of pain, suffering, and grief inflicted. Here the

---

[19] Hamber explains the psychological functions that memorial objects can have as "bridges" between the inner and outer worlds of victims and survivors, and to "mirror" back the reactions of others (Hamber 2006, 570–71).

common requirement of "proportionality" of compensation to injury appears as one aspect of what is in fact a more general feature. Except in cases of restitution of the lost object, or where what is compensated for has a determinate monetary value that it is possible to pay, even in monetary compensation "fit" is often determined, as in the case of legal punishment, relative to a standard or scale that is defined in some conventional way or that involves symbolic representations or equivalences of value. Mass reparations for gross violence can also mix material and symbolic equivalences, as when victims of illegal detention receive pensions equivalent to some rank of civil servant. They can be fitted to remedy specific physical, psychological, or legal disabilities, as when victims receive special access to rehabilitative or legal services. They can respond to fear of reoccurence with public programs of education and institutional reform, and to grief with individualized and concrete forms of memorialization. Fit can also be constructed narratively, in terms of a fitting continuation or representation of the story of grave wrongs and victims' vindication, as when a torture center is turned into a museum to educate about the abuses. For families of those disappeared, nothing short of retrieving the remains of loved ones may seem even minimally fitting. Martha Minow notes rightly that reparations "cross lexicons of value" attempting to achieve one or more kinds of fit.[20] Fit has an especially strong intuitive relation to justice: as punishment is to be proportionate to crime, compensation proportionate to loss, and reward proportionate to achievement, so to does fittingness of a reparations vehicle represent an *appreciation of the nature, meaning, and magnitude of what is "due" as a matter of justice.*

Fourth, the reparations vehicle chosen must be *effective*. The vehicle must be carefully considered, and ideally it is negotiated with victims, so that victims of wrong are likely to be *able to access and use it*. Usefulness and fit carry messages that choices are given in response to lost freedoms, powers to act given in response to having been powerless, acknowledgment given as a bulwark against denial and erasure, and opportunities to express or contain grief and anger given in recognition of the acute suffering and burden with which victims or their survivors struggle. If access to reparations, or the nature of what is provided, is not carefully considered so that victims can secure it and meet such needs, the gesture will seem careless or perfunctory. As a result, while all of the features support the message of responsibility for wrong or its repair, care for effectiveness in particular signals *seriousness and sincerity* in the task of reparation, showing that responsibility is fully taken, and that it is not just credit for the reparative gesture, or relief from continuing demands for reparations, but instead the victim's concrete experience of repair that is sought.

When reparations proposals are contested, the issue is not usually whether any of these four conditions express reasonable expectations of reparations; rather, questions about proposed reparations are usually about whether particular measures in fact fulfill these conditions, which are implicitly assumed. A reparations measure can be and seem evasive if it does not engage the wishes of victims or require consultation with them; unilateral gestures that are unresponsive to what victims

---

[20] Minow (1998, 104).

expect violate the first *interactive* condition and may aggravate the victims' sense of being disregarded. The repetitive failures of the inaptly named "comfort women" to secure the response of the Japanese government that they sought – the Diet's apology and a publicly financed compensation fund – is, among other things, a failure of interaction.[21] The second and third conditions, *usefulness* and *fit*, address whether a reparations vehicle acknowledges and expresses appreciation of the nature of the loss victims have suffered and whether what responsible parties offer seems to acknowledge, in kind and magnitude, what is due. The Lakota Sioux do not accept the proposed court-ordered compensation payment by the U.S. government for the unconstitutional taking of the Black Hills. Even were compensation to be offered as reparations with public apologies, the loss of the Black Hills is not a question of economic value for the Lakota, and payment for them does not fit the offense of cultural destruction, genocidal dispossession, and denial of sovereign nationhood.[22] A question about the *effectiveness* condition can arise when accessing or using what is offered as reparations is made too burdensome. Offering a monetary reparations payment to women in patriarchal societies in which they will have no effective control over the economic resources tendered is not effective, nor are money or services offered to female victims of sexual violence who would need to publicly identify themselves to apply for or access their reparations, where this would predictably expose them to social stigma, retaliatory violence, or exclusion.[23]

Apologies, one kind of reparations, can also be assessed for their interactive, useful, fitting, and effective features. Are they delivered directly, effectively, – and in political cases, publicly – to the victims, providing a full, accurate, detailed, and unqualified acknowledgment of the reality and wrongfulness of the act to which victims can point? The combination of explicit and complete apology and a well-considered vehicle of reparation is most likely to achieve adequacy in sending the vindicatory message, so long as all the elements cohere.

12.3   A Second Expressive Function of Reparations: Exemplification of Right Relationship

The communicative component of the expressive function of reparations needs to make the present gesture speak to the past and its continuing meaning for relationships among victims, responsible parties, and their communities. If reparations are

---

[21] The tangled history is summarized in Iida (2004). Some recent developments are reported in Onishi (2007a, b, c, d).

[22] See Tsosie (2007) and Barkan (2003).

[23] Bernstein (2009) argues that shares in microfinance institutions have unique potential truly to benefit and enhance the agency of women, especially poor women in male-dominated societies. On appropriate and effective reparations for sexual violence, see also Duggan and Jacobson (2009), and on many complexities of the little-explored area of reparations for child victims, see Mazurana and Carlson (2009).

an invitation to the hope that in turn might make renewed relations possible, a second expressive dimension of reparative acts matters. An act or program of reparations can only transcend being an incidental or isolated gesture addressing the past if it is meant and seen not only as sending the vindicatory message on this occasion, but as exemplifying the rectified relationship in the present and future that could, if sustained, become the basis for acceptable and stable moral, civil, and political relations. I call this dimension of its meaning the *exemplifying* function of an act or process of reparations.[24]

In its exemplifying function, the gesture of reparations attempts to model and exhibit the kind of relationship between victim and responsible parties that was lacking or rejected in the circumstances in which the wrong was done. The reparative interaction purports to express to victims and to society the respectful, compassionate, and responsibility-taking attitude appropriate to amends-makers by embodying that attitude. The expression of the attitude in the attempt at reparations tokens a more acceptable form of relationship in general and for the future. It is important to recognize this second, prospective meaning of reparations in order to understand the ways that reparations attempts succeed or fail in their expressive function. For it follows that all reparations measures are vulnerable to failure in *two* ways. A reparations effort may fail to achieve convincing exemplification of the appropriate attitude because of a defective vindicatory message. Or, a reparations effort can fail if the attitude successfully exemplified in the vindicatory message is not consistently adopted and displayed in *other* or *future* interactions.

Ideally, the exemplification of right relationship works with and through communication of the vindicatory message. In the best case, the amends-maker clearly communicates an intention to verify the wrong, to "own" it, and to fulfill an obligation of justice to redress it through a reparations vehicle that is interactive, useful, fitting, and effective. The attention, respect, and concern that are shown in the clarity and strength of the vindicatory message, and the appropriateness of the vehicle in and of itself, says something positive about the amends-makers' acknowledgment of wrong and harm, and their intention to do justice. The context and performance of reparative gestures can add as well to the emotional tone, the sense of gravity, or the public commitment involved in the reparations gesture. The meaningfulness of public apologies, for example, involves the locations from which and the people by which they are given, and how victims are involved and addressed, as well as what they say. Patricio Aylwin Azócar made a public apology to the nation of Chile as its first elected President in the era after the military dictatorship of Augusto Pinochet, delivered from a stadium that had been a center of illegal detention and torture.

---

[24] Exemplification as a kind of reference was introduced by Goodman (1968). An object exemplifies those among its own qualities that it is used to represent; a fabric sample, for instance, is used to represent color, pattern, weave, content, texture, and quality of a kind of fabric, but its serrated edges, nine-inch-square dimensions, or dirty finger smudges are not part of what is represented. Elgin (1983, 71–95) gives a clear and detailed exposition of exemplificational reference. I here use only the very basic idea that we use a particular instance to exhibit certain properties that are to be found in other instances of a kind of thing.

The speech literally embodied a message of candor about the reality of human rights abuse and a signal that the country had been reclaimed; it was also a part of a political transition in which Aylwin, within one month of his inauguration, created a truth commission to investigate and acknowledge cases of those who died due to human rights violations of the Pinochet regime. Despite the powerful symbolism surrounding the apology and commitment to the truth, however, Chile's National Commission on Truth and Reconciliation was limited in its mandate to investigate only those human rights violations that resulted in the death of the victims, leaving aside tens of thousands of victims of torture whose cases would not be investigated for another decade. Despite rather robust material reparations, the adequacy of the reparations as acknowledgment of severe and widespread abuses continues to be contested.[25] In another example of compromised exemplification through the reparative process itself, consider the German Federal Republic's massive program of reparations for individual Holocaust victims. Despite the fact that this program remains by far the largest transfer of money ever made in a reparations effort, the process of qualification required an examination of Holocaust survivors by German physicians. In order to receive a pension, survivors had to satisfy German experts that an adequate degree – with bizarre exactitude, at least 25% – of their ill-function could be attributed to the experience of persecution, including confinement in a concentration camp. Many survivors found the process painful and humiliating.[26]

When reparations attempts fail in the communicative dimension, defects in the vindicatory message or in its presentation can be negative exemplifications: the form of relationship revealed is one in which the amends-maker remains sufficiently out of touch with the wronged parties that the amends-maker fails to appreciate the wrong or the pain and loss of the victims, fails to grasp the effort that this understanding requires, fails to see the victims of wrong as worth the effort, or seems even now not to accept those wronged as moral and civil peers. When apologies are lame or insulting, or what is offered as a vehicle of reparations is unresponsive, insensitive, useless, unfitting, inadequate, or ineffective, the exemplification fails not only in the sense that the attempt doesn't "come off," but that it betrays that the wrong kind of relationship persists, undermining even the hope that morally adequate relationships are a real possibility. Reparations efforts can send mixed messages through compromised or questionable exemplification in the act, process, or vehicle of reparations itself.

There is another possible failure of the exemplifying aspect, however, that goes beyond the failure to enact a convincing vindicatory message in the reparations effort itself. As an exemplification of right relationship, the gesture of reparations offers itself as a sample or representative instance of the broader redeemed relationship that is sought. Interactions other than the process or program of reparations, including future ones that directly affect those to whom reparations are given, can fail to live up to the standards of rectified (or basically decent) relationship. Where they

---

[25] Lira (2006) provides detailed explanation of this complex and protracted process of reparations.
[26] Danieli (2007).

fail, and especially if they fail in ways that reflect the flaws or malignancies at the root of the original wrong, the expressive dimension is compromised or nullified. At best, the reparations effort is then reduced to a payment, a monument, an empty verbal gesture, or a report with little reparative meaning. At worst, the failure inflicts renewed insult and aggravation, possibly damaging relationships further. Depending on the relationship and wrong involved, monetary reparations, unless they are framed adequately within a reparative process, can take on counter-reparative meanings. Money can signify "paying off," the termination or dismissal of further attempts to address a wrong or to build a continuing relationship, or money can seem and be the easiest thing to give and can represent an evasion of something more difficult, such as continuing to grapple with the full truth and meaning of past wrongs and their consequences.

Examples of reparations efforts that stutter, or that fail to establish, consistently express, or sustain the improved relationship the reparations gestures exemplifies, are not uncommon. In Argentina's reparations program, families of individuals who were disappeared during Argentina's "Dirty War" were entitled to a lump sum reparations payment of over $200,000 that was given in government bonds. During a financial collapse in 2001, the government of Argentina defaulted on its debts, including its payments of interest and principal to thousands of families. The government pleaded initially that it could not "make an exception" for the families of the disappeared because it would violate legal principle and expose the government to lawsuits. A family member was quoted by the *New York Times* as saying: "They took our children and never answered our questions about what was done with them, not where how, why, or when. Then they tried to clean their consciences giving us these bonds, and now there's not even that. It's too much to bear."[27] Although the policy was revised some months later to continue payment to those who received bonds as reparations, the Argentine government's false step of treating the families of the disappeared like any other bondholders, temporarily betrayed the status of the payments as reparations for horrific wrongs. In another instance, detailed by psychologist Brandon Hamber, President Thabo Mbeki of South Africa impugned the motivations of victim groups who pressed for long-delayed reparations, while perpetrators of human rights abuses rather swiftly secured amnesty; Mbeki implied that victims and their families dishonored the freedom struggle by seeking monetary reparations.[28]

Official apologies as reparative gestures can end up at odds with popular sentiment, thus undermining the prospect of right relationship the apology portends. When Chancellor Willy Brandt fell to his knees at a memorial for victims of the Warsaw Ghetto uprising in 1970s, the gesture was widely viewed favorably as a part of Germany's reckoning with its crimes in World War II. But when President Aleksander Kwasniewski of Poland asked "pardon in my own name and in the name

---

[27] Rohter (2002) reports on the reactions of victims' families to the action. See Guembe (2006) for a detailed account of Argentina's reparations, which resulted partly from litigation and partly by legislative action.

[28] Hamber (2009, 103–108).

of those Polish people whose consciences are shocked by this crime," at a memorial to a massacre of Jews by ordinary Poles in Jedwabne in 1941, widespread resentment and backlash among Poles was reported to follow.[29] In a recent case, the Supreme Court of Hawaii relied on the remarkable 1993 apology of the U.S. Congress for the illegal overthrow of the Hawaiian monarchy to block, pending indigenous claims, a transfer of land that was ceded to the United States after the overthrow. The U. S. Supreme Court, however, rejected any legal force of the 1993 apology and allowed the transfers to occur.[30]

Reparations bear the burden of sending the right message and of opening a portal to hope for a kind of relationship that allows and builds trust, even if it is only or primarily some level of confidence that gross violence and other grave wrongs will not be repeated. The persuasiveness of exemplification rests both on the adequacy of the vindicatory message in the reparations process and also on the grounds it gives for hope that the right relationship will emerge and be sustained more generally and into the future. Reparations are not best seen as a conclusion, but rather as a beginning; reparations do not only fulfill obligations, they also make commitments.

12.4 Conclusion

The expressive burdens of reparations efforts are heavy, and we should expect that they are often not fully met. The conception of full-blown reparations with which I began might thus be most usefully seen as a best case scenario. There are at least some good instances, certainly in private life, and sometimes in public cases. The U.S. program of reparations for unjust internment of Japanese-American citizens in World War II seems to be viewed widely as one of the good instances. The reparations effort resulted from an initiative of the Japanese-American community and enjoyed strong congressional support. It culminated in a response with the authority of the U. S. Congress that offered moral, legal, and political vindication through an official report, public and individualized presidential apologies, a negotiated money payment that was clearly seen by all parties as a symbolic token of good will, and funding for a variety of educational and memorial measures. The relatively small scale of the program, the varieties of amends offered, the participation of representatives of the Japanese-American communities affected, and the fact that the initiative had unusually well-placed political advocates, no doubt contributed to a satisfactory effort.[31]

In his comprehensive taxonomy of mass reparations programs, Pablo de Greiff includes complexity and coherence as distinguishing features of reparations programs. Complex programs distribute benefits of more distinct types; greater complexity

---

[29] Fisher (2001).

[30] Liptak (2009).

[31] On the effort, see Minow (1998) and Yamamoto and Ebusugawa (2006).

introduces flexibility that might enhance the overall impact of a program. Internal coherence refers to compatibility and support among different types of reparations benefits offered by a program.[32] Greater complexity, on my analysis of the expressive function of reparations, offers both more conduits for the vindicatory message and the compelling exemplification of right relationships, but also creates more vehicles and messages that individually and in concert bear the burden of communicative clarity and convincing exemplification. Given the inevitable economic, political, and social pressures surrounding mass reparations for political violence, authoritarian repression, and historical injustice, and the practical compromises that will likely result in designing a program, it is unlikely that each and all of the messages will fully achieve expressive adequacy, although their total effect, as de Greiff suggests, might be greater than the individual parts. As de Greiff also suggests, the "external coherence" of the reparations program with other measures of transitional justice is important to avoid undermining, as well as to reinforce, the message of the reparations measures. This is a question, in terms of my account, of consistent exemplification beyond the reparations program or process itself. Even with internal coherence of reparations measures and consistent support by other measures of justice in the immediate context of reparations, problems await the exemplifying promise of reparations programs where the entrenched marginalized or unequal status of some victims, such as women or minority ethnic or indigenous populations, remains in place, leaving them vulnerable to disrespect or mistreatment despite a reparations effort for particular injustices at a particular point in time.[33]

There might also be tensions or conflicts in actual cases among the demands of different features that contribute to the expressive adequacy of a reparations offer or process. The most fitting reparations in the view of victims are often the symbolic ones involving public acknowledgment and remembrance, but monetary reparations might be seen as easily deliverable, effective, and useful, while being less socially controversial in unsettled political circumstances. Yet, in some contexts, victims have been both unsatisfied and uneasy about accepting money payments when fuller forms of public acknowledgment and recognition are what they really value. It is also likely that temptations will arise to trade off some forms of adequacy for others. For example, governments in the wake of conflict may like the visibility and concrete usefulness of infrastructure improvements and communal material investment as reparations when the communities affected by violence are very poor. Yet, attempts to get value twice-over from using investment and development in communities as a kind of collective reparation can mute or cancel the fittingness of what is offered, as victims find what they receive is perhaps only what they deserved as citizens regardless of the specific injuries they have suffered, and that the public goods offered equally benefit others who are not victims (and in some situations those who have been perpetrators).[34]

---

[32] de Greiff (2006a, 10–12).

[33] On the potential and dilemma of "transformative" reparations, see Rubio-Marin (2009).

[34] On collective reparations, see Roht-Arriaza (2004), and Verdeja (2007) on the ambiguities involved in using development as reparations.

It is also true that expressive power is not all or nothing and that the expressive power of gestures can lay in the perception and interpretation of them in context. Some instances of compensation that withhold apologies or admissions of fault, for example, can "play" as reparations to their beneficiaries or to the public, such as the State of Florida's 1994 compensation program for the white riot that obliterated the town of Rosewood in 1925. While expressly avoiding the language of reparation and offering no apology, the measure went beyond monetary payments (some uniform and some based on demonstrable losses and direct exposure to the violence) to include memorial scholarships, a recommendation for continued research, and an admission of failure to prevent the destruction. Although modest, the Rosewood Compensation Act is remarkable given the extensive, unrepaired, and largely unacknowledged history in the United States of violent racial expulsions and white riots extending well into the twentieth century.[35] The force of acknowledgment and monetary compensation in such a case can gather expressive significance against a uniform backdrop of silence, denial, and fabricated or selective history. There are deeply contextual, pragmatic, and historical elements, then, in how actions can be interpreted as reparations.

Perhaps the final moral of these complexities is that reparations attempts are best seen as negotiations among victims, parties responsible for wrong or repair, and their communities. This is not only because a negotiation is an indispensable (if not always an easy or successful) way to uncover, clarify, test, and adjust understandings, refine meanings, and coordinate expectations in pursuit of an expressively adequate reparations process. It is also because fruitful negotiation can already be part of a process of repair: for victims, one of regaining voice and control; for those responsible for wrongs or repair, one of taking responsibility and learning to attend to the experiences and concerns of victims; for communities, one of coming to understand, and possibly to transform, the sense of who "we" are.[36]

It might be that what is most important is the increasing recognition in recent decades of a moral imperative *of* reparations as a matter of justice. Next in importance might be the recognition there is no single or simple measure of justice *in* reparations, despite the natural desire for a single straight rule – such as restoring the status quo ante or making the victim whole – to guide this process. Instead, there are various features of the reparative message, vehicle, and exemplified relationship that are fraught with meaning for victims, responsible parties, and communities. The negotiation of these meanings within the range of political possibilities is precisely what reparations for massive violations involves.

---

[35] Jaspin (2007) and Loewen (2005) explore the history of expulsion and forcible segregation for African-Americans, while Pfaelzer (2007) examines the history of Chinese immigrants to America.

[36] See Walker (2006c) on the ways restorative justice processes involving direct engagement can "leverage" responsibilities. On the pressure to reflect on the political culture of Australia in the debate about an official apology for the policy of removal from Aboriginal communities of mixed race children, see Celermajer 2006.

References

Barkan E (2003) The guilt of nations. Johns Hopkins University Press, Baltimore

Bernstein A (2009) Tort theory, microfinance and gender equality convergent in pecuniary reparations. In: Rubio-Marin R (ed) The gender of reparations. Cambridge University Press, New York

Boxill B (1972) The morality of reparation. Soc Theor Practice 2:113–122

Brooks RL (2003) Reflections on reparations. In: Torpey J (ed) Politics and the past: on repairing historical injustices. Rowman and Littlefield, Lanham

Brooks RL (2004) Atonement and forgiveness: a new model for black reparations. University of California Press, Berkeley/Los Angeles

Celermajer D (2006) The apology in Australia: re-covenanting the national imaginary. In: Barkan E, Karn A (eds) Taking wrongs seriously: apologies and reconciliation. Stanford University Press, Stanford

Coleman J (1994) Corrective justice and property rights. Soc Philos Policy 22:124–138

Colonomos A, Armstrong A (2006) German reparartions to the Jews after World War II: a turning point in the history of reparations. In: de Greiff P (ed) The handbook of reparations. Oxford University Press, New York

Corlett JA (2001) Reparations to native Americans? In: Jokic A (ed) War crimes and collective wrongdoing. Blackwell Publishers, Oxford

Czitrom CG (2002) Executive summary of "Truth Commissions: An Uncertain Path?" by Victor Espinoza Cuevas, Maria Luisa Ortiz Rojas, and Paz Rojas Baeza. Association for the Prevention of Torture, Geneva

Danieli Y (2007) Conclusion: essential elements of healing after massive trauma: some theory, victims' voices, and international developments. In: Miller J, Kumar R (eds) Reparations: interdisciplinary inquiries. Oxford University Press, New York

de Greiff P (ed) (2006a) The handbook of reparations. Oxford University Press, New York

de Greiff P (2006b) Justice and reparations. In: de Greiff P (ed) The handbook of reparations. Oxford University Press, New York

de Greiff P (2008) The role of apologies in national reconciliation processes: on making trustworthy institutions trusted. In: Gibney M, Howard-Hassmann RE, Coicaud J-M, Steiner N (eds) The age of apology: facing up to the past. University of Pennsylvania Press, Philadelphia

de Greiff P (2012) Theorizing transitional justice. In: Williams M, Nagy R, Elster J (eds) Transitional justice, vol LI, Nomos. New York University Press, New York

Duggan C, Jacobson R (2009) Reparation of sexual and reproductive violence: moving from codification to implementation. In: Rubio-Marin R (ed) The gender of reparations. Cambridge University Press, New York

Elgin CZ (1983) With reference to reference. Hackett, Indianapolis

Fackler M, Sang-Hun C (2007) Japanese researchers rebut premier's denials on sex slavery. In: New York Times, 18 April

Falk R (2006) Reparations, international law, and global justice: a new frontier. In: de Greiff P (ed) The handbook of reparations. Oxford University Press, New York

Fisher I (2001) At site of massacre, Polish leader asks Jews for forgiveness. In: New York Times, 11 July

Gill KA (2000) The moral functions of an apology. Philos Forum 31:11–27

Goodin R (1989) Theories of compensation. Oxf J Leg Stud 9:56–73

Goodman N (1968) Languages of art. Bobbs-Merrill, Indianapolis/New York

Govier T, Verwoerd W (2002) The promise and pitfalls of apology. J Soc Philos 33:67–82

Guembe MJ (2006) Economic reparations for grave human rights violations: the argentinian experience. In: de Greiff P (ed) The handbook of reparations. Oxford University Press, New York

Hamber B (2006) Narrowing the micro and macro: a psychological perspective on reparations in societies in transition. In: de Greiff P (ed) The handbook of reparations. Oxford University Press, New York, pp 560–589

Hamber B (2009) Transforming societies after political violence: truth, reconciliation, and mental health. Springer, Dordrecht

Herman J (1997) Trauma and recovery: the aftermath of violence – from domestic abuse to political terror. Basic Books, New York

Iida K (2004) Human rights and sexual abuse: the impact of international human rights law on Japan. Human Rights Quart 26:428–453

Issacharoff S, Mansfield AM (2006) Compensation for the victims of September 11. In: de Greiff P (ed) The handbook of reparations. Oxford University Press, New York

Jaspin E (2007) Buried in the bitter waters: the history of racial cleansing in America. Basic Books, New York

Kort L (1973) What is an apology? Philos Res Arch 1:80–87

Lazare A (2004) On apology. Oxford University Press, New York

Lind J (2008) Sorry states: apologies in international politics. Cornell University Press, Ithaca

Liptak A (2009) Justices limit the reach of apology to Hawaiians. In: New York Times, 1 April

Lira E (2006) The reparations policy for human rights violations in Chile. In: de Greiff P (ed) The handbook of reparations. Oxford University Press, New York

Loewen JW (2005) Sundown towns: a hidden dimension of American racism. Touchstone, New York

MacCormick DN (1977–1978) The obligation of reparation. Proc Aristot Soc 78:175–194

Malamud-Goti JE, Grosman LS (2006) Reparations and civil litigation: compensation for human rights violations in transitional democracies. In: de Greiff P (ed) The handbook of reparations. Oxford University Press, New York

Mazurana D, Carlson K (2009) Reparations as a means for recognizing and addressing crimes and grave rights violations against girls and boys during situations of armed conflict and under authoritarian and dictatorial regimes. In: Rubio-Marin R (ed) The gender of reparations. Cambridge University Press, New York

Minow M (1998) Between vengeance and forgiveness. Beacon, Boston

Nickel JW (1976) Justice in compensation. William and Mary Law Rev 18:379–388

Nozick R (1974) Anarchy, state, and utopia. Basic Books, New York

Onishi N (2007a) Abe rejects Japan's files on war sex. In: New York Times, 2 March

Onishi N (2007b) Denial reopens wounds of Japan's Ex-sex slaves. In: New York Times, 8 March

Onishi N (2007c) Japan court rules against sex slaves and laborers. In: New York Times, 28 April

Onishi N (2007d) Japan's 'Atonement' to former sex slaves Stirs Anger. In: New York Times, 25 April

Pfaelzer J (2007) Driven out: the forgotten war against Chinese Americans. Random House, New York

Pierik R (2006) Reparations for luck egalitarians. J Soc Philos 37:423–440

Radzik L (2009) Making amends: atonement in morality, law, and politics. Oxford University Press, New York

Roht-Arriaza N (2004) Reparations in the aftermath of repression and mass violence. In: Stover E, Weinstein HM (eds) My neighbor, my enemy: justice and community in the aftermath of mass atrocity. Cambridge University Press, Cambridge

Rohter L (2002) Argentine default reopens 'Dirty War' wounds. In: New York Times, 12 March

Rubio-Marin R (2009) The gender of reparations in transitional societies. In: Rubio-Marin R (ed) The gender of reparations: unsettling sexual hierarchies while redressing human rights violations. Cambridge University Press, New York

Satz D (2007) Countering the wrongs of the past: the role of compensation. In: Miller J, Kumar R (eds) Reparations: interdisciplinary inquiries. Oxford University Press, New York

Sher G (1980) Ancient wrongs and modern rights. Philos Public Aff 10:3–17

Smith N (2008) I was wrong: the meanings of apologies. Cambridge University Press, New York

Tavuchis N (1991) Mea culpa: a sociology of apology and reconciliation. Stanford University Press, Stanford

Teitel R (2000) Transitional justice. Oxford University Press, New York

Thompson J (2002) Taking responsibility for the past: reparation and historical injustice. Polity Press, Cambridge

Torpey J (2006) Politics and the past: on repairing historical injustices. Rowman and Littlefield, Lanham

Tsosie R (2007) Acknowledging the past to heal the future: the role of reparations for native nations. In: Miller J, Kumar R (eds) Reparations: interdisciplinary inquiries. Oxford University Press, New York

Verdeja E (2007) A normative theory of reparations in transitional democracies. In: Card C, Marsoobian AT (eds) Genocide's aftermath: responsibility and repair. Blackwell, Oxford

Waldron J (1992) Superseding historic injustice. Ethics 103:4–28

Walker MU (2006a) Moral repair: reconstructing moral relations after wrongdoing. Cambridge University Press, New York

Walker MU (2006b) The cycle of violence. J Hum Rights 5:81–105

Walker MU (2006c) Restorative justice and reparations. J Soc Philos 37:377–395

Wenar L (2006) Reparations for the future. J Soc Philos 37:396–405

Winter S (2006) Uncertain justice: history and reparations. J Soc Philos 37:342–359

Yamamoto EK, Ebusugawa L (2006) Report on redress: the Japanese American internment. In: de Greiff P (ed) The handbook of reparations. Oxford University Press, New York

Index